Yeats and the Rhymers' Club

American University Studies

Series IV
English Language and Literature
Vol. 47

PETER LANG
New York • Bern • Frankfurt am Main • Paris

Joann Gardner

Yeats and the Rhymers' Club

A Nineties' Perspective

PETER LANG
New York • Bern • Frankfurt am Main • Paris

Library of Congress Cataloging-in-Publication Data

Gardner, Joann
    Yeats and the Rhymers' Club : a nineties' perspective / Joann Gardner.
      p. cm. — (American university studies. Series IV, English language and literature ; vol. 47)
      Bibliography: p.
      Includes index.
      1. Yeats, W. B. (William Butler), 1865-1939. 2. Rhymers' Club (London, England) 3. Authors, Irish — 19th century — Biography. 4. London (England) — Intellectual life — 19th century. I. Title. II. Series.
PR5906.G37   1989   821'.8—dc19   88-14171
ISBN 0-8204-0769-0   CIP
ISSN 0741-0700

CIP-Titelaufnahme der Deutschen Bibliothek

Gardner Joann:
Yeats and the Rhymers' Club : a nineties' perspective / Joann Gardner. — New York; Bern; Frankfurt am Main; Paris: Lang, 1988.
  (American University Studies: Ser. 4,
  English Language and Literature; Vol. 47)
  ISBN 0-8204-0769-0

NE: American University Studies / 04

© Peter Lang Publishing, Inc., New York 1989

All rights reserved.
Reprint or reproduction, even partially, in all forms such as microfilm, xerography, microfiche, microcard, offset strictly prohibited.

Printed by Weihert-Druck GmbH, Darmstadt, West Germany

For my parents

YEATS AND THE RHYMERS' CLUB: A NINETIES' PERSPECTIVE

Table of Contents

Acknowledgements	xi
List of Illustrations	xiii
Introduction	1
Chapter I: Where All Ladders Start	11
Chapter II: The Pattern in the Web	53
Chapter III: The Turning of the Gyre	93
Chapter IV: The Myth of Failure	137
Chapter V: Visions and Responsibilities	173
Works Cited	209
Appendix I: Biographical Sketches	223
Appendix II: Chronology	231
Index	243

ACKNOWLEDGEMENTS

I would like to thank Hugh Kenner and Lee Patterson for their help in the earliest stages of this project, George Mills Harper who loaned books from his library and offered sound editorial advice, Marta Harley for her photograph of the Cheshire Cheese, Deborah O'Neal and B. G. Dillworth for their photographs and photographic advice, the English Department at Florida State University for allocations from the Research Committee, and the National Endowment for the Humanities for a Travel to Collections grant. I would like to thank John Parker for his work as typesetter, Jerry Stern for his computer expertise, and numerous supportive friends: Michael, Carol, Donna, Terry, Bob, Karen, Bill; others, too, who have contributed in many ways.

Formal acknowledgement and thanks go to Richard Finneran for permission to reprint a version of Chapter IV from *Yeats: An Annual of Critical and Textual Studies*, John Kelly and Oxford University Press for permission to use excerpts from Yeats's letters, Michael B. Yeats and Anne Yeats for permission to quote from unpublished letters, Macmillan Publishing Company for permission to quote from *Autobiographies* and *The Variorum Edition of the Poems of W. B. Yeats*, the Rare Book and Manuscript Library of Columbia University for permission to quote from the Edmund C. Stedman Papers, the University of Reading for permission to quote from material in the Elkin Mathews Collection, and Mrs. Brian Read, to quote from Arthur Symons's poetry and prose.

I would also like to thank the University of Reading for its photographs of letters in the Elkin Mathews Collection, Mrs. Eva Reichmann for permission to reprint Max Beerbohm's drawing "Some Persons of the Nineties," the Victoria and Albert Museum for Aubrey Beardsley's poster for *A Comedy of Sighs* and *The Land of Heart's Desire*, and the National Gallery of Ireland for its portrait of W. B. Yeats.

Joann Gardner
Tallahassee, Florida

LIST OF ILLUSTRATIONS

1. The Cheshire Cheese Pub in Wine Office Court where the Rhymers' Club held their meetings (Harley).　v

2. Portrait of W. B. Yeats by John Butler Yeats (National Gallery of Ireland).　xv

3. Aubrey Beardsley's poster for John Todhunter's *A Comedy of Sighs* and W.B. Yeats's *The Land of Heart's Desire* (from the Victoria and Albert Museum).　92

4. Max Beerbohm's "Some Persons of the Nineties, Little Imagining, despite their Pride and Ornamental Aspect, how much they will interest Mr. Holbrook Jackson and Mr. Osbert Burdett." Figures from top left are: Richard Le Gallienne, Walter Sickert, George Moore, John Davidson, Oscar Wilde, W.B. Yeats, partial view perhaps of "Enock Soames," //Arthur Symons, Henry Harland, Charles Condor, William Rothenstein, Max Beerbohm, Aubrey Beardsley (from *Observations*, photo by Dillworth and O'Neal, permission from Mrs. Eva Reichmann).　136

5. Letter announcing the termination of the Bodley Head partnership of Elkin Mathews and John Lane, accompanied by a list of authors (University of Reading, Elkin Mathews Collection).　222

INTRODUCTION

The tragic generation, as Yeats had labelled his friends of the nineties, offered a troubling example for the writers of the twentieth century, one which they felt they had to get beyond. So Eliot created Prufrock and abandoned him to recalcitrant mermaids; Pound penned Mauberley, turning his back on his former self; Joyce took Stephen through the various stages of aesthetic posturing, purging his readers and himself of the adolescent urge. Rejecting the intimacy between art and life that the nineties had fostered, these writers adopted techniques that separated the individual who suffers from the artist who creates. The use of personae in verse established a distance between the writer and his emotions; multiperspectivalism in fiction removed the author from the center of his presentation. And because these writers were able to put the vulnerable nineties behind them (Eliot based his religious sense on intellect rather than empty mysticism; Pound developed a harder, more masculine verse; Joyce reproduced the contours of Ibsenite realism in his fiction), modern critics have felt secure in either accepting the given myths about these figures or dismissing them altogether. But Yeats came into his own during this period, and he took pains in both his critical and creative pursuits to point out its importance to him. Because of his direct involvement in this decade and because of his tendency to return to and build upon old themes, this era and the individuals who dominated it constitute important aspects of his work.

Our present notion of the Rhymers' Club comes to us primarily from Yeats, who depicted this collection of minor versifiers as a coherent if somewhat volatile force that prepared the way for the modern age. In *Autobiographies*, his introduction to *The Oxford Book of Modern Verse*, "The Grey Rock" and other writings, he stressed notions of victimage and tragedy: social or philosophical forces that contributed to the untimely ends of many talented members. Grouping the various personalities he had met into a single unit, he spoke of these poets' self-destructiveness, their championship of "poetic purity" and their uncompromising dedication to art. Their youth and intensity had assured their failure, but it had also determined their artistic nobility. Pondering the developments of his own advancing career, he came to see himself as the inheritor of a tradition of dedication and passion.

In reality, the Rhymers' Club had been much less coherent as a group, and his treatment of it as such was part of a metaphorical process whereby actuality took on the significance of a much larger idea. At the opening of *Four Years*, Yeats claims "an historian's right" over the dead, indicating that as a survivor he had earned the right to interpret and define the past according to his own instincts and recollections. With respect to the Rhymers' Club, this claim may have been justified, since relatively little was recorded by those directly involved, and all of it, with a certain amount of artistic recreation. Yet it would be wrong to assume—as many critics have—that Yeats's version was free of fantasy. *Autobiographies* itself is notoriously dubious as an historical document, and Yeats's general preference for "poetic" rather than literal truth leads one to believe that he followed his contemporaries' example in refashioning experience to fit his own artistic needs. It stands to reason then that his interpretation of the Rhymers' Club should not be taken at face value and dismissed, but analyzed for what it tells us of the writer and his milieu. Failing to do so, we lose not only an accurate grip on history but an understanding, both sociologically and poetically, of how the myth of the Rhymers' Club came about and what role it played in the ultimate success or failure of the artists involved.

Relatively little has been written about the Rhymers' Club and that which has been written bears the marks of a tradition of prevarication. This problem works its way into the critical sphere in the form of factual imprecisions and misinterpretations—when Richard Ellmann misidentifies Aubrey Beardsley as a member of the Rhymers' Club (IY, 114) or when John Unterecker, speaking of "The Statesman's Holiday," concludes that the poem is a farewell to the diction of Yeats's youth (RGWBY, 287) or, most recently, when A. Norman Jeffares posits that Lionel Johnson's courtesy "to the worst" in "In Memory of Major Robert Gregory" may be a reference to Ernest Dowson (CP, 133). These statements depend upon scanty or misleading information and contribute as well to the myth, either by promoting existing fantasies or creating from them new features. Yeats did not meet Aubrey Beardsley until after the Rhymers' Club had disbanded, although he speaks of Mabel Beardsley as being "almost one of us"; "The Statesman's Holiday" is a goodbye to or rejection of noncommittal political jargon, although Oscar [Wilde's] name is mentioned in the text; Lionel Johnson's courtesy was extended more significantly to those who misconstrued and rejected his work, even though Ernest Dowson's life had been "a sordid round of drink and cheap harlots." Without a reliable full-length study of the Club or the stories surrounding it, we are at the mercy of the poet's recreations, often interpreting his associations in such a way that the poems themselves are not served thereby.

Critics such as Morton Seiden (*The Poet as Mythmaker*), George Mills Harper (*The Making of Yeats's "A Vision"*) and Mary Helen Thuente (*W.B. Yeats and Irish Folklore*) have discussed Yeats's mythmaking activities with respect to his occult and Irish concerns, while Harold Bloom (*Yeats*) and George Bornstein (*Yeats and Shelley*) have explored Yeats's relation to the high Romantics, enterprises which inevitably touch on myth. The present focus complements their findings by examining an aspect of the poet's own experience and its subsequent incorporation into his artistic system. As Yeats informs us In "The Circus Animals' Desertion," his often lofty symbols are derived from common sources, and it is important that we keep this personal aspect of his work in mind if we are to have a truly informed view of the creative process. The Rhymers with whom he learned his trade were intensely personal writers, and their attitude toward personality had much to do with their artistic fates.

This study then intends to offer a reliable account of the Rhymers' Club and to plot the evolution of the myth surrounding it. Additionally, it addresses questions of artistic success and failure: how Yeats benefitted from his association with the Club and how he was able to succeed while others of his cenacle failed. Interestingly, the answers to these questions involve myth as well: the Masks these poets created, the difficulties they encountered, and the solutions they devised or failed to devise as *fin-de-siècle* writers. Yeats learned to control his external environment by incorporating personal experience into poetry, and so created an internal world where life's difficulties could be and were resolved. Transferring the personalities he had known into symbols, Yeats gained distance on his own experience and thus freedom from the vulnerability of a totally personal art. Lacking the same talent or commitment to the power of verse, poets such as Dowson and Johnson were controlled by visions of self-destruction or the inability to apply their formal skills to larger poetic issues. Caught in a dilemma typical of the decadent consciousness, they patterned their lives after an artistic vision that would have permanent and devastating effect on them as they moved closer to their goals.

My ideas concerning the Rhymers' Club and myth have

been formed by readings within the period, a number of which I will mention to fill out the dimensions of my concern. At one time Yeats's "sacred book of the arts," Villiers de l'Isle Adam's *Axel* is an important example of decadent writing. Through a series of denials, it describes a movement away from reality towards an ideal, thought-created universe, similar to the movement Yeats discovers in Lionel Johnson's career, or even that implicit in his own transition from passionate youth to disillusioned or disinterested old man. With the decadents, myth and art became a way of rejecting society, an exploration of inner life at the expense of outer belonging. Yeats recognized this tendency in his friends, and his attempt to understand and explain it in their careers was also an attempt to understand, explain and go beyond it in his own.

Oscar Wilde's *The Picture of Dorian Gray* moves away from realistic representation as well, into a gothic otherworld of art. The conflict between the beautiful surface of Dorian's face and the increasing corruption of his inner soul creates a tension that is crucial to Yeats's concept of the Mask and supports his view of life as drama, where reality and irreality exist in troubled but passionate association. The painting that registers the gradual disintegration of Dorian's moral sense offers an extension of Ruskin's notion (*Modern Painters*) that art reflects the moral character of the culture from which it is produced and may be related to Yeats's counterthought that art has the power to affect and change external reality. Lord Henry and Dorian derive extreme pleasure from artifice and deception, values that become increasingly *de rigeur* in decadent circles of the 1890s and are given voice in such major essays as Beerbohm's "A Defense of Cosmetics," Wilde's "The Decay of Lying" and Symons's "Being a Word on Behalf of Patchouli." The elder Yeats implicitly reaffirms these values in his continued use of symbols as well as his choice of Byzantium as a reward for mortal existence. Art, according to these sources, is superior to life because it controls and thus perfects the material with which it works. It brings our minds to contemplate the Platonic ideal of Beauty or Truth, which life itself can only approximate.

This pull away from nature and from natural objects or subjects may also be seen in Beardsley's drawings and his prose fantasy *Under the Hill*, where an intense, almost baroque attention to details of costume and artifice transforms his characters from genuine personalities to artistic types and removes them to an environment where the real and the unreal, the sensuous and the sterile, strain against each other as black against white. In Yeats's system, duality provides the essential tension for art, the successful expression of self depending on a clear and compelling vision of the anti-self. The world of artifice and the passionate world of the senses remain locked in an ongoing opposition, symbolic truth created from the largest obstacle one may confront without despair.

Walter Pater expressed this tension through a fascination with death in youth. This theme combined for him the opposing values of beauty and ugliness and generated a power analogous to Yeats's "terrible beauty." In *The Renaissance*, Pater's conviction of human ephemerality provokes a call for experience: a sensuousness and receptivity that would allow one the ultimate rewards of each moment and a notion of art where words would aspire to the condition of music, preserving eternally the instant of desire and evoking emotion rather than thought. These ideas are dramatized in *Marius the Epicurean*, along with the notions that "intensely realized memory" can bring the dead to life in our minds, that the most real world is that which we create in our imagination. The importance of this understanding to Yeats may be seen in his treatment of the poets of the Rhymers' Club, who died young and are transferred in death to the spiritual and poetic plane. Here, they enjoy a secondary, numinous existence through the very intensity of the poet's memory.

In the three-volume edition of Blake's work, Yeats and Ellis

Introduction

offer insights into Blake's mythical system and the concept that art redeems us from Nature's cycles of death and destruction; in Arthur Symons's *The Symbolist Movement in Literature,* Symons speaks of the symbolic nature of language and efforts the French have made to produce a literature "in which the visible world is no longer reality, and the unseen world no longer a dream." Together, these viewpoints argue for the richness of the subconscious mind and the power of its archetypes to counter the burdens of external experience. Yeats's own essays—"William Blake and the Imagination," "The Symbolism of Poetry" and "Magic"—sponsor the connection between poetry and the dream world, between the poet and the ancient high priest, and outline a poetic of ritualistic reenactment where symbols invoke Unity of Mind and Memory, allowing both reader and writer to return to basic instincts and understandings and to experience the world through them. This philosophical exploration complements Yeats's poems, which transpose the real world into symbolic patterns and, thus, create a system whereby the actual may be understood and controlled.

    I have taken my overall structural idea for the book from David Daiches's interpretation of Yeats's winding stair (PMW, 167-8), moving vortically from a primarily historical introduction toward an application of history to the poet's work. According to Daiches, Yeats's career is not linear, or easily divisible into discrete units, but approximates the shape of the winding staircase up which the poet climbs. Connected in an unbroken series, each step in the ascent is in line with the step below, yet brings the poet closer, vertically, to his goal. While this presentation progresses chronologically, it moves out of biographical and historical concerns into treatment of texts and art, just as Yeats's association with the Rhymers' Club was transferred out of the realm of immediate experience into the dream or symbolic world. The first chapter of the presentation, "Where All Ladders Start," examines the principal characters of the Club and their motives for association. It aims at presenting a clear view of these individuals and how they went about establishing their status as artists in the years just preceding the founding of the Club. The second chapter, "The Pattern in the Web," speaks of the early stages of organization and finds in these events features that helped determine the ephemerality, both of the Club and many of its key members. The third and fourth chapters, "The Turning of the Gyre" and "The Myth of Failure," deal primarily with the anthologies of the Rhymers' Club: the first, with regard to the phenomenon of dissolution and the attitudes expressed in the poems; the second, with regard to the early literary reviews and their role in the developing myth. In the case of the reviews, one sees Yeats incorporating both the ideas and the language associated with the Rhymers' Club into his own vision of them, and, in the books, one detects his commitment to Ireland and to the mystical power of the poet which distinguishes him from his less perspicacious contemporaries. The last chapter, "Visions and Responsibilities," deals with Yeats as a survivor of the change in taste that occurred around 1895. It examines the effect his experience of the Rhymers' Club and its members had on poems published in *Responsibilities* and after, which touches upon both conceptual and structural concerns. At each stage in the development of this history, one can see that Yeats managed to benefit from his associates while remaining essentially distinct from them, and that this distinction contributed to his eventual success. Appendices containing biographical sketches of the principal Rhymers and a chronology of the period from 1883 to 1898 have been included.

Since the chapters that follow depend upon an overall understanding of the Rhymers' Club and its activities, it seems appropriate here to provide a brief historical summary. The principal facts are available from various studies and memoirs of the 1890s and offer a starting point for our ascent of the winding stair.

Introduction

Yeats, Ernest Rhys and T.W. Rolleston founded the Rhymers' Club in 1890, apparently so that poets of their generation might benefit from mutual acquaintance and association. The earliest meetings were composed of Celtic poets whom Rolleston and Yeats had met previously in Dublin and several writers of various backgrounds, including John Davidson, Arthur Symons and Ernest Radford, whom Rhys and Yeats had encountered after their arrival in London. In 1891, the Club expanded to include a group of Oxford aesthetes: Lionel Johnson, Ernest Dowson, Herbert Horne and Victor Plarr. Primarily through the efforts of Richard Le Gallienne, the group secured close connections with Elkin Mathews and John Lane's Bodley Head publishing company, and, in addition to entertaining a core group of fairly regular members, accumulated an ample list of permanent and impermanent "guests."

Initially, the Rhymers' Club met at the Cheshire Cheese, a restaurant-pub in Wine Office Court, once frequented by Goldsmith and Johnson. Poets would dine downstairs on steak and ale, and then repair to an upper room to read their verses and engage in delicate criticisms of each other's work. As time went on, meetings were also held in Rhymers' homes. Herbert Horne, John Todhunter and Edwin Ellis, among others, hosted such eminent guests as Oscar Wilde, Francis Thompson, Maud Gonne and Paul Verlaine, and the group gradually gained a sense of sobriety and purpose. In the five years or so of the Club's existence, members produced two anthologies of verse, helped each other publish their work and engaged in an active exchange of reviews in the literary press.

Yeats's treatment of the Club as a coherent movement, however, was a fiction of his own device. Not only did other members frown on attempts to intellectualize their creative activities, but they demonstrated fairly diverse notions of their craft. The most influential members were advocates of Pater's and Rossetti's work. Some had experimented with French meters and were recognizable, according to Yeats, by their uncompromising dedication to art. Some, however, remained solidly Victorian in taste, carrying with them what Yeats called "the dreadful burden of the TCD tradition." Although reputed to be young poets, they varied in age from twenty-four to fifty-two at the beginning of their association, and they varied also in profession and literary talent.

The Rhymers' Club broke up gradually, partially due to their lack of ideological coherence, partially due to events occurring in and around 1895 which put an end to the fashion of literary decadence and the successful careers of key members. Many came to be known for their brief and intense lives, generating a legend concerning their purported dissipation and tragic unfulfillment as artists. Among these were the three most important figures to Yeats: Ernest Dowson, Lionel Johnson and Arthur Symons. With them, he had learned his trade, experiencing the passion and frustrations of the decade, and, through them, he had discovered ways of dealing artistically with these emotions. His attempt to explain their failures persisted into old age, and his acknowledgement of their importance to him is registered in both his poetry and prose.

WHERE ALL LADDERS START

The history of the Rhymers' Club begins with the phenomenon of association: how such a group could have come together and what each had hoped to achieve. Although mostly young poets, these figures had various family backgrounds, educational and professional orientations, and, while some promoted the principles of Pater's aestheticism, others remained loyal to established Victorian values. The group, in fact, had little to bind it together ideologically outside of the simple desire to write poetry, and the insubstantiality of this focus kept it from becoming a truly integrated school of writers.

Yeats, however, came to think of the Club as such, and his vision of a unified movement with specific symbolic import stands at the end of a long process of factual and conceptual transformations. He had founded the Rhymers' Club, he claimed, so that artists could work together to avoid professional jealousies (Au, 164), but, as time went on, he also remembered the spirit of competition implicit in their number. "None of us can say who will succeed," he recalled having said one evening, "or even who has or has not talent. The only thing certain about us is that we are too many"(Au, 171). Prophetically echoing Hardy's Father Time, Yeats speaks ominously of the Rhymers' future and establishes the mythical framework for subsequent discussions. Elimination would come—in most cases, long after the Rhymers' Club had ceased to meet—and the nature of these individual failures reinforced their symbolic potency. Despondent in his love for a Polish restaurant keeper's daughter, Ernest Dowson died of tuberculosis and pneumonia at age 33. Lionel Johnson, whose alcoholism and psychological guilts had led him into a pattern of social withdrawal, died at 35 of a massive brain hemmorhage. Oscar Wilde died in exile in Paris at age 46. Arthur Symons went mad at 43. John Davidson, aged 52, jumped from the cliffs of Penzance, never to be seen again. Some few, like Victor Plarr and Richard Le Gallienne, lived on to ripe but ineffectual old age. Yeats alone survived, both as a man and an artist.

The notion that Yeats developed in his *Autobiographies*, that the Rhymers were compelled to live out their tragic fates, is at once supported and deflated by a conscientious reconstruction of the past. The creative strengths and weaknesses of these individuals as well as their practical understanding of the values of fellowship brought them together, while differences in talent, ideology and personal loyalties eventually pulled them apart. Artistically, they failed for virtually the same reasons: lack of sufficient talent or adherence to self-limiting principles that would not survive beyond the turn of the century. Yeats's mystical treatment of these poets must be questioned in light of specific details of personality and circumstance, and the difference between his and a more rational approach to history is seen as a measure or manipulation of available information. As William Rothenstein pointed out in "Yeats as a Painter Saw Him," Yeats comprehended both perspectives, and he used his mysticism to his best professional advantage. "For in Yeats," said Rothenstein, "there was a solid kernel of wisdom, a shrewd judgement of men, and of the material side of life; he was well aware of the value of an aloofness and mystery, which he cultivated" (GET, 40).

The present chapter goes back to the beginnings of the mythologizing process, to the years 1884-1890 that precede the founding of the Club. It attempts to gain an accurate understanding of who these poets were and what they were doing before their identities became part of a cultural myth and to perceive how much of their future course could be apprehended from early events and reactions. It also examines how these poets came to be associated with one another, to what extent they exercised conscious strategy in establishing their literary careers or were simply carried along by a romanticized vision of "the artistic way of life." In terms of ultimate success or failure, practicality played an important role, allowing those who possessed it a clear understanding of what should and should not be done to advance their careers. Yeats, more than the others of the group, was an organizing mind whose practical abilities existed on a par with his poetic instincts. Joining these disparate personalities into a group was not, as his *Autobiographies* might have us believe, a coincidence or mystical phenomenon, but part of the poet's desire to associate with and benefit from others whose interests were similar to his own. Possessing an admittedly self-dramatizing personality, he recognized the importance of playing his role well and thus gained influence over his surroundings. Having apprehended the value of personal connections, he systematically went about creating a context for his work.

I. Yeats and the Contemporary Club

Yeats's first model for the Rhymers' Club was the Contemporary Club, an association of Dublin artists and intellectuals brought together by Charles Hubert Oldham in 1885. For two years preceding his family's move to London (1885-7), he and his father attended the Saturday night meetings at 116 Grafton Street and benefitted from the opportunity to discuss "the political, social and literary questions of the day" (Roster of Rules, qtd. in Harry Nicholls's "Memories of the Contemporary Club," IT [20 December 1965]: 10). Then an art student, the young Yeats found in this organization the opportunity to test his rhetorical skills against some of the most distinguished minds of Ireland, and the spirited, often heated, atmosphere of these debates gave him valuable social experience, teaching him composure even in extremes of verbal adversity:

> I had begun to frequent a club founded by Mr. Oldham, and not from natural liking, but from a secret ambition. I wished to become self-possessed, to be able to play with hostile minds as Hamlet played, to look in the lion's face, as it

were, with unquivering eyelash. In Ireland harsh argument which had gone out of fashion in England was still the manner of our conversation, and at this club Unionist and Nationalist could interrupt one another and insult one another without the formal and traditional restraint of public speech. (Au, 93)

Yeats's "secret ambition" to play with hostile minds stemmed from a practical estimation of what would be required of him in life—the development not only of a private self, but of a public individuality that would enable him to confront and effectively control social situations. His identification with Hamlet suggests his natural theatricality and gives us insight into an artistic self-image that gained significance as his association with the decadents developed.[1] By creating a Mask for the public's eye, Yeats not only enhanced his own mysteriousness, but insisted upon artistic precedency and control. Creating a double that improved upon nature, he turned life into a stage for his own best soliloquies.

Despite the fact that "harsh argument" had gone out of style in England, Yeats reaped benefits from the Contemporary Club that would continue to influence his career even after he had left Ireland. From his participation in the Club, he became acquainted with many distinguished Irish intellectuals and learned the practical advantages of literary fellowship. From his confrontations with such rhetorical giants as John F. Taylor, he developed an artistic presence and self-confidence that would distinguish him not only in present circumstances but in future encounters as well. Taylor was an advocate who was called to both the English and the Irish bars, and while Yeats admitted to their mutual antipathy, he also spoke with admiration of his adversary's rhetorical skills. "When Taylor spoke," Yeats writes in *Reveries Over Childhood and Youth*, "it was a great event . . . . Verses that seemed when one saw them upon the page flat and empty caught from that voice, whose beauty was half in its harsh strangeness, nobility and style"(Au, 99). Yeats evidently learned from Taylor's delivery, for we find in future descriptions of his speaking style similar attributes. Edgar Jepson recalls him at the Rhymers' Club, "wearing . . . the air of a Byronic hero, long-haired and gaunt, and delivering his poems in a harsh and high chanting voice"(MV, 235). And Ezra Pound records in Canto LXXXIII Yeats's penchant for incantation:

>   so that I recalled the noise in the chimney
> as it were the wind in the chimney
>   but was in reality Uncle William
> downstairs composing
> that had made a great Peeeeacock
>   in the proide ov his oiye.
>   (EPC, 569)

A successful Hamlet, Yeats gained the respect of his associates at the Contemporary Club, both as an intellect and as a poet. They came to attribute his personal idiosyncracies to a kind of raw genius and freely exercised whatever literary influence they had on his behalf.

Charles Oldham and John O'Leary offered the most direct professional assistance, providing him with publishing outlets and further personal contacts. Oldham published Yeats's first poems in the *Dublin University Review*[2] and introduced him to Katherine Tynan, a poet to whom Yeats would propose marriage in 1888. O'Leary helped him place work in the *Gael*, the *Providence Sunday Journal* and the *Boston Pilot*[3] as well as editing *Poems and Ballads of Young Ireland* (1888) and helping to collect subscriptions for his volume *The Wanderings of Oisin*.

The most important personal contact to come from this association was Maud Gonne. With an introduction from John O'Leary, she visited the Yeats family at Bedford Park in January 1889, immediately capturing the young poet's heart. Soon, she became his model for passionate yet unattainable love, a dynamic player who brought him close in spirit to Ernest Dowson and others of the aesthetic school. Ernest Rhys's report of her arrival at the Rhymers' Club demonstrates that Maud Gonne's spell was effectively cast on all who met her:

> It must have been in the first years of the nineties, one dark and wet winter evening, that I caught a first glimpse of the intrepid Irish heroine who had already become part of Yeats's legend. He was then living at Woburn Buildings, the dingy court behind St. Pancras Church, that reminded one of the slums round St. Patrick's Cathedral in Dublin. Imagine a tall, a very tall, figure in emerald green, a gold torque round her neck, with a most queenly head. Sometimes she was attended by an Irish wolf-hound, and then her favourite posture was a reclining one, with her wolf-hound at her feet. A wet black winter's night when Yeats had his party at Woburn Buildings, and as it was impossible for her hansom to get any nearer than the end of the court, Yeats darted out of his doorway through the rain to receive his Irish princess, and when she dismounted, a gleaming figure, dressed as if for a state function, a dozen dirty little ragged boys who had gathered in the rain were so astonished that they cried out in shrill admiration. When she was seated on a couch before a bright blazing fire, with tall candles at her elbow, she seemed to fill the room with her presence. She had a generous, gracious way of making you enter into her proud belief that Ireland was the Land of Destiny. (WEW, 172)

Rhys's account does not wholly agree with factual probabilities and assumed dates for the Rhymers' Club,[4] but it does point to the intoxication that Ireland and things Irish produced in literary circles at that time. Maud Gonne, especially, inspired in her audiences an almost worshipful respect, and Yeats was careful to present her in the most dramatic light possible. A stately, elusive beauty, she kept the poet seeking reward, and—like Elizabeth Siddal and Jane Morris for the Pre-Raphaelites—became in his mind an archetype for mysterious womanhood. Yeats's intimacy with Gonne and the equally dynamic old Fenian leader John O'Leary provided a cast for his Celtic identity and an area of expertise that had fascinated the English from Matthew Arnold onward. In this way, his connections at the Contemporary Club not only allowed him to move comfortably within Irish circles but prepared the way for acceptance into the larger context of literary London.

II. T. W. Rolleston[5]

Another young poet who attended the Contemporary Club and benefitted from his experiences there was T. W. Rolleston. Rolleston, whom Rhys mentions as a founding member of the Rhymers' Club, became editor of Oldham's *Dublin University Review* in August 1885 and published much of Yeats's early creative work. He also published in *Kottabos*, a literary journal sponsored by Trinity College (Dublin) and containing poems by A. C. Hillier, G.A. Greene and other future Rhymers. Having become friendly with John O'Leary through meetings at the Contemporary Club, Rolleston joined his Young Ireland movement, and, when *Poems and Ballads of Young Ireland* was published in 1888, his poems appeared alongside those of Yeats, Katherine Tynan, John Todhunter and Douglas Hyde. These experiences eventually provided a context for his later participation in the Irish Literary Society and other specifically Irish projects, but his ultimate success as an artist was hampered both by a lack of poetic genius and an over-regard for traditional methods and attitudes. Yeats stated in *The Trembling of the Veil* that Rolleston was always sadly out of place in artistic company (Au, 170), but he was more likely unable to affect the emotional extremes necessary to compete with Yeats for the limelight. Certainly, Rolleston was a more sober, less vitally imaginative personality, whose professional choices brought him less success than Yeats enjoyed. In the controversy at the Irish Literary Society (1892) over whose work should be chosen to represent the new cultural movement, Rolleston sided with the somewhat reactionary Charles Gavan Duffy and his nationalist view of art. He thus alienated himself from Yeats and the new breed of poets who would come to characterize the Irish literary renaissance. Supplied with the same practical advantages that Yeats had had at the beginning of his career, Rolleston fell far short of his contemporary's achievements. His notably handsome face led others to believe in greater artistic substance beneath, but his strained and rollicksome verse perpetuated the worst aspects of an already dying mode.

III. Yeats and William Morris

In April 1886, William Morris visited the Contemporary Club, expanding its members' hopes for cultural exchange beyond the usual parochial concerns. Morris had by this time become engrossed in the political activities that were to occupy his final years, and this journey to Ireland was part of a larger campaign to establish support for the emergence of a unified Socialist party. Earlier in the day, he had spoken at a working men's club and had been largely unsuccessful in converting them to his ideas. He met with similar resistance at the Contemporary Club, but a small group of compassionate Irishmen managed to take him aside and engage him in less incendiary topics. Whether this reprieve was actually what Morris wanted is somewhat to be doubted, but it obviously helped him survive the evening, and it helped those who detained him establish contact with a recognized literary father figure. Stephen Gwynn, a member of the Club, recalls the event:

> Three or four clever young political barristers fell upon him, and from their exceedingly different points of view worried the poor great man with arguments and statistics; made him contradict himself, and having demonstrated clearly that he was a very puzzle-headed old gentleman, returned to the more congenial task of quarrelling about the latest Land Bill. Three or four of us

> who cared more about other things than Land Bills succeeded in drawing him into a corner, where he discoursed upon sagas to Yeats and upon stained glass to Walter Osborne, whose names, then unknown, are now sufficiently familiar. (GELM, 43-4)

Yeats's kindness on that occasion, his interest and knowledgeability in areas traditionally close to Morris's heart, undoubtedly made their impression on him and provided Yeats with access to yet another society of artists and intellectuals. Soon after his arrival in London in 1887, he began attending Morris's socialist meetings at Kelmscott House in Hammersmith—a spot where most of literary and artistic London gathered at one time or another, to discuss issues pertaining to socialism or simply to be seen among the artistic *élite*.

Socialist League lectures were generally given in the longhut at the top of Morris's garden. After these meetings, Morris would occasionally invite a select group of members to dine at his house and discuss the issues of the day. Yeats himself was invited to join this group with the hope that he would commit himself to the political effort, but the young poet was more interested in Morris as a literary figure than as a political activist and quietly resisted the opportunity that was being forced upon him. On June 25, Yeats wrote to Katherine Tynan, indicating both his intoxication with and reluctance concerning this new affiliation:

> Last Sunday evening I had supper at Morris's. Pictures by Rossetti all round the walls, and in the middle much Socialistic conversation. Morris asked me to write for the Commonweal on the Irish Question. However, though I think Socialism good work, I am not quite sure it is my work.
> (TFY, 269)

Yeats's association with Morris promised rich professional

rewards, although the most significant benefit he would reap from this pursuit—that of making the acquaintance of Ernest Rhys and Ernest Radford, future members of the Rhymers' Club, or of Frances Fahy, founder of the Southwark Literary Club,[6] are different from his initial expectations. Morris had many literary contacts, but provided no outlet for Yeats's interests in folklore and religion, nor did he write reviews of Yeats's work. With the exception of the pages he might solicit for socialism, Morris, indeed, offered few contributions to Yeats's career, and it was becoming evident to the younger man that even the ideological bond that existed between them was not as firm as he had once assumed. Proof that Yeats's association with Morris had been at least partially practical may be seen in an anecdote concerning conditions "shortly before" Yeats left the Socialist League. In this scenario, Yeats assumes the validity of his own entrepreneurial attempts while implicitly berating Morris's fascination with and appreciation of details of *décor*:

> I had sent my *Wanderings of Usheen* to his daughter, hoping of course that it might meet his eyes, and soon after sending it I came upon him by chance in Holborn—"You write my sort of poetry," he said and began to praise me and promise to send his praise to the *Commonwealth* [sic] the League organ, and he would have said more had he not caught sight of a new ornamental cast-iron lamp-post and got very heated upon that subject. (Au, 146)

This event evidently cured Yeats of whatever expectations he might have had *vis à vis* the former Pre-Raphaelite, and it certainly prepared him for his ultimate rift with the Socialists. The decision to break with that group came after an impassioned outburst over religion, which Yeats delivered with all the commitment and rhetorical skill he had learned at the Contemporary Club. To his surprise, Morris cut him off in mid-sentence, and the young poet, stung by the callousness and lack of vision of his mentor, never returned again.

Yeats learned that evening of the limited use of "heated argument" and thereafter trimmed his temper to fit his audience's expectations more closely. His relations with W. E. Henley, a Scotsman of notorious irascibility, were more deferential and, thus, more professionally rewarding than with Morris, and his demeanor at the Rhymers' Club, if not always acceptable in terms of aesthetic practice, was based on the principle that one should persuade one's audience through the subtlest means available. "Violent energy," he would say with regard to John Davidson, "which is like a fire of straw, consumes in a few minutes the nervous vitality, and is useless in the arts" (Au, 318). From that moment onward, he would nurture patience and craft, as Hamlet had done, using his play to catch the conscience of the king.

IV. Edwin Ellis and John Todhunter

In addition to the Contemporary Club and to William Morris's Socialist League meetings, Yeats's home environment provided an important precedent for the Rhymers' Club and an opportunity to meet other father figures. At Terenure (Ashfield Terrace, Dublin), the family's lodgings had been too small to entertain guests, but after moving to the artistic community of Bedford Park (3 Blenheim Road, London) in 1888,[7] John Butler Yeats kept his home vibrant with enquiring minds and intellectual conversation. Here, he renewed old acquaintances with Edwin J. Ellis—a friend from his days at Heatherley's Art School—and John Todhunter—a doctor turned playwright whom he had known from his law school days at Trinity College Dublin. He also made new friends, primarily through the local club The Calumet, to which Todhunter and Yeats's neighbor Elkin Mathews belonged. Willie Yeats, as he then was called, participated in many of these evenings, deriving much of his literary education from discussions with more informed individuals and meeting people who would be helpful to his career. He had learned the importance of social contacts, and he cultivated these friendships as he would those of his peers.

Both Ellis and Todhunter had married women whom the elder Yeats found difficult to tolerate, and as his relationship with these individuals became strained, his son's ties with them became more secure. Todhunter, who had followed W. B. Yeats's career from the beginning,[8] was devoting himself full-time to poetry and drama, and his experiments in poetic drama must have intrigued the young man, who had patterned his speech and actions after Hamlet and who later brought his own poetic talents to the stage.[9] With Ellis, conversations tended towards William Blake, a figure whom the English painter had long worshipped and who had provided the spiritual focus for his and J.B. Yeats's earlier association, The Brotherhood. Yeats's mystical beliefs and occult experiences, as well as his efforts to include them in his poetry, corresponded naturally with his interest in Blake, and before long he and Ellis had begun editing Blake's work, a project that was to culminate in the three-volume edition of February 1893. When Yeats helped organize the Rhymers' Club in 1890, Edwin Ellis and John Todhunter, although both ssignificantly older than the poet, came along as original members. Neither brought as much artistic talent into the group as Yeats, but each offered expertise in areas crucial to Yeats's future development.

V. Ernest Rhys

Ernest Rhys, a co-founder of the Rhymers' Club and editor for Yeats's *Fairy and Folk Tales of the Irish Peasantry* (1888), came to London from Newcastle-on-Tyne in January 1886. A mining engineer by training, Rhys had acquired literary ambitions along the way, and eventually decided to abandon his coal mining activities in favor of a career in letters. In London, he was introduced to artistic and political societies by his boyhood friend Percival Chubb and met at these meetings individuals who would play a significant role in his immediate future. He also became general editor for the Camelot series, a new series of shilling reprints that would provide employment for many of Rhys's early associates. At the Fellowship of the New Life, an organization that patterned itself after the cultural idealism of

Whitman and Thoreau, he met Havelock Ellis. At Fabian meetings, he would get to know Ernest Radford, another future Rhymer, and at William Morris's Socialist League meetings in Hammersmith, he would make the acquaintance of W. B. Yeats.

Rhys speaks of his initial encounter with Yeats in the *Fortnightly Review* ("W. B. Yeats: Early Recollections," FR [July, 1935]: 52-7) and in his memoir *Wales England Wed* (91ff), and, although some of the details of this account are inconsistent with verifiable facts, one can derive from it a clear picture both of the young Yeats and of the easily-captivated Rhys. According to both sources, Rhys had attended a lecture given by Morris on "Useful Work and Useless Toil," after which Morris had complimented him on his recently published *Malory's King Arthur and the Quest of the Holy Grail* and had invited him to dinner. Around the great Pre-Raphaelite's table at Kelmscott House sat Prince Kropotkin, "most urbane of revolutionaries," dramatist George Bernard Shaw, and "a very pale, exceedingly thin, young man with a raven lock over his forehead" (FR, 52). This figure turned out to be Yeats, introduced after supper as "an unknown Irish poet...whose first poems were about to appear."[10] Rhys and Yeats settled into an extended conversation and at the end of the evening left Morris's together, the latter exuding all manner of ingenuousness and Celtic charm:

> It was getting late and Yeats missed his train at Hammersmith station. But he did not mind that at all, and seemed to regard trains as things that came and went at random. He talked eagerly, continuously, in a soft Irish voice, quite content, late as it was, to walk on towards Chelsea with me. On the way he regaled me with two Irish stories in which I noticed how he relished the names, putting "a leaf on his tongue" (as the Welsh say) and lengthening out words like TIR-NAN-OGUE. We stood talking until midnight under a lamp-

post at the end of World's End Passage and when
we parted he was uncertain which way to go.
(FR, 52-3)

This meeting between the two young writers answered some of the social and professional needs of both parties and provided a friendship whereby they could exercise some control over their literary environment. In addition to securing a plausible outlet for his work, Yeats found in Rhys an enthusiastic audience, one who could accept and appreciate his poetic attire and histrionic poses. For his own part, Rhys gained another writer for the Camelot series and reaffirmed his sense of belonging to the artistic community.

A willing correspondent for Yeats's self-dramatizing personality, Rhys reveals in his rendition of the evening the same tendency toward factual omissions characteristic of mythical accounts: Eardley Crescent, where the Yeatses then resided, was within walking distance of Hammersmith Station and in the general direction of Rhys's Chelsea address.[11] Since both the poet and his family were poor, it seems unlikely that he intended to spend money on a train or would be concerned with their comings and goings. Midnight was not an unreasonable hour for a young man of twenty-two to be out in London, especially if he had just met a companion who not only shared his literary interests but who was in a position to offer practical assistance to the development and publication of those interests. And if Yeats seemed uncertain of the precise direction home, so would almost anyone who had as yet lived only a few months in the city. Rhys's account blurs these considerations, not simply because he has forgotten the details of the event but presumably because he wishes to enhance its taleworthiness. Written some years after Yeats had established himself as a poet, this rendition also anticipates the reader's expectations, confirming Yeats's image as a unique or somehow charmed personality who would fulfill the promise suggested by his idiosyncracies. Details of the evening have faded, but the overall excitement and awe—the sense that Rhys had once been intimate with greatness—remains. Whether he ever saw beyond the Mask to Yeats's true personality is doubtful, since he himself was so wrapped up in the Mask. Like so many of his contemporaries, he needed the mythical construct to justify or support his own estimation of himself.

Yeats's account of Rhys, on the other hand, omits such literary spell-binding, and one assumes that, privately at least, he accurately judged the talents and usefulness of his associates. In a letter to Katherine Tynan, 18 May 1887, he contrasted his new friend's straightforward personality with the glib insincerity of the literati he had met, quickly pointing to the advantages both of Rhys's Celtic enthusiasms and of his literary connections. "I recommended your poems to him strongly," he said, "... a friend of his is editing for the Canterbury poets' a book of Irish songs."[12] In another letter to Tynan on 31 May, Yeats alluded to Rhys as "a not brilliant but very earnest Welshman"; and in June he characterized the two basic types of London literati, placing Rhys in the more favorable group of sound but undirected intelligence:

> London literary folk seem to divide into two classes; the stupid men with brains and the clever ones without any. Sparling, I fear, belongs to the latter; Ernest Rhys and possibly Mr. Ranking, to the first. The latter is the most numerous—young men possessing only an indolent and restless talent that warms nothing and lights nothing.
> (To Katherine Tynan [25 June 1887] in L, 41)

Yeats's estimation was not totally out of keeping with Rhys's actual progress to that point. He had got the job as editor of the Camelot Classics at least in part because the publishers had mistaken him for the Oxford don and Celtic scholar, John Rhys. His first publishing opportunity, as an editor of George Herbert's poems—had come to him through the offices of his old friend Joseph Skipsey. He had not worked his way up in the world of art, nor had he delineated the specific path his ambition would take, but had stepped more or less directly from mining engineer to man of letters, without experiencing the obligatory hunger for success. Unlike Yeats, he lacked the need to think of his artistic "adventure" in absolute practical terms and, thus, did not develop the entrepreneurial shrewdness that would have helped him improve his fortune or continue as an artist once that fortune ran out.

Yet Rhys had a genuine sense of the nobility of his craft and stood ready to do what he could to further the cause of art. In typical careerist fashion, Yeats took advantage of this willingness and saw in it an extension of his own impulses and needs. On 24 January 1889, he wrote to John O'Leary concerning the project Rhys had undertaken for him and hinting at the projects he would eventually be called upon to complete:

> He is going to do an article on my book called "New Celtic Poetry" and I do not see why he should not say a good word for the ballad book. Besides it would just suit him to discover a school of writers—he is always searching for schools in most unlikely places, especially Celtic ones being a most truculent Welshman.[13]

Rhys's interest in Celtic matters, his connections with the London publishing world and with London artists compensated for his limited poetic talents and made him an important associate in Yeats's mind. Not only could he promote the books that were crucial to the Irish cause, but he could appreciate the need for artistic fellowship that led to the founding of poetic schools. His gregariousness and enthusiasm ultimately made the Rhymers' Club possible, and if this group did not come to constitute an actual school, it did offer a forum for Yeats's Celtic interests and provided the support necessary for continued publications and increased critical attention.

VI. Herbert Horne

Rhys seems to have met Herbert Horne almost immediately

upon his arrival in London.¹⁴ Horne, who had been apprenticed to Arthur Mackmurdo in architecture and who had recently (1885) become his partner at the Century Guild, had a studio at the end of Paradise Walk, not far from Rhys's abode at 59 Cheyne Walk. Rhys's memoirs indicate that he became close friends with Horne's family as well, and a letter from Selwyn Image to Herbert Horne, dated September 1886, shows that he knew the principal members of the Century Guild at least by that date (Letter to Churchill Osborne, 12 November 1884, AS, 33). This connection proves crucial in terms of the Rhymers' Club, since the Century Guild and later the Fitzroy Establishment provided both spiritual influences and actual membership for the expanded and reconstituted Rhymers' Club of 1891. Rhys attended the literary gatherings at the Fitzroy Establishment—very likely at Horne's invitation—and met there such future Rhymers as Lionel Johnson, Ernest Dowson and Victor Plarr.

By March 1888, when Dowson was just arriving in London, Yeats was sufficiently well-acquainted with Horne to write letters from his office, and, although he claims in *Autobiographies* that he never became intimate with Horne (Au, 168), the circumstances and substance of his letter indicate that the two were at least on business terms:

> I have been busy these last two days making up material in the British Museum reading room for a story about Father John O'Hart.
>
> Horne has just come in and tells me that your poem will be in the next *Hobby Horse*.
>
> I was at the Southwark Literary Club last night. Crilly lectured on Miss Fanny Parnell.
>
> I must finish this now as I want to talk to Horne.
>
>   Your friend,
>   W. B. Yeats
> (To Katherine Tynan, in L, 65)

Part of Yeats's business involved placing Katherine Tynan's poems in the *Hobby Horse*, a favor which she returned by selling subscriptions for *The Wanderings of Oisin* and which Horne furthered by including her in his widening circle of literary associates. Yeats's determination to keep Tynan involved in his developing drama acknowledged the advantages of cultural exchange and the increasing attractiveness of Irish art in English circles.

The Fitzroy Street connection exposed Yeats to major ideas and trends in contemporary culture, and its obvious Oxford ties provided him with a less parochial audience than he had previously known. Both Mackmurdo and Image had been students of Ruskin, who was, from 1869 onward, Slade Professor of Fine Art at Oxford. Lionel Johnson, a *protégé* of Walter Pater, was an accomplished classicist at New College. Ernest Dowson, whom Johnson had met while Dowson was at Queens, had left the University without a degree, but had acquired valuable understanding of classical and continental literature and exercised strong technical gifts in poetry. Victor Plarr, who graduated from Worcester College with a degree in Modern History exerted less of a direct literary influence than the rest, but his continental heritage and conscientious attitude toward craft made him worthy in his own right. Yeats came to know these individuals through his connections with Rhys and Horne, and he made the most of the opportunity, realizing that their knowledge and willingness to share what they knew would have to compensate for his own lack of university training.

VII. Arthur Symons

Rhys introduced Yeats to Arthur Symons early on in the poet's residence in London, and the latter went on to become not only a central figure at the Rhymers' Club but a very close literary friend. Like Yeats, Symons had a shrewd business sense and was able to make the most of his personal contacts almost from the beginning of his career. His poetic abilities, however, were more limited than Yeats's, and he was able to command an appreciative audience only for that period of time in which decadence enjoyed a degree of popularity. His attack of madness in 1908 put an end to his artistic hopes, but his field and degree of achievement had been determined long before that date.

Symons was still living at home with his family in Nuneaton, Coventry, when he wrote the article on Frederei Mistral that would launch him on his literary career. In November 1884, the *National Review* accepted the article, and, when it was published in January 1886, it attracted the attention of Havelock Ellis, then the general editor of the Mermaid Series. Delighted with Symons's style and having heard that the young writer was editing some plays of Shakespeare,[15] Ellis wrote to invite him to do a similar task with Philip Massinger's plays for the Mermaid Series. Symons accepted and began work in July of that year. The two exchanged letters concerning the project, and, after a short time, arranged to meet at the National Gallery during one of Symons's visits to London.

Not long afterwards, Symons met another editor on the steps of the British Museum, where he was conducting research for the Shakespeare and Massinger projects. Ernest Rhys, who had met Havelock Ellis at the Fellowship of the New Life, sought editors for future editions of his Camelot Classics and, learning of Symons's experience in the field, engaged him to compile a volume of Leigh Hunt's essays. Whether Rhys's friendship with Ellis had anything to do with this meeting or the subsequent agreement is not known, but the two men seem to have established an immediate rapport. On 16 October 1886, Symons wrote to his former teacher Churchill Osborne, alluding to his editing responsibilities and offering an estimation of his new employer's literary capabilities:

> Don't abuse Ernest Rhys, the esteemed editor of the Camelot Classics for whom I am at present toiling and moiling over Leigh Hunt. He isn't much of a fellow as a writer; I can't stomach his style; but he is very friendly disposed.
> (AS, 41)

The friendly dispositions of both Rhys and Ellis allowed

Symons to come in contact with the rising stars on London's literary horizon, including future Rhymers Herbert Horne, Ernest Radford, John Davidson and W. B. Yeats. His friendship with Ellis also provided the occasion for his earliest visits to France in September 1889 and Spring 1890, where he met such important figures as Auguste Rodin, Stéphane Mallarmé, Paul Verlaine and Joris-Karl Huysmans. During his travels, Symons gained first-hand knowledge of the artistic innovations occurring in France and, thus, the authority to speak of them before an English audience. His interest in and study of French symbolism made him indispensible to his contemporaries and to future generations alike—but especially to the first major poet of the new century, W. B. Yeats, whom he dubbed in his dedication to *The Symbolist Movement in Literature* (1899) "the chief representative of that movement in our country" (SML, v).

A gifted entrepreneur, Symons established early contact with an important literary father figure, one who would determine the course of his future career. In 1886, he published *An Introduction to the Study of Browning* and sent a complimentary copy to Walter Pater. On 2 December, Pater wrote back thanking him for his "very interesting and useful volume," and expressing his desire to meet the author should he one day be able to stop by and see him at his London address. Pater also expressed his admiration publicly, writing in the *Guardian* on 9 November 1887, that Symons demonstrated "real refinement and grace" and enthusiastically calling "for work from his hands of larger scope than this small volume" (1709). This gesture of friendship resulted in concrete professional aid for Symons. Not only did he gain an apologist for his early work, but he found in Pater an able and dedicated critic, one who could provide valuable inspiration and advice. In addition, his association with Pater made him an acceptable member of the Rhymers' Club, especially to those of the Fitzroy group (Johnson, Dowson, Horne) whose literary views were uncompromisingly Paterian.

In the interim between their first correspondence and their actual meeting in December 1888, Symons sent Pater a constant flow of work and ultimately sought his advice concerning the proper course for his career. His answer came in a letter of 8 January 1888, with Pater noting that he had poetic talent, remarkable "for precise and intellectual grasp on the matter it deals with," but advising Symons to seek his livelihood in prose:

> The young poet comes into a generation which has produced a large amount of first-rate poetry, and an enormous amount of good secondary poetry. You know I give a high place to the literature of prose as a fine art, and therefore hope you won't think me brutal in saying that the admirable qualities of your verse are those also of imaginative prose; as I think is the case also with much of Browning's finest verse. I should say, make prose your principal metier as a man of letters, and publish your verse as a more intimate gift for those who already value you for your pedestrian work in literature. (LWP, 121-2)

Pater's estimation of Symons's prospects was borne out later in his career. Symons continued to write and publish verse throughout the nineties, but it never progressed beyond the level of good secondary poetry, and it appealed mostly to those who knew and approved of his larger critical stance. His prose, however, earned him a name in the tradition—specifically, his efforts to make the principles and techniques of French symbolism available to the English mind. By the time of his breakdown in 1908, he had written several volumes of verse, as well as numerous critical essays, and had served as contributing editor to the *Savoy*. But his key work, *The Symbolist Movement in Literature* survived these attempts at greatness, attracting the attention of poets such as Eliot and Pound, who built new systems upon the notions it espoused. One cannot know if Symons would have achieved greater poetic fame had he not been stricken by madness, but he seems to have been cut out for a minor, supporting role in the poetic revolution of the new century.

VIII. W. B. Yeats and W. E. Henley

W. B. Yeats met William Ernest Henley in the summer of 1888, approximately one year after he had moved to London. Editor of the *Scots Observer*, Henley stood at the center of a group of journalists who frequented Solferino's Restaurant in Rupert Street, held Thursday night debates at the home of the artist Joseph Pennell and met Sunday evenings at Henley's own home, not far from Bedford Park on the Richmond Road.[16] Henley's Tory imperialist politics and anti-Pre-Raphaelite attitudes were contrary to Yeats's most basic instincts, but this discrepancy did not alter his admiration for the man or his willingness to align himself with his circle once relations with Morris had broken down. Indeed, Yeats placed his first loyalty in his art, and he subordinated political and even aesthetic differences to considerations of prospective professional reward. In return, Henley offered him enthusiastic verbal support, access to new literary contacts, as well as direct and indirect publishing opportunities.

The immediate circle of writers who gathered around Henley and whom Max Beerbohm would name "The Henley Regatta" consisted of such figures as Charles Whibley, R. A. M. Stevenson, Gilbert Parker and Kenneth Grahame.[17] For the most part, these "journalists" held little interest for Yeats, and, as he wrote to Katherine Tynan on 30 August 1888, he would not have associated with them at all had it not been for his essential regard for Henley. "They have ceased to be self-centered," he complained, "... have given up their individuality"(L, 83). This failure to be "self-centered" had deprived these writers of whatever uniqueness they might have had and made them as a group devoid of dramatic or intellectual interest. With the exception of Henley, they inspired little professional or personal confidence and gave him none of the rewards he expected from literary fellowship.

Yeats's interest in Henley, however, much like his interest in Rhys, had little to do with his respect for his mentor's artistic abilities. In the letter to Katherine Tynan, dated 30 August 1888, he spoke of Henley's book (*A Book of Verses*, May 1888), as "a wonderful affair if it was not so cobwebby"(L, 83), and in a later letter to Tynan, dated after 6 September 1888, he repeated his comment, comparing Henley's work to that of Meredith:

> Lately I have read much of George Meredith's poems. They are certainly very beautiful, and have far more suavity and serenity than I had expected. Henley is very cobwebby after them and not very spontaneous. To me Henley's great fault is his form. It is never accidental but always preconceived. His poems are forced into a mould. I dislike the school to which he belongs. A poem should be a law to itself as plants and beasts are. It may be ever so much finished, but all finish should merely make plain that law. (L, 86)

Yeats later claimed that he objected to Henley's verse primarily because it was written in *vers libre* (Au, 125), but here he seems to be arguing from the opposite point of view. "Cobwebby" in this text evidently refers to forced or archaic diction, encouraged by the poet's attempt to make his thought fit a preconceived form, and the argument that a poem "should be a law to itself" is clearly a statement in favor of formal adaptability, remarkably similar to Pater's idea of organic form. The opacity of Yeats's terminology, however, and the inconsistency of his later justification with reasons given contemporaneously make one wonder if he knew precisely why he objected to Henley's verse or what methods he would have used to achieve the preferred effect. In *Reveries Over Childhood and Youth*, he admits having had difficulty with meter in the early stages of his career,[18] and his later complaint concerning *vers libre* may be a mark of his initial confusion or of the transitional state in which he had been working. "Years afterwards," he notes, "when I had finished *The Wanderings of Oisin* . . . I deliberately reshaped my style . . . I cast off traditional metaphors and loosened my rhythm, and recognising that all the criticism of life known to me was alien and English, became as emotional as possible but with an emotion which I described to myself as cold"(Au, 67).

The process of loosening and casting off, however, began somewhat earlier than Yeats admits. Reacting to early reviews of *Oisin*, he wrote to John O'Leary and depicted himself as a revolutionary in matters of style. "If my style is new," he explained, "it will get plenty more such for many a long day. Even Tennyson was charged with obscurity, and as to charges of word torturing etc. the first thing one notices in a new country is its outlandishness, after a time it's [sic] dress and customs seem as natural as any others"(3 February 1889, MS 5925, NLI). It seems that Yeats did not respond naturally to the requirements of traditional meter or the accepted modes of poetic presentation, but had a sense of what he liked in verse and sought ways of obtaining it. The forced or artificial diction characteristic of Henley's lines did not please him, and he turned away from this example towards a more ingenuous means of expression. The urge for new forms and the receptivity to Paterian directives were both present, waiting for the proper catalyst to fire them, and Yeats clearly understood Henley's comparative uselessness as an artistic advisor.

If Yeats did not find in Henley the example he sought, he did gain through him an outlet for his Irish studies, as well as other paying literary occupations at a time when cash was scarce. Henley recommended him to the editor of *The Dictionary of National Biography*, who commissioned him to write an essay on the blind Gaelic poet Hefernan; as well as to the editor of *Chambers's Encyclopaedia*, who was to consider him an expert on Irish subjects. In addition, he made the pages of the *Scots Observer* available to Yeats's essays, stories, poems and reviews, beginning with the publication of "Scotch and Irish Fairies" in March 1888. Unlike Morris, Henley was willing to praise his *protégé* for his literary successes, and he reviewed *The Wanderings of Oisin* as a volume written by one who could "speak out with the right heroic accent, and kindle the blood with tales"("A New Irish Poet," SO [9 March 1889]). However narrow-minded Henley may have been politically, he was sufficiently liberal in an artistic sense to promote Yeats's own interests, and the sheer practical rewards of this relationship made it more valuable to Yeats than his association with Morris. Significantly, the younger poet had cultivated his relationship with Henley despite the ideological differences between them, and his willingness to put up with Henley's journalistic friends indicates the extent and strength of his careerist ambitions.

IX. Oscar Wilde

One frequenter of Henley's evenings whom Yeats did not disdain and who would exercise an important spiritual influence over the Rhymers' Club was Oscar Wilde. Wilde and Henley had met several years earlier through the introduction of Edwin Bale, a mutual friend at Cassell's, and they continued to associate with each other until July 1890, when the *National Observer* initiated hostilities between them with an antagonistic review of *The Picture of Dorian Gray*.[19]

In December 1888, well before the rupture took place, both Yeats and Wilde happened to be at one of Henley's Sunday night meetings, and Wilde, very much in character, captivated his young listener with his usual host of *bons mots*. In *The Trembling of the Veil*, Yeats remembers that Wilde effusively praised Pater's *Studies in the History of the Renaissance*, labelling it his "golden book,"[20] and proclaiming that it was "the very flower of decadence." The volume in question had proved a touchstone of aesthetic criticism since its first publication in 1873, and Pater's demand that the critic possess "the power of being deeply moved by the presence of beautiful objects" had sent his followers out to seek "new experiences, new subjects of poetry, new forms of art"(PR, 2). "The last trumpet should have sounded the moment it was written," Wilde announced with histrionic vigor to those around him (Au, 80)—unaware that for some the last trumpet had sounded, that their pursuit of this goal would leave them vulnerable to desires they could neither control nor satisfy. The same histrionic sense and desire for experience would lead Wilde himself to the dock at Old Bailey and ultimately to his personal and professional destruction at the hands of Victorian

Society.

At the time of his first meeting with Yeats, Wilde was already acquainted with several of the artists who would eventually compose the Rhymers' Club, and, if he was not personally responsible for introducing him to Fitzroy, he did make that association firmer by serving as a much-admired, mutual friend. By the time he had left Oxford, Wilde's sexual preference for young males had been established, and his intimacy with such figures as Frank Miles and Arthur May had initiated a lifestyle that would not be broken with his marriage to Constance Lloyd in 1884 (See ULOW). This is not to say that his relationship with the poets of the Rhymers' Club stemmed from purely sexual motives, but that social and artistic affairs were often conflated in his mind and much of his entrepreneurial activity in artistic circles took on the flavor of elaborate courtship. Wilde's charm, wit, natural generosity and professional success made him a focus of interest to young artists in the city, and if some particularly talented young man failed to seek him out first, Wilde usually managed to draw him into his circle of influence. He and Herbert Horne had been acquaintances at least since August 1886, when they planned to establish a memorial plaque to Thomas Chatterton.[21] Richard Le Gallienne attended his lecture on "Personal Impressions of America and Her People" in Birkenhead, December 1883, and several years afterwards sent him a complimentary copy of his poems (*My Lady's Sonnets*, privately published 1887). Greeted with enthusiastic thanks and extensions of hospitality, Le Gallienne visited his mentor in September 1887, and returned in June of the following year to spend three days at Tite Street.[22] "With Oscar Wilde," Le Gallienne's commemorative poem begins, "A summer-day/Passed like a yearning kiss away . . . ". Arthur Symons's work on and interest in Walter Pater had attracted Wilde's attention by October 1887, to the extent that Wilde began asking about him to a mutual friend, Olive Schreiner (Letter, Arthur Symons to J. D. Campbell, 8 October 1887, BM Add. Ms. 49522). By December of the same year, Symons was contributing to Wilde's *Woman's World* and receiving appreciative notes from its editor. Ernest

Dowson made Wilde's acquaintance after leaving Oxford in 1888, most likely through his connections at Fitzroy. When evidence of Dowson's poetic talent began to make him a figure of some promise, Wilde invited him to luncheon at the Cafe Royale, an honor reserved for the most distinguished of guests. Yeats encountered Wilde at Henley's, probably after having heard a great deal about him from his Irish and Fitzroy Street connections. Wilde invited him to Christmas dinner and afterwards reviewed his Fairy and Folktale book and *Oisin* charitably in both *Woman's World* and the *Pall Mall Gazette*.[23] Coming into Yeats's life as he did, at a time when the younger man was hungry for examples, Wilde offered him an approach to art and experience that fit his dramatic and poetic instincts, as well as direct support for his career in the form of literary reviews. Yeats's identification with Pater's aestheticism, although never as fully developed as that of Symons, Johnson or Dowson, took him away from Henley's influence, closer to those attitudes that would dominate at the Rhymers' Club. A charismatic personality and an Irishman as well, Oscar Wilde played an important role in this process.

X. Oscar Wilde and Lionel Johnson

Another role-player in the Yeatsian drama was Lionel Johnson. Instrumental in determining the direction the Rhymers' Club would take and in Wilde's ultimate tragedy, he too had sought a conceptual father, but the solutions he found were appreciably different from Yeats's and the cost to him personally was high. As Wilde had been in the seventies so was Johnson in the eighties a disciple and favorite of Pater. After leaving Oxford, Wilde kept in touch with his former master, and when Pater spoke to him about one of his students who wanted to model his life after *Marius the Epicurean*, his curiosity was aroused. Wilde's relationship with Johnson was perhaps more directly sexual than any of the other Rhymers mentioned and, for this reason, was more psychologically damaging once time and moral position came between them.

Wilde met Johnson on a visit to Oxford in February 1890.

He had come up from London to visit Pater, oversee a production of Browning's *Strafford* and get his first glimpse of Pater's young Epicurean disciple. Johnson records the event in a letter to Arthur Galton:

> On Saturday at mid-day, lying half asleep in bed, reading Green, I was aroused by a pathetic and unexplained note from Oscar; he plaintively besought me to get up and see him. Which I did: I found him as delightful as Green is not. He discoursed, with infinite flippancy, of everyone: lauded the *Dial* laughed at Pater: and consumed all my cigarettes. I am in love with him. He has come to visit Pater; and to see Strafford.
> (OWL, n., 254-5)

Innocently expressed, Johnson's proclamation of love presaged the agony of future events. At Winchester School, he had belonged to a homosexual circle of young boys, exploring inclinations that would continue to influence his life at Oxford. But Johnson was also a strongly religious individual, and he would affirm that religiosity with his baptism into the Catholic Church, 22 June 1891—shortly after having introduced his long-time friend Lord Alfred Douglas to Oscar Wilde. Johnson's initial delight over Wilde's irreverence and charm, his expression and experience of love, would evolve from that point into a more complicated state of mind, as his moral code began to conflict not only with his own sensual drives but with those of others. Johnson wrote a review of the *Strafford* productions, published in the April 1890 edition of the *Hobby Horse* and later in the year wrote a poem in praise of the author of *Dorian Gray*. A metrical imitation of the *Stabat Mater*, this poem includes Johnson himself in its appreciation and depiction of the decadent spirit:

In Honorem Doriani Creatorisque Eius

BENEDICTUS sis, Oscare!

Qui me libro hoc dignare
  Propter amicitias:
Modo modulans Romano
Laudes dignas Doriano,
  Ago tibi gratias.

Juventutis hic formosa
Floret inter rosas rosa
  Subito dum venit mors:
Ecce Homo! ecce Deus!
Si sic modo esset meus
  Genius misericors!

Amat avidus amores
Miros, miros carpit flores
  Saevus pulchritudine:
Quanto anima nigrescit,
Tanto facies splendescit,
  Mendax, sed quam splendide!

Hic sunt poma Sodomorum;
Hic sunt corda vitiorum;
  Et peccata dulcia.
In excelsis et infernis,
Tibi sit, qui tanta cernis,
  Gloriarum gloria.[24]

This ode to one "who discerns so well" was countered a year later by a poem anticipating the scandal of Douglas and Wilde's relationship. "The Destroyer of a Soul" speaks of sin that is no longer sweet, no longer fierce with beauty, but cold and corrupting, as Johnson now blames Wilde for depriving Douglas of his goodness and innocence:

  That I should dare forgive a sin so great,
  As this, through which I sit disconsolate;
  Mourning for that live soul, I used to see;

> Soul of a saint, whose friend I used to be:
> Till you came by! a cold, corrupting, fate.
> (LJP, 74)

Finding in Wilde behavior he now deplored, Johnson struggled in a conflict between love and hate. The tragedy rested not only in Wilde's indulgence in forbidden pleasures but in Johnson's inadvertant complicity in corrupting an innocent friend. Suddenly, the sins which had made for such excitement and sweetness in art took on a new and threatening cast in life, and the inconsistency between the two domains—between provocative artistic expression and acceptable social behavior—generated a dilemma which Johnson could not ultimately resolve.

The meeting with Johnson had affected Wilde as well, provoking in him further curiosity concerning the young man's character. After returning to London, he penned Johnson an apology for not having seen more of him and expressing the desire that they get to know each other better:

> Dear Mr. Johnson, I was so sorry I could not get back, to see you again, but I was dragged to the theatre to see the realization of some suggestions I had made, and could not get away till just before my train started.
>
> I hope you will let me know when you are in town. I like your poetry—the little I have seen of it—so much, that I want to know the poet as well.
>
> It was very good of you getting up to see me. I was determined to meet you before I left Oxford.
>   Believe me, yours very truly,
>   OSCAR WILDE
> (c. 16 February 1890, [OWL, 254-5])

Wilde's interest in Johnson was artistically genuine, brought about by Pater's statement that he was a talented young poet and a follower of the aesthetic school, but it was also influenced by his basic, libidinous impulses and the fact that Johnson was a diminutive though strikingly handsome young man. Somewhat narcissistically, Wilde needed to have such individuals around him, and he exerted a great deal of energy securing their attention. He flattered them, appealed to their literary ambitions, thrilled them with his own verbal dexterity and with his notoreity, and they in turn doted on him with all the mysterious abandon of impressionable youth. It is doubtful that Wilde and Johnson's relationship was ever physically consummated, but the effects of this infatuation penetrated into and influenced the atmosphere at the Rhymers' Club. Victor Plarr, whose own sense of sobriety gave him insights that others did not have, affirmed the aura of splendor that Wilde enjoyed and the power he had over various members:

> And round Oscar Wilde, not then under a cloud, hovered reverently Lionel Johnson and Ernest Dowson, with others. This must have been in 1891, and I marvelled at the time to notice the fascination which poor Wilde exercised over the otherwise rational. He sat as it were enthroned and surrounded by a deferential circle.
> (EDP, 64)

Like Dorian Gray, or perhaps more justly, Dorian's mentor, Lord Henry Wotton, Wilde would toy with and explore the fascinations of the homosexual underworld, finding in what was then socially unacceptable behavior an excitement that could transform simple life into art. Intoxicated with his growing circle of young men and with the elaborate Masks and falsehoods he established to shock and mislead the masses, he forgot the distinctions to be drawn between art and truth—distinctions that would not be overlooked by the unimaginative bourgeoisie. The cloud that Plarr referred to would eventually overtake him, and, when it did, many of the most dedicated aesthetes would run for cover, leaving the great instigator to face the storm alone.

Richard Le Gallienne

Richard Le Gallienne was one devotee who, like Johnson, eventually deserted Wilde. Before doing so, however, he allowed himself to benefit from his friendship, without ever going so far as to engage himself physically.[25] The son of a businessman, Le Gallienne—or Gallienne, as the family's name was properly called—studied accountancy to please his father and gain some hope of financial stability later on in life. But Richard was a poet in temperament, and his poetic good looks helped him escape the prospect of businesses and office life. James Lewis May recalls with awe his "pale chiselled features, shadowed by long, wavy, raven-black hair"(PTW, 168), which made him such a striking presence at the Bodley Head bookstore, and Stephen Gwynn attests to the general sensation he would cause at parties, inspiring in others the conviction that he must be either a poet or a god:

> His good looks were dazzling; the profuse black hair with a ripple in it, parted in the middle and combed out sideways in medieval Italian fashion, set off his fine regular features and wide eyes. Beauty so obvious and so cultivated is rather disconcerting in a man, and Le Gallienne's looks were discussed in his presence as if he were some beautiful woman. (GELM, 138)

At a time when literary dandyism was fashionable, a poet's physical appearance was crucial, and Le Gallienne was able to the make most of his. Wilson Barrett, the actor, was his first conquest, having met him in September 1887 after a performance of "Chatterton" at the Royal Court Theatre in Liverpool (*Critic*, [9 June 1894]: 399-400). Impressed by the young man's carriage and beautiful eyes, Barrett proclaimed his desire to get to know him and eventually brought him to London as his personal secretary from February to October 1889. As Barrett's secretary, Le Gallienne came into contact with much of London's artistic and literary community, including Algernon Charles Swinburne, who was by that time a literary legend.

Le Gallienne also exercised the usual professional strategies. *My Lady's Sonnets* appeared in August 1887, and he forwarded copies to Oscar Wilde and other influential people. Wilde invited him to visit him at Tite Street, which he did in September 1887 and in the following year (June 1888), thus establishing a friendship that would open the doors to literary London. Wilde took him the rounds of the restaurants, theatres and cafes frequented by the artistic *élite*, gave him an introduction to Charles Sayle—and, thus, to Sayle's friends at Fitzroy[26] —as well as to the other remaining representative of the Pre-Raphaelite Movement, William Morris. Wilde also took an active concern in Le Gallienne's poetic future, serving on various occasions as an able professional advisor. His motivation for befriending the young man may have been attributable to an apprehension of his talent, but it certainly included an appreciation of his physical presence as well. Writing a note of thanks for a copy of Le Gallienne's second book of verse, Wilde reveals the more-than-professional dimension of his interest:

> My dear Le Gallienne, The lovely little book has just arrived, and I must send you a line to thank you for so charming a gift. Written by your own hand it has the very quintessence of grace and beauty, and the page on which I find my own name set daintily in dainty music is a real delight to me, for I think often of so young a poet who came here so wonderfully and so strangely, and whose memory is always with me.
>
> I hope to see you in London soon. I often think of your visit. Tomorrow I hope to read your book over. It shall be a day of gold and marked with a white pearl. But the singer should

> be here also. Bother space and time! they spoil
> life by allowing such a thing as distance.
> Ever Yours
> OSCAR WILDE
> (Postmarked 25 Oct. 1888 [OWL, 230-31])

While securing Oscar Wilde's favor and devotion, Le Gallienne proceeded with other aspects of his career. The editor of the *Academy* awarded him books to review on the strength of his first collection of verse, and John Lane, having read of the aspiring poet in the pages of that journal, wrote to him asking if they could meet.[27] From that encounter, came Le Gallienne's second book of poetry, *Volumes in Folio*, published March 1889 by the Bodley Head, an outlet for many future projects.[28] By January 1892, he had become such a trusted part of that establishment that he was asked to serve as Mathews and Lane's first reader. This connection proved important for the Rhymers' Club, since it secured the association between that group and its major publishing organ and it gave Le Gallienne a more-or-less permanent position in London's literary mainstream. Le Gallienne had negotiated the first difficult stages of his career with relative ease, benefitting from his ability to play the part of the poet and offering his verses to the appropriate sources of influence. It remained to be seen if he could grow in the role he had chosen for himself, developing his talents and good fortune to the point where they equalled his physical appearance.

By February 1890, Yeats had met many of the poets who would come to be associated with the Rhymers' Club. This process, however, was not as simply or as innocently achieved as he would have liked readers of his *Autobiographies* to believe, but was the result of a conscious and continual effort to make contact with individuals whose interests were similar to his own and to benefit in whatever way possible from their acquaintance. Others of the group had demonstrated similar instincts for self-dramatization and artistic control, but it was their practical understanding of how to advance in the world, rather than any mystical or cosmic magnetism that had brought them together and allowed them some hope of a literary career. Those who exercised the least amount of practical awareness set themselves up for tragedy later on, and those who developed entrepreneurial skills without the same degree of poetic talent delayed failure only until such time as tastes evolved or professional criticism was leveled at their work. Yeats's early successes, more potent than he realized, rested in his ability to *use* both sides of his nature, to assume the role of a poet or a Hamlet while remaining aware of professional opportunities and the necessity of manipulating his environment to his best advantage. A socially quiet and somewhat cold personality, he showed in his gregariousness and energy during this period how far he was willing to go to secure an artistic career, and he developed friendships with a number of individuals who not only offered him publishing outlets but who helped him develop new ideas concerning art. That he was well aware of the value of such experience is evident in advice he gave to another young artist seven years after the Rhymers' Club had disbanded. Written to James Joyce in 1902, these words depict Yeats's sophisticated understanding of the nature of success and failure, and the limitations inherent in a purely romantic view, either of history or oneself:

> . . . men have started with as good promise as yours and have failed, and men have started with less and have succeeded. The qualities that make a man succeed do not show in his work, often, for quite a long time. These are much less qualities of talent than qualities of character—faith (of this you have probably enough), patience, adaptability (without this one learns nothing) and a gift for growing by experience, and this is perhaps rarest of all.
> I will do anything for you I can, but I am afraid that it will not be a great deal. The chief use I can be, though perhaps you will not believe

this, will be by introducing you to some other writers, who are starting like yourself, one always learns one's business from one's fellow-workers, especially from those who are near enough one's own age to understand one's own difficulties.

(Letter [18 December 1902] qtd. from Stan Joyce, 209)

NOTES FOR CHAPTER 1

[1] See Yeats's allusion to Hamlet with regard to the Rhymers' Club in OBMV. Quoted in Chapter IV (*The Myth of Failure*). See also Au, 47, for his reaction to Irving's Hamlet at age 10 or 12.

[2] "Song of the Fairies" and "Voices" appeared in the March 1885 issue.

[3] The *Gael* was the organ of the G. A. A. (Gaelic Athletic Association). UP1, 21, indicates that all copies of this journal have disappeared, but John Kelly claims otherwise. See his article in *Yeats: An Annual of Critical and Textual Studies* (1984: 75-143, also his edition of Yeats's letters (volume 1), 11n. The *Providence Sunday Journal*, edited by Alfred Williams, was a paper to which Katherine Tynan also contributed. See TFY, 279: "In the *Providence Sunday Journal*, a very wilderness of a paper, one discovered the stars in the English literary sky while they were yet only on the horizon." The *Boston Pilot* was a Catholic weekly edited by John Boyle O'Reilly. Yeats contributed to it from 1889-1892.

[4] Yeats did not move to Woburn Buildings until 1896—not, as Rhys speculates, "in the first years of the nineties." By that time, the Rhymers' Club had virtually ceased to meet, casting doubt on the probability that this event was actually a Rhymers' Club meeting or the first time that Rhys had met Maud Gonne.

[5] For a complete list of and biographical information concerning individual Rhymers, see Appendix I.

[6] Herbert Sparling, editor of the Socialists' paper *Commonweal* and *fiancé* of Morris's daughter May, introduced Yeats to Fahy.

Yeats subsequently attended meetings and gave lectures at the Club. Later, he founded the Irish Literary Society from its membership.

[7]The Yeatses lived for about a year at 58 Eardley Crescent in Earls Court before settling into more comfortable surroundings at 3 Blenheim Road.

[8]Todhunter had assessed "The Island of Statues" as being "not on the highest level," but wrote glowingly of *The Wanderings of Oisin* to Edward Dowden (See PF, 144). Judging from a letter from Yeats to Katherine Tynan (14 Mar. 1888), Todhunter had something to do with Yeats's submission of *The Wanderings of Oisin* to Kegan Paul. See L, 63.

[9]Yeats's first production, *The Land of Heart's Desire*, played at the Avenue Theatre, London, 1894, alongside Todhunter's *A Comedy of Sighs*. (See illustration.)

[10]FR, 52. *The Wanderings of Oisin and Other Poems* was submitted to Kegan Paul in March 1888, but was not published until January of the next year. Judging from Yeats's *Letters*, this meeting between Rhys and him must have occurred somewhat before mid-May 1887.

[11]Rhys mentions that Yeats lived in Bedford Park, but if this account is indeed of their first meeting, then the Yeatses would still have been at Eardley Crescent. In a letter to Katherine Tynan, 18 May 1887, Yeats recalls having met Rhys. His family moved to Blenheim Road in April 1888.

[12]William Sharp and Joseph Skipsey, both friends of Rhys, edited the Canterbury Poets series for Walter Scot & Co.. I am unsure what volume, if any, Yeats may be referring to, but it could be *Romantic Ballads and Poems of Phantasy*, edited by Sharp and appearing in 1888 and 1889.

[13]MS 5918, NLI. Original owned by William Roth, Yale Library. The books in question are Yeats's *The Wanderings of Oisin* and *Poems and Ballads of Young Ireland*.

[14]ER, 97: "At one of Mrs. Bell Scott's parties, I met a silent,

dark young man, with a long smooth raven lock over his forehead—Herbert Horne, who she said was a disciple of Ruskin, architect, painter, and poet."

¹⁵Symons edited editions of *Henry V, first quarto, Henry V, second quarto* and *Venus and Adonis*—all in 1886.

¹⁶PF, 155, prints a map indicating that Henley lived on the road to Richmond. This information is corroborated by Yeats in Au, 124. If Henley's Addiscombe Anna, the Chatelaine, is meant by this, these meetings could not have begun until September 1892, when the home was purchased.

¹⁷Charles Whibley was Henley's right-hand man for the *National Observer*. He was responsible for that review's scathing indictments of Oscar Wilde's *The Picture of Dorian Gray* in 1890. Cousin of Robert Louis Stevenson, R. A. M. Stevenson was a noted art historian. Gilbert Parker wrote prose, became a member of Parliament in the 1930s. Kenneth Grahame is the author of *The Wind in the Willows* and other children's books.

¹⁸Au, 40: "My lines seldom scanned, for I could not understand the prosody in books, although there were many lines that taken by themselves had music. I spoke them slowly as I wrote and only discovered when I read them to somebody else that there was no common music, no prosody."

¹⁹Henley was editor of Cassell's *Magazine of Art* until 1886, and Wilde began his editorship of *Woman's World* in 1887. Edwin Bale, painter and manager of Cassell's art department from 1882, invited them to dinner so that they could meet. See HC, 152: "Wilde and Henley were radically antipathetic in manners, habits and aesthetic beliefs; but Bale, who admired qualities in both, determined to bring them together. He had them and other celebrities to dine at his house. 'Wilde completely won over Henley, the latter insisting that Wilde should drive home with him to Chiswick, and at three o'clock in the morning they left together in a hansom cab. I saw Wilde the next day and he told me that they had 'sat and babbled' at Chiswick till nine

o'clock.'"

[20]ME 40, Chapter V, "The Golden Book": "What they were intent upon was, indeed, the book of books, the 'golden' book of that day, a gift to Flavian, as was shown by the purple writing on the handsome yellow wrapper."

[21]In late November/early December, Horne traveled with Wilde to Colston's School, Stapleton, Bristol, in the hope of erecting a plaque in honor of Thomas Chatterton, once a student there.

[22]Wilde and his family lived at 16 Tite Street, Chelsea.

[23]*Fairy and Folktales of the Irish Peasantry* was reviewed February 1889 in *Woman's World* and July 1889 in *The Pall Mall Gazette*. Yeats claims in Au, 134, that the Christmas meeting occurred sometime after the publication of *Oisin* and before the publication of "The Decay of Lying," but *Oisin* was published in January 1889 and Wilde's "The Decay of Lying" appeared in *Nineteenth Century* in the same month and year—with subsequent publications in the *Eclectic Magazine* (Feb.) and *Intentions* (1891). A letter from Yeats to Katherine Tynan (24 Jan. 1889, L, 102) indicates that he and Wilde had at least some contact, direct or indirect, before 1891 and concurrent with the period in which the reviews were being written: "Fairy book is reviewed in February's Woman's World by Oscar Wilde, who promises to try and get reviewing of poems for Pall Mall." It seems likely that Yeats and Wilde met in December 1888, and that Wilde thereafter wrote to him and promised reviews.

[24]In Honor of Dorian and His Creator:

> You, Oscar, singing in the Roman fashion
> in this book, ought to be honored for
> thinking me worthy of such a book.
> You, singing in a Dorianesque fashion
> praise me, you judge me worthy.
> To you I bear thanks.

This finely wrought rose of youth blooms
among the roses.
Until suddenly death comes.
Behold the man! Behold the god!
If it could only be thus, my merciful genius!

With beauty the hungry one loves his
strange and wonderful lusts;
with beauty the ferocious one devours
the strange and wonderful flowers.
How great the blackness of the soul grows,
so much more bright the countenance shines.
Though counterfeit, yet it is more
magnificent than the truth.

Here are the fruits of the Sodomites
Here the essence of moral
transgression.
So sweet a crime.
Glory of all glories to you
in the highest and in the lowest
who discern so well.

—translation by Steven Lally

[25] This is, of course, speculation, based on the fact that Rupert Croft-Cooke has little to say about him in this regard and that Le Gallienne is better known for his wives and womanizing later on in his career.

[26] Charles Sayle, another Oxonian, was acquainted with Johnson, Dowson and Plarr. Yeats mentions him in a letter to Katherine Tynan, c. 10 October 1889 (L, 138), indicating that he had met him by that date.

[27] Lane was then Elkin Mathews's silent partner for the Bodley Head bookstore and publishing firm.

[28]Lane had engaged him to write a book on George Meredith and a collection of essays to be called *Oblivion's Poppies: Studies in the Forgotten.* At about this time, he co-authored a collection of stories with Robinson Kay Leather entitled *The Student and the Body-Snatcher and Other Trifles,* and he began his autobiographical novel, *The Book Bills of Narcissus,* all with Lane's firm as a probable outlet.

THE PATTERN IN THE WEB

The Rhymers' Club was founded, as Yeats claims in *Autobiographies*, so that poets of the nineties could work together to avoid professional jealousies. This process involved acquainting oneself with other writers and their poetic undertakings, exchanging with them professional favors and ideas. The Club began somewhat inauspiciously as a loose association of literary dilletantes—as Victor Plarr expressed it (PED, 63), "a small group of Dublin poets"—but with the injection of talent from the Fitzroy Establishment, a domestic settlement arising from the ranks of the Century Guild, it became a serious and productive association of artists. The process of growth from an unremarkable collection of poetic enthusiasts to an historically relevant literary phenomenon involved Yeats's considerable skill as an entrepreneur. Threatened by John Davidson's attempt to introduce four of his burly Scottish friends into the assembly, the Club nearly disbanded within months of its founding. The move to disrupt proceedings and turn the organization away from the aesthetic interests of Fitzroy was quickly if somewhat hysterically defeated, however, and Yeats's efforts saved it from a threatened early demise. The single thread of communality between these two stages of Club development was its members' tendency to romanticize their roles, seeing themselves as poets who confronted history, society and unspeakable odds in their bid for literary achievement. Closely associated with this mood of defiance was a tendency in many to conflate life and art, and the urge to live intensely as Pater had commanded contributed to the untimely ends of several key members. Arthur Symons's treatment of Ernest Dowson reflects the self-destructive fascinations of the aesthetic temperament; Dowson himself, its less than salubrious effects.

The present chapter examines the principal stages in the founding of the Rhymers' Club: the early meetings of 1890 and the introduction of poets from Fitzroy in 1891. It also analyses the threat to organization caused by John Davidson and his friends and depicts the mythmaking tendency that affected Dowson's and others' careers. Because the Club kept no formal records and because much of the information that survived is either incomplete or contradictory, mythmaking plays an important role in the critical process as well: complicating questions of authority, creating colorful though unsubstantiated claims which must ultimately be set right. Success for these Rhymers would have involved an ability to control the myth rather than allowing it ultimately to control them. Yeats perceived its value without becoming bound by its extraordinary demands. He exercised control not only of his own public image but of the evolving character of the organization in an effort to gain maximum entrepreneurial and artistic rewards.

I. Early Meetings

The precise date of the founding of the Rhymers' Club has been a matter of speculation for some time, and the nebulousness of this event reflects the overall uncertainty concerning its earliest phase. A debate was staged in the early 1970s between Daniel Rutenberg, Karl Beckson and R. K. R. Thornton (ELT 12.3; ELT 13.1; ELT 14.1) concerning its probable founding, and although Thornton had the last word, his assertions did not entirely put the question to rest. Today, it seems clear that the Club existed in two stages: the early "Rhymesters' Club," which consisted primarily of Celtic members, and the later-formed "Rhymers' Club," which added to that body the aesthetic poets

The Pattern in the Web

of Fitzroy. Whether one accepts 1890 or 1891 as the correct founding date, however, depends upon the importance one attaches to actual membership and the subsequent definition of "Club identity." A variety of individuals frequented both stages of these meetings with different levels of enthusiasm, for different lengths of time, and since they kept no records and no code of membership was devised, it is difficult to ascertain whether these groups were considered part of an ongoing movement or as two separate entities. Treating them as belonging to the same whole is inevitably a scholarly convenience as Thornton suggests, but it also acknowledges a process of self-definition which seems to have been inherent in the facts of association. The necessary tentativeness of such a conclusion, however, underscores the uncertainty of the event; lack of information opens even the simplest statements to imprecision and ultimately to myth.

The first unequivocal evidence we have, then, concerning the Rhymers' Club in any form is offered by Ernest Rhys in a letter, 9 July 1890, to E. C. Stedman. In this communication, Rhys speaks at length of the Marlowe night, and the cast of those on hand is markedly different from those we now associate with the group:

> You ask about our "Rhymesters' Club"; we had a very jolly meeting last Friday,—a sort of *Marlowe* night, as that afternoon a benefit performance for the Marlowe Memorial had been given at the "Shaftesbury". John Davidson—author of "Scaramouch in Naxos" and other most original plays, lately much discussed; Willie Yeats, a young Irish poet; T. W. Rolleston, another Irish poet, or rhymester, to use the Club term; Nettleship, the painter; O'Leary, the old Irish rebel; and two or

three others less notable were there. Not a large gathering, you see; but a right jovial and friendly one. (CUS)

With the exception of Davidson, who was Scottish, and Nettleship, who was English, the guest list reads like an advance roster of the Irish Literary Society and gives some indication of how these individuals may have come together. One of the "less notable" figures whom Rhys fails to mention was probably G. A. Greene, the promulgator of commemorative evenings (LED, 95), and also an Irishman. An associate of T. W. Rolleston at Trinity College Dublin, Greene, like many of his fellow expatriates, naturally sought artistic community and friendship once having settled in London. Yeats speaks in *Autobiographies* of this Irish contingency, claiming that they dispelled the awkwardness and tedium of these early meetings. "I think," said he, "that but for its Irish members, who said whatever came into their heads, the club would not have survived its first difficult months" (Au, 167). The predominantly Irish character of the group as well as the role these poets played in keeping conversations alive led Plarr to identify it as "A small group of Dublin poets." Although his statement is not strictly correct, it does point to the ethnic bias of the Club as well as to its seemingly parochial ambitions.

Conspicuously absent from Rhys's list are representatives of the Oxford contingency—poets like Ernest Dowson, Lionel Johnson, and Victor Plarr who were associated with Horne's Fitzroy Establishment at 20 Fitzroy Street. This omission strongly suggests that they had not yet joined the organization, although Rhys had been friendly with Horne from early on in his London career. Dedicated aesthetes, these poets would have objected to any frivolous treatment of art, and their presence would have commanded some form of comment. Rhys's failure to mention them, coupled with his account of the evening's

The Pattern in the Web

frivolity, seems to underscore their absence and reinforces the claim that they belonged to a later and much different phase of the Club.

The chief feature of this occasion—the reading of each other's verses—was done "to a Bacchanalian accompaniment of whiskey," which, says Rhys, "kept the fun going merrily." Having failed to bring along a verse in honor of Marlowe, he was "exiled to a far corner with a glass of crystal fluid at his elbow, and bidden compose a quatrain there and then, or—die!" The commemorative lines he eventually penned were calculated to affront the egos of his bohemian brothers. These also were written in a spirited (though not seriously artistic) vein:

> With wine and blood and reckless deviltry,
> He sped the flames, new-fired our English verse:
> Bethink ye, rhymesters! what your praise shall be,
> Who in smug suburbs put the Muse to nurse?

When read, the quatrain produced "an uproarious scene." And Rhys, "feeling his life in Danger, escaped incontinently into the rain without; and so home!" He ends his account of the evening by quoting in full his ballad concerning the Club. Like the Marlowe quatrain, it was reproduced in *The Book of the Rhymers' Club* and perpetuates the robust image we now associate with Rhys, Davidson and most of the Irish members:

> Set fools unto their folly!
>   Our folly is pure wit,
> As 'twere the Muse turned jolly:
> For poets' melancholy,—
>   We will not think of it.
>
> As once Rare Ben and Herrick
>   Set older Fleet Street mad,

With wit not esoteric,
And laughter that was lyric,
    And roystering rhymes and glad:

As they, we drink defiance
    To-night to all but Rhyme,
And most of all to Science,
    And all such skins of lions
That hide the ass of time.

To-night, to rhyme as they did
    Were well,—ah, were it ours,
Who find the Muse degraded,
And changed, I fear and faded,
    Her laurel crown and flowers.

Ah rhymers, for that sorrow
    The more o'ertakes delight,
The more this madness borrow:—
If care be king to-morrow,
    To toast Queen Rhyme to-night.
        CUS; BRC-1, 1-2)

    The solemnity about which Yeats and others later complained was evidently the product of personalities like Johnson and Horne who had not yet exercised their influence on the group, but one can see the incipience of such an attitude in the closing two stanzas of the poem. Here, Rhys touches upon the problems and responsibilities of his generation compared with those of his literary forebears, Herrick and Jonson: the fact that poetry no longer attracted much interest or esteem. A note of sadness enters the verse when he considers this situation, but the cavalier attitude returns with the compromise at the end. Implicit in the poet's alleged madness is the sense that these verses will not fulfill posterity's demands. Doomed to ineffectuality and silence, Rhys and his fellow Rhymers must celebrate their art nevertheless.

Rhys mentions other writers in his letter to Stedman, but the extent of their involvement in the Club is not known. Henry Harland, the American writer and future editor of the *Yellow Book*, was on hand at an earlier meeting. Four "rhymesters," Rhys tells us, had just published a book of poetry together, two of whom he identified as Manmohan Ghose and one "Phillipps." The book in question, *Privmavera* (Oxford: B. H. Blackwell, 1890), lists four individuals as authors and, thus, helps identify four other possible non-Irish members: Stephen Phillips, a poet who, at twenty, had already published a volume of his own verse (*Orestes and Other Poems* [London: private printing, 1884]); Arthur S. Cripps, a student at Trinity College, Oxford, and soon to become an Anglican priest; Lawrence Binyon, a skilled Orientalist and later a poet of some repute; and Manmohan Ghose, another Oxonian, mentioned by Dowson in 1891 as a possible contributor to *The Book of the Rhymers' Club* (Letter to Victor Plarr, c. 9 June 1891, EDL, 203). Rhys also speaks of George Douglas, "a notable young Scots tale-writer and rhymester"; and Arthur Symons's name appears in the text—although Rhys fails to say whether he has yet joined or attended the Club. Aside from Ghose and Symons, these individuals are not alluded to elsewhere in relation to the Rhymers' Club, and two of them—Harland and Douglas—were primarily writers of prose. That they stand in Rhys's mind as "rhymesters" indicates the loosely-defined notion of membership at this point and the difficulties involved in generalizations concerning the Club as a whole. Little else served to confirm or deny membership outside of individual inclination and opinion, and there was no obvious sense or statement either of unity or purpose.

The Club seems to have undergone a transformation in January 1891, expanding to include a wider range of talent than it previously had known. In the early days of the month, Ernest Dowson wrote to his friend Arthur Moore to say that he would go to Horne's on Saturday, "to meet Oscar and a select assembly" (2 January 1891, EDL, 181). The editors of Dowson's letters assume that this engagement marks the first meeting of a reconstituted Rhymers' Club, and certainly the names that begin to appear in documents thereafter are more centrally associated with it than those that had come before. There seems to have been at least one other meeting in that month, before a large group of prospective Rhymers gathered at Horne's for the evening. On or around January 19, Yeats wrote to Horne to confirm his proposal:

Walter Crane was at our last and read verse. Have you his address? I have not but could get it.	3 Blenheim Rd. Bedford Park Chiswick

My dear Horne,

    I find that next Thursday week would suit the Rhymers very well for next meeting and that they would be very glad to accept your invitation to 20 Fitzroy Street. I enclose a list of names. If Thursday does not suit you I have no doubt that any other day about the same date would serve them equally.

                              Yrs.

                              W. B. Yeats[1]

Although Yeats's list has not been preserved, one can guess that it included poets who had been on hand on previous occasions: T. W. Rolleston, Ernest Rhys, Arthur Symons, John Davidson, G. A. Greene and John Todhunter, among others. For his part, Horne invited a group of Oxonians who either frequented Fitzroy or actually lived at that address, and whose aesthetic values eventually proved a potent influence on the Club as a whole. Lionel Johnson, Ernest Dowson, Victor Plarr and Oscar Wilde offered a degree of sophistication and artistic ability that the Rhymers' Club had hitherto lacked. Their Oxford training made available to the group the most current literary trends—most importantly the influence of Walter Pater, who was preaching art for art's sake and the value of intense sensual experience. This influx helped transform the group from a collection of literary dilletantes to an association of serious-minded poets. Selwyn Image, an Anglican churchman and an architectural associate of Horne's, also took part in the group's activities. When *The Book of the Rhymers' Club* came under critical fire, Image wrote a spirited defense of it, and, on at least two other occasions, he exercised his fatherly concern in support of Rhymers' welfare.[2]

The move to hold meetings at members' homes, and the decision to hold this particular meeting at Herbert Horne's Fitzroy Street address, seems to have been motivated by a desire to give the Club a more substantial or respectable image. Yeats's position with regard to this determination is suggested by his role in making the arrangements and by his acknowledgement that he had attempted on earlier occasions to lure Oscar Wilde into the fold. "It had been useless to invite [Wilde] to The Cheshire Cheese," he notes in *The Trembling of the Veil*, "for he hated Bohemia"(Au, 165), and Victor Plarr indicates the power Wilde had over younger, genuinely talented poets such as Dowson and Johnson (PED, 64. See Chapter I for quotation). Yeats must have understood that taking advantage of Horne's hospitality meant associating with an already respected group of artists and craftsmen (The Fitzroy Establishment), as well as with a periodical (the *Century Guild Hobby Horse*) dedicated to "maintaining Originality of Thought" and "making Thorough all workmanship involved in its reproduction" (Title page, January 1886). It also meant attracting the dynamic Oscar Wilde into his circle, a figure who could give the organization an interest and bond it previously had lacked.

Wilde's effect on the impressionable young men of that gathering may be seen in the aftermath of the meeting of January 29. Recounting the events of the evening in a letter to Campbell Dodgson, Lionel Johnson reserved his praise for Wilde:

> We entertained the other night eighteen minor poets of our acquaintance: from Oscar Wilde to Walter Crane, with Arthur Symons and Willie Yeats between. They all inflicted their poems on each other, and were inimitably tedious, except dear Oscar.
> (5 Feb. 1891, BM Ad. MS 46363)

And Ernest Dowson wrote in the same vein to Arthur Moore (2 February 1891), capping his account with a dazzling image of his paragon:

> Thursday at Horne's was very entertaining; a most queer assembly of "Rhymers"; and a quaint collection of rhymes. Crane (Walter) read a ballad: dull! Ernest Radford, some triolets & rondels of merit: "Dorian" Gray some very beautiful & obscure versicles in the latest manner of French Symbolism; and the tedious Todhunter was tedious

> after his kind. Plarr and Johnson also read verses of great excellence; and the latter, also, read for me my "Amor Umbratilis"; And Oscar arrived late looking more like his Whistlerian name, in his voluminous dress clothes, than I have ever seen him. (EDL, 182-3)

It is interesting to note that Wilde, unlike the others, did not have to read his poems in order to be judged a valuable presence. He had only to arrive late in the costume of Mr. Mantalini in order to captivate his audience.[3] His youthful followers also benefitted from their association with Wilde. "Dorian" (John) Gray, one of his early *protégés*, predictably wrote *"beautiful* and *obscure* versicles in the *latest* manner of French Symbolism." Plarr and Johnson, Dowson's friends and also Wildean followers, presented poems of "great excellence." The others fared less well. Walter Crane, a forty-six-year-old poet not associated with Wilde's circle was peremptorily dismissed as "dull"; Ernest Radford, an early member of the Rhymers' Club, had simple "merit"; and John Todhunter, another elderly presence, was tagged "tedious after his kind." Dowson was not sufficiently impressed with either Yeats or Symons even to mention them in his account (Dowson could not even remember having met Symons on this occasion), and his own contribution was consigned to Johnson to read—not because of any doubt concerning its value, but because of his habitual shyness, which kept him from reading the poem himself. However unreasonable and subjective, Dowson's report demonstrates the enormous popularity Wilde enjoyed with the Oxford poets. His presence would go far to assure their attendance and alleviate the boredom that kept them aloof from the rest of the group. In Dowson's and Johnson's minds at least, Oscar could do nothing wrong, nor could those who exercised his taste for "beautiful and obscure versicles in the latest manner of French Symbolism."

In March, Lionel Johnson read again for Dowson. The poem—*"Non sum qualis eram bonae sub regno Cynarae"* ("I am not as I was under the Reign of Good Cynara")—was to be his first contribution (April 1891) to the Century Guild Hobby Horse, and its reading would mark a crucial turning point in the Club's history. Representative of a genre of expression for which the Rhymers' would eventually become known, it moved them to realize not only their individual ability but their potential importance as a literary group. Its subsequent success in the public sphere led some to create legends about it, romanticizing the event of its first reading or the subject on which it was supposedly written. Yeats himself listened to this now well-known poem, finding in its rhythms and images a mood that would haunt him for years to come:

> Last night, ah, yesternight, betwixt her lips and mine
> There fell thy shadow, Cynara! thy breath was shed
> Upon my soul, between the kisses and the wine;
> And I was desolate and sick of an old passion,
>   Yea! I grew desolate and bowed my head;
> I have been faithful to thee, Cynara! in my fashion.
>
> All night upon my breast I felt her warm heart beat;
> Night-long within mine arms in love and sleep she lay:
> Surely the kisses of her bought, red mouth were sweet?
> But I was desolate and sick of an old passion,
>   When I awoke, and found the dawn was grey:

> I have been faithful to thee, Cynara! in my
>   fashion.
>
> I have forgot much, Cynara! gone with the wind;
> Flung roses, roses riotously with the throng;
> Dancing to put thy pale, lost lilies out of mind;
> But I was desolate, and sick of an old passion,
>   Yea! all the time, because the dance was
>   long!
> I have been faithful to thee, Cynara! in my
>   fashion.
>
> I cried for madder music, and for stronger wine;
> But when the feast is finished, and the lamps
>   expire,
> Then falls thy shadow, Cynara! the night is thine;
> And I am desolate and sick of an old passion,
>   Yea! hungry for the lips of my desire:—
> I have been faithful to thee, Cynara! in my
>   fashion.
>
>   (BRC-2, 60-61)

Edgar Jepson perpetuated the rumor that "Cynara" referred to Dowson's largely unrequited love for "Missie," a Polish restaurant-keeper's daughter,[4] but a cursory examination of the facts casts doubt on strict biographical interpretations. Dowson had only known "Missie" for at most a year and a half when he wrote the poem,[5] and she did not ultimately refuse his affections until 1897, years after it was first seen in print. Furthermore, she was only thirteen years old when Dowson met her—certainly not the sophisticated woman referred to in the Latin title and certainly not the subject, yet, of an "*old* passion."

But Dowson's enterprise was very likely inspired by what "Missie" as a mysterious and beautiful child could become as a mysterious and beautiful young woman, and her inability at this point to comprehend or play along with his dream engendered the need to create an artistic counterpart. The personal aspect of this expression rests in Dowson's transformation of mundane biographical facts into a romantic vision and his subsequent attempts to live life emulating that vision. What we know of him at the time—a shy and deferential young man who preferred not to read his own verse in public—contrasts startlingly with the impassioned speaker of the poem. Yet it aptly fits the legend of the later Dowson: the tortured lover who, after his mistress ran off with and married a German waiter, drank excessively and "desired whatever woman chance brought, clean or dirty" (Au, 311).

Biographical information aside, the poem stands as a touchstone of decadent expression. Its rhythms reflect the alternately languid and violent moods of frustrated passion, and the pleasure of unfulfillment heightens the poem's sensual conflict. Cynara's attractiveness depends at least partially on her unattainability, her imperfectly perceived (and thus idealized) form interceding between the speaker and the "bought red lips" of the whore. This tension between physicality and the physical ideal is subtly reversed in the refrain, where Cynara becomes the compromised element and the poet's loyalty is instantaneously and bathetically defused ("I have been faithful to thee, Cynara!.. in my fashion"). The shock of these lines rests in the speaker's inability to remain faithful to an admittedly superior goal—a willingness to defile spiritual commitment with carnal indulgences that will not ultimately satisfy—and the emotional pattern of strong beginnings followed by weak ends offers a premonition of where such compromises will lead. Fixed in a moment of heightened sensibility, the expression conveys its own fragility: the instable mood on which it is based; the laxity of human resolve.

In reviewing the *Century Guild Hobby Horse* for the May 14

edition of the *Star*, Richard Le Gallienne devoted most of his energies to praising "Cynara." In so doing, he indicated the prestige that Dowson's poem had already received and the kind of attention it was likely to attract from future critics. Although Le Gallienne and Dowson had not yet met, Dowson had heard enough of his reviewer (identified in the *Star* column by his pseudonym "Log-roller") to understand that he was "Oscar's friend & a 'rhymer'" (Letter to Arthur Moore, 18 May 1891, EDL, 198-99). The connection proved sufficient for both poets to benefit from it: Dowson gained important critical exposure, and Le Gallienne had the opportunity to talk authoritatively about a new poetic discovery. In later years, Le Gallienne's desire to be an authority was so strong that it led him to believe that he had been on the scene when "Cynara" was read. "Certainly no poem is more associated with the period," he recounts in *The Romantic '90s*, "and perhaps of all the poems then written it is the one still found most often to-day on the lips of youth. I remember well hearing Dowson recite it, fresh from his pen, on one of those nights at the Cheshire Cheese"(RN, 186). But Le Gallienne was still living in Liverpool at the time the poem was read, and existing evidence negates his story. Dowson himself remembers that Lionel Johnson read the poem a month before Le Gallienne's arrival,[6] and Victor Plarr in his biography of the poet substantiates that Dowson "refused ever to recite his verses at the Rhymers' meetings, declaring that he had no gift that way"(PED, 66). One suspects that Le Gallienne's sense of the poem's value led him to misremember his relationship to it, or to inflate the truth until it equalled his emotional response. Like all of Wilde's followers, Le Gallienne saw life as an occasion for art, where beauty was to be valued over truth, and it seemed much more beautiful to claim that he had heard it read than to admit he had not.

    The young Yeats, too, was struck by the quality of Dowson's lines, but was moved to preserve the experience in quite another way. In a copy of *The Book of the Rhymers' Club* sent to Lady Gregory, he revealed the design that "Cynara" and other poems had placed in his mind: "This little book was put together at my suggestion. I suggested it because I wanted to have copies of Dowson's poems. He had read them to us at the Cheshire Cheese" (L-K, 273n). Yeats repeated the message several years later in a copy sent to John Quinn (March 1904), underlining the truth of his claim: "I got the Rhymers to publish this book because I wanted copies of Dowson's verse"(B, 264). Although "Cynara" itself did not appear until the second Rhymers' Club anthology, Yeats's impulse upon hearing it seems obvious: he wanted to preserve and be able to reinvoke the experience of these early meetings, and he wanted to be able to study the lines that had impressed him, to gain from them structural and thematic insights.[7] Significantly, he did not—as Le Gallienne had done—single Dowson out for praise in his critical excursions of that period, but included him in a project that allowed for his own professional advancement and the greater stability of the Rhymers' Club as a whole. Since, as Ernest Rhys claims (ER, 106), Dowson was then considered to be the most talented member of the group and since Yeats himself obviously admired him, it seems odd that he would not promote him critically—especially in an essay like "The Rhymers' Club," which was ostensibly written to call attention to the literary merit of this fledgling organization.[8] One can only conclude that he felt threatened by Dowson's ability and the attention he was beginning to receive and that he did not wish to promote his rival at his own expense. Thus, he put off developing his own version of the Dowson myth until after the latter had ceased to be a threat to him professionally.

"Cynara" survives in Yeats's poetry, however, both as an example of the youthful passion that characterized the decadent age and as a type for the process of transforming life into art. The older poet, looking back upon the past, commemorates

Dowson's type of poetry in "The Scholars"—depicting it as an outpouring of genuine emotion, violated by scholarly analysis:

> ... bald heads
> Edit and annotate the lines
> That young men, tossing on their beds,
> Rhymed out in love's despair
> To flatter beauty's ignorant ear.

Young men create from frustrated passion, while old men, without the capacity to experience that passion, perform meaningless analyses of their work. The allusion fits Dowson's situation better than Yeats's own: writing for a beauty who was not only ignorant but indifferent to his effort; inheriting from unsympathetic and incomprehending critics their purposeless commentary and scorn. Although Yeats did not remain consistently hostile to scholars as a group, he did continue to associate the sexual vision of the decadent artist (young men tossing on their beds) with poetic vitality itself and often contrasted this immediacy with the sterility of intellectualism or old age as he himself grew old. Thus, in "After Long Silence" he equates bodily decrepitude with wisdom and claims that "young We loved each other and were ignorant"; thus, in "A Prayer for Old Age," he asks to be protected from "thoughts men think in the mind alone."

Moreover, Yeats's poetic treatment of his unhappy love affair with Maud Gonne bears a striking resemblance to Dowson's transformation of "Missie" into a literary figure: transferring her to a poetic environment where feelings can be symbolically defined and, thus, in some way controlled. Yeats's theme of unrequited love, the elevation of Maud Gonne to the status of classical heroine, appear in poems from *The Wind Among the Reeds* onward—turning the poet's life into a dream which, as he informs us in "The Circus Animals' Desertion," takes "all my thought and love." Although devoid of Dowson's sordidness, Yeats's poem "The Arrow," written in the same year Maud Gonne became intimate with John MacBride, may be seen as an analogue to "Cynara." In it, we find the same tension between good and bad, the same theme of loss in which memory overwhelms the more palpable rewards of physical presence:

> I thought of your beauty, and this arrow,
> Made out of a wild thought is in my marrow.
> There's no man may look upon her, no man,
> As when newly grown to be a woman,
> Tall and noble but with face and bosom
> Delicate in colour as apple blossom.
> This beauty's kinder, yet for a reason
> I could weep that the old is out of season.
>   (VP, 199)

As the reference to apple blossoms informs us, the poem concerns Yeats's unrequited feelings for Maud Gonne,[9] but it is a depersonalized, archetypal Maud Gonne whom he addresses and who inspires the passion noted here, rather than an actual or clearly identified woman; and it is the arrow, or passion itself, that is the true focus of the poet's concern. Like Dowson, Yeats establishes a tension between conflicting values—between the beauty he cannot have and the beauty which is accessible—and creates from it a dramatic situation, holding time in a momentary balance. Again, he depends upon a pairing of sensuousness and pain, the woman's face and bosom, "delicate in color as apple blossom," inflicting the sharp and painful stroke of the arrow; and he manipulates the same kind of turn in the last two lines of the poem, establishing the value of his present situation ("This beauty's kinder"), then defusing it with the inevitable qualification ("yet . . . I could weep that the old is out of season"). Rhythmically, too, Yeats's lines adapt to the emotion, speeding up to capture the suddenness of recollection, slowing down to contemplate face, bosom and the consequent regrets. And they confirm Dowson's basic understanding concerning the power of unrequited love, a motif which resonates throughout Yeats's love poems and which he finally confronts in lines included in "The Tower." ("Does the imagination dwell the most/ Upon a woman won or woman lost?").

The difference perhaps between the two dramatic situations is that Dowson's dream precedes the reality whereas Yeats's reality dictates the need for the dream. In keeping with decadent practice, Dowson patterned his life after an artistic vision that would consume him and succeeded as a poet to the degree that he failed in life. Yeats, on the other hand, used his art to control experience and succeeded as a poet to the degree that he created solace and refuge from the world. In *Autobiographies*, Yeats excuses himself from championing Dowson's art, saying his best verse was immortal but that generally "he was too vague and gentle for my affections" (AU, 312). Although vague, distant and dim, "Cynara" is anything but gentle, and it has made its claim on posterity, surviving untarnished into the present age. Johnson's reading of the "Cynara" poem and similar readings in 1891 must have impressed Yeats with the change that had come over the Club, stimulating in him the urge to preserve and learn from what he had heard. Realizing that the Rhymers had genuine literary potential, he wanted to create a record of their productivity, both for the immediate end of publishing a book and for the long-term, historical reward of remembering and testifying to their importance as a group. As the rising star of the Club, Dowson may have posed a threat to Yeats, whose theatrical instincts made him prefer to be the center of attention, but he used Dowson's talents to great mutual benefit, and he learned from his example what he needed to know about being an aesthetic poet. Dowson's "Amor Umbratilis," "Carmelite Nuns" and "Cynara" helped establish him as a serious and promising young artist and helped give the Rhymers' Club anthologies the literary interest they enjoyed.

III. John Davidson and the Four Scotsmen

Another mark of the changes that were taking place within the Rhymers' Club may be seen in an altercation that occurred in April of the same season (1891). John Davidson, an early member of the Club and a practitioner of a kind of poetry that was very different from Dowson's, attempted to introduce four of his more robust Scottish friends into the assembly, and in so doing, caused a disruption that nearly brought the Rhymers to a premature end. Like any myth, this story has evolved from contradictory evidence and hearsay to acquire a number of elaborations, and it is difficult to render a complete account of the meeting without calling into question the integrity of one's own narration.[10]

A survey of the available sources suggests both the possibilities and impossibilities of interpretation. Patricio Gannon, a later historian, depicts a scene that is telling but suspiciously inconsistent with other facts. In his book *The Poets of the Rhymers' Club*, he picturesquely reveals that, when John Davidson insisted that the Scotsmen read their rhymes aloud, Dowson and Johnson were discussing "the beauties of 'la rime riche'" and "the occult virtues of the alexandrine." Gannon, however, takes his diction (and most likely his story) from Plarr, who speaks of Dowson's and Johnson's interests in a more general way:

> Dowson constantly insisted that *the "rime riche" is a beauty* in poetry. A brutal philistine pointing out to him that the "rime riche" is a bore in French and an imbecility in English versification, he so far acquiesced as seldom to use it. In common with Lionel Johnson he found *an occult virtue in the Alexandrine*, but again did not press his

admiration to the point of using it overmuch.
(PED, 26. My emphasis)

Dowson himself undermines the authenticity of Gannon's story, alluding to the meeting in a letter to Arthur Moore (28 April 1891), but in a way that makes one suspect he is hearing of events second-hand: "How foolish of the immortals to crown these impossible Scotchmen: when the divine Albert was there." About all one can discover from Dowson's account (outside of his absence) is that the recipient's uncle, Albert Moore, had been on hand when hostilities broke out and that "the Immortals" (that is, the established members) had voted to accept the Scotchmen into the Club.

Yeats speaks in *The Trembling of the Veil* (Au, 317-18) as if he had been present on the occasion, but Morely Roberts, who attended the meeting and recorded his version in an essay entitled "The Rhymers' Club" (JOL), claims that he did not meet Yeats until afterwards at a dinner at Davidson's house. If one feels inclined to accept Roberts's account as the one unassailable rendition of the story, one must first deal with Plarr's characterization of him as "a brilliant weaver of fancies"(PED, 64). And if one is moved to take Yeats's account as the most accurate, one must take into consideration a body of critical work that points to the process of fictionalization in the *Autobiographies*, of which this story is a part.[11] The two primary sources for the story—Roberts's essay in *John O'London's Weekly* and Yeats's section on Davidson in *The Trembling of the Veil*—are sufficiently biased to have caused substantial critical confusion. Yet they provide the only in-depth treatment of the event and stand as an example of the polarization that was occurring within the membership. For these reasons, it seems useful to relate them in some detail.

Roberts recalls that he had met Davidson at the home of Henri Van Laun,[12] and the older man invited him to a meeting of the Rhymers' Club at the Cheshire Cheese. Roberts was required to bring along a poem of his to read aloud, and he was somewhat concerned about his ability to do so successfully. But Davidson's indifference to the opinions of the young poets of that cenacle encouraged his young friend, and Roberts proceeded to choose from his collection of verses lines "which might possibly appeal to a set of semi-moribund geniuses." The poem he chose had something to do with worms and graveyards, and, according to him, it was received, "if not with applause, at least with more or less approving grunts." Davidson's poem, he remembers, "was certainly the best piece given us that night," but it was not received charitably. Roberts posits that the negative reaction to Davidson had caused the Rhymers to resolve, immediately after their departure, to elect no more new members and to reserve their association as "a sacred and forbidden place of resort and consolation for pure poets." The news did not seem to disturb the undauntable Davidson, who relayed the information to Roberts, "not without laughter."

According to Yeats, however, Davidson was annoyed by the "delicate, laborious, discriminating taste" of poets like Johnson and Dowson, and he attempted to change the spirit of meetings by introducing four of his Scottish friends into the assembly. They read poems calculated to offend their audience—one, about a life boat and another about a quarrel with an Australian miner concerning the rotundity of the earth. Yeats remembers little about the other recitations, "except that they excelled in argument." When Davidson insisted upon his friends' immediate election into the organization, the Rhymers—gentlemen to the end—complied. Yeats reports that they secretly resolved, however, never to meet again, and he was forced to organize, with great difficulty, another meeting in which the Scotsmen were voted out.

Whether Davidson had consciously tried to disrupt the meeting—as Yeats suggests—or simply had attempted to gain a more sympathetic audience for his own verse—as Roberts's story seems to imply—is not certain. What is clear from both versions of the event is that an ideological split had occurred within the membership, and that Davidson had found himself very much in the minority. When called upon to take sides, Yeats had placed his loyalties where his poetic beliefs were—with those whom he considered the true craftsmen. Interestingly enough, his idea of craft meant more than the simple manipulation of poetical skills. It included the artist's approach to life—his philosophical goals and strategies—and in this sphere he found Davidson seriously lacking. He was capable of producing volatile scenes, but incapable of understanding their significance or of providing for them a justifiable cause. To Yeats, Davidson's actions seemed senseless and arbitrary, and his encounter with the poet several days later is meant to demonstrate this attitude: "He was full of amiability, and when we parted shook my hand, and proclaimed enthusiastically that I had 'blood and guts'"(Au, 317-18). "Blood and guts" becomes the Yeatsian term for Davidson's literary and existential motivation: a natural, unreflecting enthusiasm that pushes past all opposition and seeks to establish itself, irrespective of quality or right. In summarizing his account, Yeats by-passes Davidson's perceptive appreciation of his (Yeats's) verse and focuses instead on the appreciation he should have had for others of the group:

> I think he might have grown to be a successful man had he been enthusiastic instead about Dowson or Johnson, or Horne or Symons, for they had what I must lack always, scholarship. They had taught me that violent energy, which is like a fire of straw, consumes in a few minutes the nervous vitality, and is useless in the arts. Our fire must burn slowly, and we must constantly turn away to think, constantly analyse what we have done, be

> content even to have little life outside our work, to show, perhaps, to other men, as little as the watch-mender shows, his magnifying glass caught in his screwed-up eye. Only then do we learn to conserve our vitality, to keep our mind enough under control and to make our technique sufficiently flexible for expression of the emotions of life as they arise. (Au, 318)

As difficult to understand and as potentially misleading as this paragraph is, it sheds real light on Yeats's mythical formula. He credits Dowson, Johnson, Symons and Horne with keen scholarly objectivity—the ability to treat even the most personally troubling circumstances as possible material for art. The fire or passion that can consume life is used instead to refine it, forging from experience the poetic creation. That Dowson's and Johnson's deaths were as tragic, or Symons's madness as acute as Davidson's does not disturb the contrast in Yeats's mind, nor do the realizations that Symons's and Dowson's levels of scholarship were vastly overrated,[13] and that Yeats himself tended to portray these figures as passionate and ingenuous youths. Their poems remain for him the product of painstaking analytical consciousnesses, able to adjust technique to fine changes of emotion.

Yeats's political alignment with the aesthetic poets arose from a commitment to their literary ideals, and part of his esteem had to do with what he needed to see in them. He had inherited the responsibility of being an Irish poet at a time when the political situation in his country required a national literature, and he realized that the artist attempting to define Ireland's spirit would not only have to capture his country's passion and variety, but be able to control these attributes through language. Dowson, Symons, Johnson and Horne had shown him the value of the exotic in art and had impressed him with their ability to govern emotion: their experiments with French forms allowing them to develop a tempered cadence which paid heed to natural pauses. Davidson's rollicking verse, like his rollicking personality, remained insensitive to a whole depth of expression, and his lines seemed driven by artificial impulses rather than serving, themselves, as the driving force of the poem.

In "To Ireland in the Coming Times" (first published in 1892), Yeats presented measure or metrics as a viable control for the "rantings and ravings" of Nature. His country's heart had been set beating by the swift violence of Time, but the poet could alter those cadences—first in art, then through art's example, in life. Offering a mythical formula for the historical situation, Yeats speaks his cure in the form of a blessing:

> *When Time began to rant and rage*
> *The measure of her flying feet*
> *Made Ireland's heart begin to beat;*
> *And Time bade all his candles flare*
> *To light a measure here and there;*
> *And may the thoughts of Ireland brood*
> *Upon a measured quietude.*
>
> (VP, 138)

Benefitting from a more or less traditional sense of the poet's mystical powers, Yeats structurally imitates the condition he wishes to invoke. The winding down of the tempo in the last two lines of the stanza actually achieves the "quietude" about which he speaks and, thus, offers an artistic model through which his goals can be realized. The experience of the poem, therefore, is an experience (in small) of the general transformation, and the work as a whole becomes an example of a spiritual ideal.

Yeats goes on to distinguish himself from those great Irish poets, who, like Davidson, had failed to perceive the artist's full powers and responsibilities. His willingness to face the undisciplined forces of Nature, to attempt to find for them proper poetic expression, becomes a way of tempering and controlling the emotions they evoke, which in turn elevates the poetic activity to a kind of (sympathetic) magic:

> *For the elemental creatures go*
> *About my table to and fro,*
> *That hurry from unmeasured mind*
> *To rant and rage in flood and wind;*
> *Yet he who treads in measured ways*
> *May surely barter gaze for gaze.*
>
> (VP, 138-9)

Yeats may be speaking metaphorically here, but he believes in the reality of these "elemental creatures" as well as in his own ability, through poetic measure, to tame them. His commitment to his work and belief in its mystical power to control and transform reality exceeds even that of his aesthetic contemporaries, who had the craftsmanship to perform such psychological miracles, but consciously exercised Paterian ideas of creating art only for art's sake.[14]

Whether or not Yeats's criticism of Davidson was just, it reflected his deepest poetic commitments, and, whatever the philosophical shortcomings of the aesthetic poets, he had found in their poems an interest and importance that Davidson's verses lacked. Tension between good and bad, between ecstasy and suffering, held such expressions as "Cynara" in a beautiful balance. Yeats could identify in that situation the shape of his own image for Ireland, and he could learn from its perpetrators how best to produce it on the page. When Davidson nearly put an end to his plans, he was swift to act—placating Johnson and his circle while driving the unruly Scotsman further towards self-exile.

IV. The Conflation of Life and Art

The myth of the Rhymers' Club grew out of two basic tendencies: the tendency of journalists to promote a romantic and often tragic image of the poet and the tendency of the poet to attempt to live up to that image. This fictionalizing process affected the followers of Pater with greatest severity because of their commitment to intense artistic experience and because of their eventual inability to distinguish between their legend and the somewhat less dynamic reality behind it. Arthur Symons's treatment of Ernest Dowson's career reflects the self-destructive fascinations of the aesthetic temperament and the power of rhetoric in altering future attitudes and events. The urge to myth-making, coupled with the kind of myth these poets adopted, may not have been singly responsible for their failure, but it encouraged a life-style and frame of mind that contributed to premature demise.

Arthur Symons forgets precisely when he met Ernest Dowson. "It must have been in 1891," he said, "at one of the meetings of the Rhymers' Club"(MAS, 84). But Dowson remembers clearly and records the event in a letter to Arthur Moore, 29 May 1891: "I met Arthur Symons last night: do you know of him? He is a standing dish with the 'Academy' and knows his Paris well: but on the whole, I was not greatly impressed"(EDL, 201). Dowson's lack of enthusiasm for Symons was probably fostered by the latter's social rather than artistic presence, although, with the decadent artists, one feature tended to be mistaken for the other. In a room full of quick-witted conversationalists, Symons was not a skilled talker, nor did he have the compensating good looks of a Le Gallienne. Nevertheless, he attempted to play the bohemian-artist role, and his performances continued to strike his audiences as somewhat inauthentic. Edgar Jepson remembers meeting him in The Crown, after he had acquired the post of music hall critic for the *Star*. Even at this stage of his progress, the trappings of his trade did not sit naturally upon him:

> He was wearing the longish hair of a poet and
> a top hat on it, and a black coat, and was carrying
> as I remember, an umbrella; but they were some-
> how incongruous with his face and failed to give
> him the poetic air. He was plainly thrilled at be-
> ing a Bohemian in such Bohemian surroundings,
> and I learnt later, that some years before he had
> renounced nonconformity. (MV, 214)

"Michael Field"[15] claimed to have found him charming, but an excerpt from *Works and Days* catches Symons in what must have been a characteristic moment of discontent. The evening in question was Pater's lecture on Prosper Merimée given at the London Institution. All of the illustrious personalities were there—including Oscar Wilde, who "gave to the tiers of faces his lambent eyes." Symons, unaccompanied and poetically solemn, entered last. "He was charming to watch," sighed "Field," "with the crossness of isolation on his brows and mouth" (WD, 120).

If other aesthetes indulged in romantic fantasies, they were not subtly ostracized for it, but Symons's affectations, because he had not sufficiently integrated his suburban character with his poetic role, often offended those he met. Oscar Wilde, who was uncharacteristically calm in Symons's presence, insisted always that he could not pronounce his own name. Wilde, of course, would season the insult by pronouncing the name phonetically: "SIGHmyns," rather than "SIMMyns," for that, according to Wilde, was the way it was spelled. Somewhat later, Victor Plarr (*Ernest Dowson*) and Edgar Jepson ("The Real Ernest Dowson") would take exception to Symons's romanticized treatment of Dowson, which had first appeared as a "literary causerie" in the August issue of the *Savoy* (1896). Dowson himself treated Symons's exaggerations with patience and indulgence, but demonstrated a realistic understanding of the damage such transmutations could do. The letter deserves to be quoted in full because it offers a list of requests from which later comments will spring:

> You are right in assuming my complete indifference to what things may be said of me over yonder, & I am content to be found of sufficient interest personally, to be the subject of your chronique. Would you, however, mind, toning down certain phrases of the 3rd page of your proof which I return forthwith to you—sentences which would—if the veil of your article were penetrated—give an erroneous & too lurid account of me: for have I not been peacefully rusticating these five months en pleine campagne? The sentence "Abroad in the *shadier* quarters of foreign cities etc down to "Gay" to him" [sic] is the one which I have in mind & suggests the too hopelessly disreputable. *Could you, without spoiling your article,* change that sentence into an expression of the fact that my wanderings have long since outgrown mine old "curious love of the sordid", and am grown the most pastoral of men? I should be grateful if you would do this, not so much for my own feeling, as for the benefit of sundry of my friends, who might otherwise be needlessly pained (as for instance Image, who heard exaggerated rumours of my life in Paris & was at the pains to write a most kind grieved paternal letter.). If at the same time you would suppress a too alcoholic reference to the cabman's shelter—(for the "refused admittance" was to outsiders generally and not personal) substitute

"readier means of oblivion" or some such phrase for "oblivion of alcohole", & if you *could* possibly find a less ignoble word than "very dilapidated", there is nothing in your article which I have any objection to your publishing.

It is always of curious interest to get any genuine idea of the manner in which others see you, & and I am especially charmed with the sympathy & tact with which you touch on what you call my "supreme sensation". And for your conclusion I take off my hat to the compliment—the "genius" is perhaps too partial and beacoup trop flatteur, but, as no one is better aware than myself, I have always had, alas! too much of that "swift,/disastrous & suicidal energy" which destroyed our dear & incomparable Verlaine.

(5 July 1896, EDL, 371-2.)

A tacit understanding seems to exist between these two writers that the truth must be altered in order to make it taleworthy, or that the truth the artist wants lies somewhere beyond the strictures of fact. Dowson's mention of "the veil" of Symons's article refers to the knowledge that nowhere in the text does the author identify his subject by name. Yet the term goes further to define a strategy of presentation representative of the age and the individuals involved. *"Nommer un objet,"* said Stéphane Mallarmé, *"c'est supprimer les trois quarts de la jouissance du poème."* And Verlaine used the veil to create a tension between observer and observed:

> *Et, dans les longs plis de son voile*
> *Qui palpite au* brises d'automne,* *[sic]
> *Cache et montre au coeur qui s'étonne,*
> *La vérité comme une étoile.*

> (And in the long folds of her veil
> That trembles in the autumn breezes,
> She hides and reveals to the surprised heart
> Truth like a star.)[16]

Verlaine, of course, was talking about a woman and Mallarmé, about a poem; but the lessons they had to teach were absorbed into Symons's prose. To suppress a name meant to subject the reading mind to a new focus of interest, and the decision to do so was based upon an understanding that we had become too attached to names, had begun to assume that we knew all there was to know about a subject if we could simply affix to it a suitable proper noun. Mallarmé vexed his reader into discovering new dimensions of reality or of rediscovering essential traits behind the textbook definitions of words. By disengaging his subject from all of the expected labels, he released it from the specific into the universal. Symons, leaving out Dowson's name, turned actuality into ideality: the individual poet became a representative of the movement as a whole and a working element of Symons's personal myth. Verlaine's image of the woman benefitted from an archetypally-accepted sense of enigma and was easily translatable into other terms. The crucial concept lay in the veil: a fibrous barrier that allowed the eye to see and not see its object—the not-seeing encouraging us to imagine greater visions than the one that actually lay behind or beyond. Whistler's paintings offered a similar sensation, with their misty atmospheres and dark, half-perceived figures shimmering in the distance. Yeats, of course, understood the principle well, importing the symbol into his own account of history, naming his chapter on the nineties "The Trembling of the Veil."

Symons's "literary causerie" on Dowson informally and confidentially narrates the story of a young poet whom he had "the privilege to know somewhat intimately." The facts remain sufficiently close to the events of Dowson's life so that the author felt the responsibility to send him the galley sheets and ask for his approval. Yet the treatment of these facts—the words used, the nostalgic tone and the somewhat willful interpretation of events—twists the story to the point of misrepresentation. Dowson recognized all this, and voiced his exceptions almost apologetically: *"Could you, without spoiling . . .", "could* you possibly find . . ." At the same time, his concern for reality and respectability leads him to ask for alterations. As he thinks further on the subject, his list of requests grows. At first, he restricts himself to the final page of Symons's article in which he speaks of Dowson's present life in "the ship-wrecked quietude of a sort of self exile" (by which he means Dowson's residence in France). Then he moves back to earlier scenes where his patronage of cabmen's shelters is discussed, and then back even further to where Symons describes him as having "a pathetic charm, a sort of Keats-like face." Dowson does not even raise the point that Jepson and Plarr find especially disturbing—that Symons did not know Dowson intimately, that their relationship never really matured beyond the original indifference, that Symons had no business writing about an individual whom he was bound, through ignorance, to misinterpret. Dowson understood, it seems, that the real personality did not matter in art, and he was also flattered by his biographer's attempt to turn him into a literary figure—"It is always of curious interest to get any genuine idea of the manner in which others see you."

As far as Symons's commitment to reality is concerned, one need only examine what he made of Dowson's requests. "Abroad in the *shadier* quarters of foreign cities" has been dropped, but one suspects that the remainder of the segment has not appreciably changed. Dowson is still credited with a "curious love of the sordid," and if his present life has achieved any pastoral sense, it depends heavily upon notions of resignation and defeat:

> So the wilder wanderings began, and a gradual slipping into deeper and steadier waters of oblivion. That curious love of the sordid, so common an affectation of the modern decadent, and with him so expressively genuine, grew upon him, and dragged him into yet more sorry corners of a life which was never exactly 'gay' to him. And now, indifferent to most things, in the shipwrecked quietude of a sort of self-exile, he is living, I believe, somewhere on a remote foreign seacoast. (93)

Symons knew perfectly well where Dowson was living, but in a tribute of this kind it would not have been appropriate to offer his address. By way of compensation, the segment on the cabmen's shelter had been extensively revised. Instead of having been refused admittance, the poet and his friends "were welcomed, cordially and without comment." "I used to think he was at his best in a cabmen's shelter," explained Symons, "Without a certain sordidness in his surroundings, he was never quite comfortable, never quite himself . . . ." Dowson's suggestion of "readier means of oblivion" has taken the place of "oblivion of alcohole," but it accompanies specific reference to more *risqué* behavior:

> At Oxford, I believe, his favourite form of intoxication had been haschisch; afterwards he gave up this somewhat elaborate experiment in visionary sensations for readier means of oblivion; but he returned to it, I remember, for at least one afternoon, in a company of which I had been the gatherer, and of which I was the host . . . . (92)

Finally, Symons revised his assessment of Dowson's appearance, changing "very dilapidated" to the infinitely more respectable "somewhat dilapidated." He still insisted, however, upon Dowson's bohemian image, his homeless and haunting ways, and his own inability to recall when he first met him:

> I do not remember the occasion of our first meeting, but I remember seeing him casually, at railway-stations, in a semi-literary tavern which once had a fantastic kind of existence, and sometimes, at night, in various parts of the Temple, before I was more than slightly his acquaintance.
>
> I was struck then by a look and manner of pathetic charm, a sort of Keats-like face, the face of a demoralized Keats, and by something curious in the contrast of a manner exquisitely refined, with an appearance generally somewhat dilapidated.
>
> (91)

Symons's vision of the nineties emphasized the waywardness of its poets and their sense of romantic self-destruction. This estimation of reality repelled Jepson and Plarr because, in Dowson's case at least, it altered history's apprehension of the poet and, very likely, the poet's apprehension of himself. The consequences of such creations may be deduced from style and effect. This "literary causerie" reads curiously like an obituary, and Dowson, who had been impressed by his own similarity to Verlaine (his "swift,/disastrous & suicidal energy") managed to fulfill the articles' prophecy by dying four years later. One cannot say that Symons's article killed the poet, but his dream and Dowson's temptation to believe it indicated a pattern of behavior that necessitated fulfillment in death. Yeats said that Symons "could slip as it were into the mind of another" (AU, 319), and, if he eventually slipped into Dowson's mind, it was to plant there an idea of tragedy in which he (Dowson) would be the principal character.

Any study of the Rhymers' Club and its members must in some ways be a study of myth. Poets such as Dowson, Le Gallienne and Yeats made of their lives a literary experience, and whatever truths may be drawn from their work (memoirs as well as poems) must be considered as conceptual rather than factual truths. Casual historians have taken imprecise information from these primary sources and, in efforts to compensate for lack of information or conflicting information, have perpetuated or aggravated the problem in later accounts. But factual imprecisions are not the only impediments to an accurate characterization of the Club. The aesthetic poets as a group present literary history with a collection of potential contradictions: poems that at once are and are not biographical, a philosophy of art that nevertheless denies philosophy and a legend of poetic immediacy that coexists with a concept of conscious craft. Dowson and Johnson in particular suffered as a result of these confusions, exercising powerful poetic talent but not realizing the ways in which that talent could be or was being channelled. Yeats learned from these artists' experience, using his poetic skills to build a national literature for Ireland. His unwavering belief in the power of language to order and control experience allowed him to continue to develop his craft, whereas the uncompromising ideologies, psychological inadequacies and simple lack of practical understanding severely limited poets like Rhys, Davidson, Dowson and Johnson. Even in the earliest documents concerning the Club, one perceives the subtle frictions that developed between members, the tendency to conflate life and art, the self-destructive attitudes that would determine not only the brevity of the Club's existence but the professional failure of some of its most promising poets.

NOTES FOR CHAPTER 2

[1] In YS, I (1971): 203, Ian Fletcher says that "P.M. 19 JA. 91." was written in under the address by Horne, but it is more likely an addition made by Yeats. The nineteenth of January was a Monday, and the "Thursday next" mentioned would have been the twenty-ninth. Johnson's and Dowson's letters concerning the meeting are appropriately dated early February.

[2] Arthur Symons submitted *London Nights* to him for inspection, and Ernest Dowson received a solicitous letter from him concerning his lifestyle in France. See Chapters III and II respectively.

[3] Flower and Maas report in a footnote that Whistler once said to Wilde, "Never let me see you . . . in the combined costume of Kossuth and Mantalini" (EDL, 183). Kossuth was a Hungarian patriot who took refuge in England during the reign of Victoria. Mr. Mantalini is a somewhat extravagant (and dishonest) fop in *Nicholas Nickleby*.

[4] A friend of Ernest Dowson, Edgar Jepson identified her as "Missie, the little lady of Dowson's heart and the Cynara of the Poem" (MV, 219). Her real name was Adelaide, and she was the daughter of Joseph Foltinowicz, owner of "The Poland" restaurant in Soho.

[5] He mentions her in a letter to Arthur Moore, 9 November 1889, EDL, 114.

[6] Letter to Arthur Moore, 18 May 1891, EDL, 190: "I have seen the proofs of my 'Cynara' poem for the April Hobby. It looks less indecent in print, but I am still nervous! though I admire Horne's audacity. I read it, or rather Lionel did for me, at the last Rhymers..."

[7] The metrical similarity between Yeats's "Innisfree" and Dowson's "Cynara" has led Hugh Kenner to conclude that

Yeats had "Cynara" in mind when he wrote his poem, but "Innisfree" was published in December 1890 (in Henley's *National Observer*), and "Cynara" was not written until 7 February 1891. The real link in this process may have been Lionel Johnson, whose enthusiasm for Alexandrines may have spurred his associates to experiment with that meter and whom Dowson names in relation to "Cynara" (EDL, 184). See CE, 53.

[8]"The Rhymers' Club" was originally published in the *Boston Pilot*, 1892. It speaks at length of Symons, Davidson and Todhunter, and it alludes also to Le Gallienne, Greene and Rolleston. Dowson is not mentioned.

[9]See comments and quotation on "The Song of Wandering Aengus," CP, 53-4.

[10]Benjamin Townsend, Davidson's biographer, found the available evidence so confusing that he presented the story as if it were two separate events. See JD, 144-5.

[11]See, for example, Stanley Weintraub's "Autobiography and Authenticity: Memoir Writing Among Some Late Victorians," *Sources for Reinterpretation: The Use of Nineteenth Century Literary Documents; Essays in Honor of C. L. Cline*. Austin: University of Texas Press, 1975. 1-21. Also James Olney's "Some Versions of Memory/Some Versions of Bios: The Ontology of Autobiography," *Autobiography: Essays Theoretical and Critical*. Princeton: Princeton University Press, 1980. 236-67; and Ian Fletcher's "The 1890s: A Lost Decade," *Victorian Studies* 4.4 (June 1961): 345-54.

[12]Dutch polyglot and translator of Molière into English.

[13]Symons had no higher education at all; Dowson left Oxford without a degree because he knew he could not pass his exams.

[14]See "Hopes and Fears for Irish Literature," *United Ireland* (15 October 1892), reprinted in UP1, 248-50. Here, Yeats speaks of the dependence "of all great art and literature upon conviction and upon heroic life." He also speaks of the decadent artists, whose craftsmanship he recognizes but whose art remains

limited by purely aesthetic goals. "—Can we but learn a little of their skill, a little of their devotion to form . . . we may make all these restless energies of ours alike the inspiration and the theme of a new literature."

[15]Composite pen name for poets Katherine Bradley and Edith Cooper.

[16]Lines from Verlaine's essay "My Visit to London," printed in SA (August 1896): 119-135. (My translation).

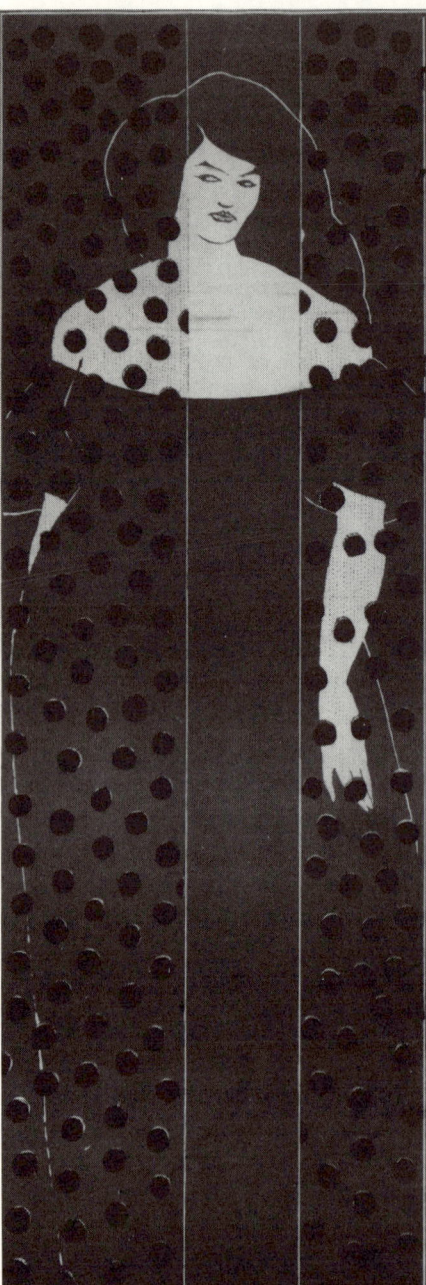

THE TURNING OF THE GYRE

Just as there has been some mystery concerning the founding date of the Rhymers' Club, so has the paucity of primary material generated questions concerning its demise. For a long time, it was thought that the Club disbanded in 1894, just after the publication of its second anthology, but as Beckson points out in "New Dates for the Rhymers' Club" (ELT, 13.1), the group met in some form well into 1896. Whether or not one accepts Beckson's conclusions concerning formal terminal dates depends again on concepts of membership and Club identity, and lack of sufficient information fosters similar opportunities for imprecision and myth. Dramatic changes were occurring in the cultural mood midway through the 1890s, and the Rhymers' Club was caught in a series of events that made its ideals and goals eventually redundant. This process took place during the period from late 1894 onward, and the meetings attested to in 1896 were probably vestigal efforts by remaining members to overcome the difficulties of the age. As with founding dates, absolute endings ignore both the limitations and complications of our knowledge, and it seems more valuable to focus on the evolution of change rather than attempt to represent it as sudden and complete.

Three primary factors contributed to the break-up of the Rhymers' Club during this period: the dissolution of the publishing partnership of John Lane and Elkin Mathews, the trial and conviction of Oscar Wilde, and the personal misfortunes and ill health of various key members. Appearing at stages before these events, the Rhymers' Club anthologies provide evidence of the emotional and artistic inclinations that led first to the disintegration of the Club and finally to the personal and professional disintegration of individual members. From amongst these writers, W. B. Yeats distinguished himself, demonstrating commitment to a cause more complex than beauty, exercising crucial though rare instincts for poetic survival.

I. Dissolution of the Lane-Mathews Partnership

At the sign of the Bodley Head in Vigo Street, Elkin Mathews and John Lane had produced a number of quality books by minor poets and had sponsored not only *The Book of the Rhymers' Club* and *The Second Book of the Rhymers' Club* but various works by individual Rhymers.[1] This profitable and increasingly popular business, however, was undermined by personality differences between its two principals, and the eventual dissolution of the partnership in September 1894 took its toll on writers who had depended on the firm for its publishing opportunities. Troubles began to surface shortly after *The Second Book of the Rhymers' Club* appeared in June 1894. Mathews, who had been a reluctant partner from the start, found himself edged out of the firm's affairs by the more aggressive Lane, and, although he preferred solitude to the political and social maneuverings necessary for a successful business, he felt he could no longer support the systematic exclusions Lane had exercised. Lane attempted to disregard personal problems while he wooed and won promising writers, but Mathews's lack of gratitude for his achievements fostered irrepressable bitterness.

Those who claim the split was amicable say less than the truth. In a letter to T. N. Brushfield, Mathews spoke with exasperation of Lane's having insinuated himself into the partnership, of his failure to put up funds for his half of the business and of his haste to win over authors once it became evident that the partnership would not survive. "I decided," said Mathews, "he was an impossible man to get on with—a man who was simply working for his own hand" (7 February 1895, EMC MS 392/1/1, ff 727-34). For his part, Lane suffered impatiently with Mathews's social ineffectuality and comparative literary conservatism. Le Gallienne had tried to assure him that "silly and ungrateful as from every point of view he is, he cannot do you or the business any real harm" (Letter, 17 January 1893, JLC), but harm evidently was done and grew too virulent to be ignored. The swiftness with which Lane took his business to quarters across the street from Mathews's offices indicates not only his lack of regret but his actual animosity towards his erstwhile partner.

The Rhymers' Club was caught in the middle of this dispute—not only as a group of individual writers who had to choose which publisher most deserved their works, but as an organization (one might recall, a highly tenuous organization) of poets that had published together two successful anthologies and looked forward to bringing out a third. The dissolution of the Lane/Mathews partnership not only threatened to end a mutually-acceptable publishing outlet, but promised to eliminate the only working bond the Club had ever had.

Much was at stake, and tempers flared as each poet rallied to support his respective favorite. G. A. Greene, in his capacity of secretary, wrote to Ernest Radford announcing the impending necessity:

> Writers in the 2nd Rh. Bk. have to decide whether Mathews or Lane is to be publisher. Will you kindly send me your vote at earliest convenience? If discussion at a meeting is preferred, please let me know at once.
> (17 September 1894, EMC 392/1/1, f706)

Radford's reply came two days later and demonstrates the political furor that threatened over this call for loyalties:

If others feel as strongly as I on the relative claims to respect of our publishers—there will be a row amongst members when we meet at the Cheshire Cheese.

Please therefore register my vote for Mathews.

I shall certainly withdraw from the Club if a third Book is offered to Lane. (19 September 1894, EMC 392/1/1, f 707)

Chroniclers attempt to gloss the difficulties involved in the decision-making process by saying that the Club voted, almost to a man, to keep anthology rights with Mathews ("A Note on the Reputation of Elkin Mathews," EMPP, n. p.; EN, 275; MOB, 9-10), but the controversy that raged concerning what status other of their works should receive indicates the political volatility of the situation. While Lane was canvassing the impressionable mass of Mathews sympathizers, Mathews was trying to engage Lane's followers in his own new business ventures. "I have elected to allow [Lane] to have my stock," John Davidson replied, "and to read for him what MSS he sends me. I shall also in all probability offer him my next book" (13 August 1894, EMC 392/1/1, f698). Thus, he categorically refused Mathews's propositions, placing his loyalties squarely behind Lane. Richard Le Gallienne remained loyal to Lane as well, entrusting to him his full creative output. Continuing to serve as Lane's first reader, Le Gallienne ultimately secured the work of other former Rhymers, including Ernest Rhys's *A London Rose* and Victor Plarr's *In the Dorian Mood*.

On the other hand, many poets felt strongly that Mathews deserved a larger share of the profits. Ernest Radford was prepared to mount a campaign in his defense and felt assured that Yeats would side with him instead of Lane. "In that case," he noted in a letter to Mathews, "his name would bear weight" (13

September 1894. EMC 392/1/1, ff704-5). Yeats and Johnson clearly sympathized with Mathews, but they eventually settled for a compromise. Yeats, who had heretofore published nothing with the Bodley Head (with the exception of his contributions to the Rhymers' Club anthologies) offered Mathews *The Wind Among the Reeds*.[2] Lionel Johnson split the responsibility for his material as well, having been worried into such a position by Lane's persistence. On 5 September 1894, he made his final decision, designating editorial responsibilities for upcoming collections of his poems and revealing to Mathews the consternation he felt concerning Lane's stipulations:

> I have written to Lane telling him of my decision and offering him the second volume of poems. I have told him that if he declines to publish for any one, who also publishes with you, I don't understand or sympathize with that state of mind, and shall offer everything to you exclusively. (EMC 392/1/1, ff 701-3)

Johnson's impatience with and Radford's sense of outrage at the controversy between Lane and Mathews offers sufficient evidence of the impact the dispute had on individual Rhymers, and the fact that members took opposite sides and staunchly defended their respective editor indicates the political tensions that must have affected the Club during this period. Even if members voted almost unanimously to keep their anthologies with Mathews, Lane still came away with the largest number of authors,[3] and the third collection of Rhymers' Club verse, originally planned for Mathews, never materialized. Although one cannot confirm that internal conflicts alone caused this failure, one must suspect that a lack of cooperation between authors had played an important role.

II. The Wilde Trials

A short five months after the termination of the Lane/Mathews partnership, another major series of events helped spread the seeds of dissolution even further. On 18 February 1895, the eighth Marquess of Queensberry, father of Lord Alfred Douglas, left his calling card at the Albemarle Club for Wilde, writing upon it "For Oscar Wilde posing as a somdomite" [sic]. On the second of March, Queensberry was arrested and formally charged with libel, and on the third of April, the trial against him began. What was to start out as a carnival was to end up as a tragedy, as evidence of Wilde's own guilt stacked up against him. Upon Queensberry's acquittal, the prosecuting party was arrested and charged with twenty-five counts of gross indecency. The first trial ended in a hung jury; the second, found Wilde guilty of seven of the original twenty-five counts and sentenced him to two years imprisonment and hard labor.

Having been Wilde's publishers, both Lane and Mathews were implicated in his debacle, and the Rhymers' Club, whose members were either associated with Wilde, his publishers or both, felt the pressure of rising public hostility towards literary decadence in general. When Wilde was arrested, he took with him a copy of Pierre Louÿs's *Aphrodite*, which was bound in a yellow cover. Journalists mistakenly identified this volume as *The Yellow Book*, then published by Lane's Bodley Head and constituting the principal organ of the decadent school of writing. The (mis)identification was sufficiently powerful to induce a mob to stone Lane's offices and ultimately to cause the firing of that magazine's art editor, Aubrey Beardsley, whose only known offense was to have illustrated Wilde's *Salome*.[4] Mathews was called to the stand during the second trial to answer questions concerning Wilde's relationship with Edward Shelley, a former office boy at the Bodley Head. Anxious to defuse potential misapprehensions concerning the moral rectitude of his business, Mathews testified that when he learned of Shelley's association with Wilde he had dismissed him. Shelley himself later claimed that he quit because others had teased him about the situation, and Rupert Croft-Cooke, in *The Unrecorded Life of Oscar Wilde* indicates that their teasing had been somewhat justified (129ff).

Although the case concerning Shelley was ultimately dismissed, the connection between Bodley Head affairs and possible homosexual or "immoral" activities had been established. Publishers as well as authors affiliated with the firm hastened to make their respective loyalties clear. Following Beardsley's dismissal, most of the Rhymers who had contributed to *The Yellow Book* ceased doing so. Le Gallienne and Davidson, adherents of a less questionable or more robust notion of art, were exceptions, and under their influence that periodical changed drastically in tone and quality. Lane, who had lost all taste for the *avant garde* in the Beardsley controversy, practiced similar exclusions in subsequent literary decisions; and Mathews, who professed continued interest in such authors, began to exercise unconscionable delays in bringing their work before the public. Nobody, of course, published Wilde's work. His books disappeared from publishers' circulars, and his plays were withdrawn from the theatres.[5]

The ferment over literary decadence and its bearing on concepts of morality and life in general had been stirring in individual minds for some time, and Wilde's trials provided the focus for, or perhaps merely the measure of, public hostilities. The effect of this process on Rhymers who adhered to aesthetic principles may be seen in the difficulties one member encountered in maintaining an outlet and audience for his work. During the winter of 1894-5, when Queensberry's assaults on Wilde were becoming increasingly difficult to ignore, Symons's *London Nights* went in need of a publisher. Having submitted the manuscript to Lane, Symons was shocked to discover that Lane wanted no part of it. He received a similar rejection from William Heinemann, leading him to wonder about the sudden undesirability of his work. "The refusal of Lane and Heinemann," he wrote to Edmund Gosse on 26 February, "was to me so inexplicable that I have just had the MS read by my very fairminded and judicious friend, Selwyn Image, offering to omit anything to which he himself took exception on the ground of taste and morals"(AS, 123). Image, a stable churchman and an associate of the Rhymers' Club, replied that it was "the extremely *personal* side which has shocked people"(AS, 124), indicating that intimacy between life and art which Yeats would later identify as the strength of Rhymers' Club verse.

When the book appeared in the early summer of 1895, under Leonard Smithers's imprint, the reviews bore out Lane's and others' predictions.[6] Coming as it did on the heels of Wilde's debacle, this volume could not hope to receive the treatment it deserved, and the almost unilateral hostility of the reviewers' comments reflected their sense of impunity in attacking this particular genre of verse. For Symons, the proper criterion for judgement was still the aesthetic pleasure afforded by art, rather than its adherence to established moral concepts, but the prevailing mood of the public at this time was one of hostility towards a movement that had rejected their own values and had stood in open contempt of their supposed needs. "All art, surely, is a form of artifice," Symons complained, "and, thus, to the truly devout mind, condemned already, if not as actively noxious, at all events as needless" ("Being a Word on Behalf of Patchouli," S, xi). Yeats offered a similar explanation of Wilde's downfall. It was not, as he argued, simply a matter of his purported immorality, but of his indifference to the common lot, their limited perceptivity and sensitivity:

> The rage against Wilde was also complicated by the Britisher's jealousy of art and the artist, which is generally dormant but is called into activity when the artist has got outside his field into

> publicity of an undesirable kind. This hatred is not due to any action of the artist or eminent man; it is merely the expression of an individual hatred and envy, become collective because circumstances have made it so. (Quoted from OWB, n. 232)

Following the Wilde debacle and Beardsley's dismissal from *The Yellow Book*, a small group of aesthetes—several of whom were Rhymers' Club members—began to plan their strategic response. With Arthur Symons as general editor and Leonard Smithers as their controversial but courageous publisher, this group launched the *Savoy*, a periodical that aimed to satisfy London's literary audience "by not being original for originality's sake, or audacious for the sake of advertisement, or timid for the convenience of the elderly-minded" (SA Prospectus, 1895). Still, the *Savoy* reflected an attitude of defiance: by assuming the name of the hostelry where Wilde had allegedly seduced his young followers and by employing as its art editor Aubrey Beardsley, the *enfant terrible* of *The Yellow Book*.[7] Had the venture worked, it would have offered an outlet for those Rhymers who continued to ascribe to aesthetic principles and who thrived on literary fellowship, but its illustrations, stories, poems and essays failed to attract even minimal public support. In December 1896, scarcely a year after it first appeared on the stands, the *Savoy* ceased publication. Symons attributed its demise to his having offered too much for too little, to having abandoned the quarterly system for monthly publications and to having assumed that "there were very many people in the world who really cared for art" ("By Way of Epilogue," SA, December 1896). In reality, it seems that the public's idea of art had changed and that continued efforts to promote the decadent cause were doomed to failure.

The rise in public hostility towards literary decadence,

which culminated in the fury expressed over Oscar Wilde's private life, left individual Rhymers with the problem of adjusting their art to a new set of cultural imperatives. For some, the situation created a barrier which they could not get beyond; for others, it encouraged a return to facile and outdated modes, unchallenged by differing critical views. Symons and Dowson, who had identified most closely with literary decadence, could not embrace the moral certainties implied. Richard Le Gallienne, protected by Lane and middle class attitudes and tastes, lapsed into the coy preciosity that had constituted the worst aspect of his earlier work. Yeats alone found sufficient substance to continue growing artistically, his Irish subject matter giving him a unique perspective on the world, while avoiding too intimate a connection either with his own private griefs or the unseemly aspects of decadence. His mystical convictions championed the magical power of poetry; his search for an artistic philosophy promised intellectual substance and control.

III. Personal Misfortunes

A third factor contributing to the dissolution of the Rhymers' Club involved developments in the lives of individual members—especially those whose talents had once promised to reap substantial rewards, but whose work was now failing to live up to that promise. Part of the difficulty had to do with the sudden turn in public and critical opinion, but part also had to do with the psychological and physical burdens these poets had to bear and the way in which they chose to bear them. Dowson was unhappily in love with "Missie" the Polish restaurant keeper's daughter, but he also bore the scars of his parents' deaths, by suicide, in 1894 and 1895.[8] Inheriting their self-destructiveness, their tendency to consumption as well as their debts, Dowson left England for France in 1895, returning only periodically thereafter in various attempts to raise money to live on.

Lionel Johnson suffered emotionally from the Oscar Wilde

controversy, not only as one who had encouraged Wilde's prodigality but as one whose religious sense now found such activities repulsive. Where once he had written a spirited benediction to the author of *Dorian Gray*, he now found fault with the attitudes that had characterized that author's work, accusing him in "The Destroyer of a Soul" of bringing about Douglas's destruction and depriving him (Johnson) of a friend. Thus alienated from his once-close circle of associates, he turned increasingly to an inner world of religious contemplation for the fellowship and persuasion he lacked.

Johnson had also been subject to severe physical ailments from at least 1891 onward[9] and had developed a growing dependence on alcohol as a means of dulling his discomfort. Having been ousted from his lodgings at 20 Fitzroy Street because of the danger he posed to others, he moved in September 1895 to Gray's Inn Square, and thence to Lincoln's Inn and Clifford's Inn, leaving old friendships and frustrations behind. Edgar Jepson reports an incident he had heard from Victor Plarr in which Johnson and Dowson, after an evening of heavy drinking, fell downstairs in each other's arms, "their progress illumined by a terrifying flame from the lamp which rolled with them"(MV, 248-9), and Yeats substantiates in his *Autobiographies*, describing the steps of Johnson's withdrawal: " . . . he shifted from Charlotte Street, where, I think there was fear that he would overset lamp or candle and burn the house to Gray's Inn to old rambling rooms in Lincoln's Inn Fields, and at last one called to find his outer door shut, the milk on the doorstep sour" (Au, 309). Johnson's increasing physical debilitation, often interpreted by his peers as simple debauchery, cut him off from his associates and from the artistic world in general. Absenting himself from the Rhymers' Club, he spent his last years in isolation, his creative potential all but exhausted.

With Dowson and Johnson gone, with Yeats and Symons devoting most of their time to the *Savoy*—and, in Yeats's case, to

Lady Gregory and the cause of the Irish Theatre—the Rhymers' Club met less frequently with less real purpose.[10] The meetings in 1896 evidenced by post cards and letters were probably scattered attempts to gain political ends: to convince Mathews to keep the possibility of future anthologies in mind, to fashion the illusion of artistic solidarity in the wake of the Wilde trials, to assess the level of agreement and cooperation that they actually did have.

But there was little solidarity among them. The best talents had ceased to lend their efforts to the organization, and they lacked sufficient cooperation to produce a collection of their work. Yeats continued to host literary gatherings at his rooms in Woburn Buildings, but the faces and goals of these meetings had changed: following the demise of the *Savoy*, such individuals as Florence Farr, Edward Martyn, George Moore and Lady Gregory turned conversations away from decadent art towards the concerns of Irish drama. The Paterian aesthetes, anxious to make individual gains in the literary world, had been supplanted by the Irish Nationalists, bent upon establishing a sense of literary tradition and achievement for their country.

When Dowson died of consumption in 1900 and when Johnson collapsed in the Green Dragon Pub in 1902, the age to which they belonged had already passed, and the Rhymers' Club had ceased to function. Symons's madness in 1908 and Davidson's suicide in 1909 reinforced a sense of the tragedy and futility of these poets' careers and caused the survivors to look back upon that era with new seriousness and understanding. The two anthologies which the Rhymers' Club had produced became legacies by which to know these largely unknown writers, and the one remaining talent of that group became, himself, a valuable legacy—one who had undergone the ordeal that society had imposed upon him and who had lived to speak for those whose gifts had given out.

The books of the Rhymers' Club today constitute the most direct and extended statements we have from the group and, as such, serve as important documents in the discovery of these poets' abilities and aspirations. Although the creative enterprise itself forbids us from taking its products strictly biographically, one can derive from these poems a sense of the Rhymers' position in history and the end towards which they precipitously moved. Harold Bloom claimed that the aesthetic poets failed because they could not put their faith completely in art (Y, 51), but their poems also indicate that they failed because they were artistically intoxicated with failure. One finds in Rhymers' Club verse an increasing preoccupation with death, an attitude of cultural and social withdrawal that ultimately determined the obscurity of their art. As Yeats himself had recognized in "Hopes and Fears for Irish Literature" (UP1, 248-50), their unwillingness to deal positively with issues of contemporary, topical or even human importance made them virtually irrelevant to their prospective audience. Adhering to what many construed as a meaningless or morally offensive art, they had little hope of establishing themselves as important literary figures.

The remaining pages of this chapter examine the phenomenon of failure with respect to the poems of the Rhymers' Club anthologies—not so much in terms of quality, but in terms of the attitudes and tendencies that contributed to these poets' ends. In the case of Dowson's, Symons's, Johnson's and Plarr's work, failure seems almost incongruous, given its seeming promise, but one can see in these entries the direction in which these poets moved and the reputations they would inherit as tragic figures. In both Rhymers' Club anthologies, but increasingly in the second, one perceives an attitude of withdrawal that ultimately negates the act of poetry. Yeats, too, indulged in escapism, but his retreats from the world were directed towards spiritual understanding, and his treatment of death was generally conducted from the point of view of a survivor. While he sought a greater expressive range for his Irish subject matter, his contemporaries gradually narrowed themselves, moving closer to apprehensions of self-extinction and silence.

The Book of the Rhymers' Club opened with a toast, celebrating "Queen Rhyme" in defiance of all other gestures. *The Second Book of the Rhymers' Club* opened with a dirge and dealt increasingly with the theme of death. This difference outlines a regression of attitude from simple ungovernability towards confirmed negation—in other words, away from a state of "artistic promise" towards a private, self-consuming art. Others of that era identified with the notions of loss that these poets depicted, but, by the time the second volume had appeared, they wanted more than a statement of the cultural need. The Rhymers denied responsibility for cultural answers in an adolescent urge for simplicity and "purity" in verse. Those who might have met the challenge refused to do so, turning their backs on "philosophy," "science" and "public demand."

The Second Book of the Rhymers' Club nevertheless demonstrated an awareness of the cultural problem and offered an implicit reaction to it in its editorial arrangement and poetic preoccupations. The initial poem of the volume, John Todhunter's "In Westminster Abbey," commemorates Tennyson's death in October 1892, calling attention to the end of a long and important era:

> In her still House of Fame her Laureate dead
>   England entombs to-day, lays him to rest,
> The leaves of honour green around his head,
>   Love's flowers fresh on his breast.
>
> Mourn him in solemn service of high song,
>   Music serene as breathed in his last breath,
> When, to the soundless ocean borne along,
>   He met majestic Death.
>
> Mourn him with grief's most fair solemnities,

> Ritual that with an inward rapture suits,
>   While in stern pomp the mind's grave companies
>   March, as to Dorian flutes.
>
> If tears we shed, 'tis but as eyes grow dim
>   When some rich strain superbly rolls away,
> For like the close of an Olympian hymn
>   Ended his golden day.
>
> Bear him in pride, like a dead conqueror
>   Brought home to his last triumph in sad
>   state,
> Over him his Country's Flag, who in life's war
>   Was victor over fate.
>
> We saw him stand, a lordly forest tree,
>   His branches filled with music, all the air
> Glad for his presence; fallen at last is he,
>   And all the land is bare.
>
> So, with old Handel thundering in our ears,
>   His mighty dirge marching from breast to
>   breast
> In sorrow's purple pageant, with proud tears
>   We leave him to his rest.
>
>   (1-2)

This lament and its position at the opening of the volume implicitly acknowledges the responsibility these poets shared as continuing artists. Yet it and the poems that follow suggest that the Rhymers were less able than ever to accept the challenge. In the case of Rolleston, Ellis, Radford or Greene, it was simply a lack of sufficient talent. In the case of Dowson, Symons or Johnson, it was more an inability to sustain beliefs by which to embrace experience and ultimately to justify their work.

While not fully characteristic of the variety of expressions to be found in the book, "In Westminster Abbey" underscores the essential difficulty plaguing Rhymers' Club verse. Acknowledging the passing of an age and implying that a new order must ensue, Todhunter's lines remain stylistically and conceptually bound by the past. Projecting a certain Tennysonian sonorousness, they are acceptable as far as imitations go, but fail to move beyond what Yeats had dubbed "the dreadful burden of the TCD tradition." Phrases like "Mourn him with grief's most fair solemnitites" or "If tears we shed, 'tis but as eyes grow dim," echo familiar Victorian sentiment while failing to convey genuine emotion or a sense of where poetry might go from here. In the end, the elegiac mode turns to self-mockery, as Handel's "thundering" is seen marching "from breast to breast," creating within "sorrow's purple pageant" the depersonalized condition of "proud tears."

Other Rhymers bore other but similarly crippling burdens in their attempts to achieve success. Unable to see new possibilities in the forms they inherited, they remained part of the artistic past rather than its future. Todhunter's poem, thus, speaks symbolically to the reader on two different levels: of Tennyson's death and the end of an age; of imitation and the lack of substantial talent to replace the loss.

I. Ernest Dowson

Ernest Dowson had much to offer poetically and did so, except that his contributions did not address the challenge implicit in the passing of England's laureate. For him, as for most decadents, rebellion found its expression in poetry that stated the problem but made little attempt at answers. So, while his technical achievements were admirable, his subject matter never rose to the level of social or philosophical engagement. Of the six poems that were eventually chosen for the second Rhymers' Club anthology, only one ("Growth") refrained from ultimate rejection of worldly interests and values. The others ("Extreme Unction," "To One in Bedlam," "Cynara," "The Garden of Shadow" and *"Ah, dans ces mornes séjours"*) gained their power from situations or moods generally thought undesirable—melancholy, disappointment and death offering ultimate spiritual reward. The one poem that attempted a resolution to its own conflicts—and, thus, a tentative reintegration into the affairs of life—nevertheless bore a distinct decadent stamp and gave subtle indication of the crippling psychological obsessions behind Dowson's art. The poem, "Growth," concerns the poet's regret for a young girl's development into maidenhood, a situation that finds obvious parallels in Dowson's own attitude toward "Missie." His ambivalence toward maturity and the maturing process becomes in this poem a reluctance to accept change, and, despite its female subject, recalls Pater's nostalgia for the delicacy and purity of ephemeral youth:

> I watched the glory of her childhood change,
> Half-sorrowful to find the child I knew,
>   (Loved long ago in lily-time)
> Become a maid, mysterious and strange,
> With fair, pure eyes—dear eyes, but not the eyes
>   I knew
>   Of old, in the olden time!

The inevitable intrusion of time on this phase of the girl's development disturbs the poet more thoroughly than it might have done had he been able to appreciate fully-realized beauty. But his adolescent mind balks at the incipience of change in the same way that Pater's narrator turns away from mature themes and focuses on the pathos of dying youths. Dowson expresses similar fears in a letter to Victor Plarr (Autumn 1894), depicting a process of sensual disengagement which ultimately limits his art:

> *Die Kleine* instead of changing, altering, repelling, as I feared/hoped might happen, in the nature of things, seems to grow in grace and favour daily. What a terrible, lamentable thing growth is! It 'makes me mad' to think that in a year or two at the most, the most perfect exquisite relation I ever succeeded in making must naturally come to an end. Yes, it makes me mad. One ought to be able to cease caring for anyone exactly when one wishes; it's too difficult: or one ought to be able to live directly in the present. (EDP, 204)

Part of Dowson's fear seems to lie in the nature of change itself and the inability of the individual to achieve or control perfection because of it. The urge to live in the present or to cease caring "exactly when one wishes" is related to the urge for permanence and freedom from time—a withdrawal from or rejection of life's processes in favor of a more stable, less threatening state. Strangely enough, this adolescent reluctance finds explanation in the decadent-aesthetic adaptation of Platonism. Acknowledging the inherent imperfections of life, one turns away from organic existence towards artifice or art, where time can be eliminated and perfection imaginatively achieved. In poetry and in life, this drive is translated into an intense experience of the moment and is dramatically based on a tension between what is and what could or will be. One thinks of "Cynara," in which the speaker clings to past or unattainable purity in the face of present physical reward, or of Dowson's French predecessor Jules Laforgue, who celebrated potentiality over achievement, childhood over adult love.

The poem itself attempts to resolve the conflict between art and reality by pointing out that the change the poet so resisted is, after all, more rewarding (beautiful, kind) than the state he wanted so impotently to preserve. What he achieves is another moment, an instant of awe and realization as fragile and mysterious as the first:

> Till on my doubting soul the ancient good
> Of her dear childhood in the new disguise
>   Dawned, and I hastened to adore
> The glory of her waking maidenhood,
> And found the old tenderness within her
>   deepening eyes,
>   But kinder than before. (83)

This is certainly not withdrawal of the sort one expects from Dowson, but it remains decadent in its pull against life and its apprehension of the ephemeral. The celebration to be gained from the conclusion is not of the young woman (or of womanhood itself) but of the moment, which is but a stage in a process that will defeat it. Acknowledgement that the woman is now "kinder than before" expresses the wonder and fear she inspires rather than any new sense of intimacy, and the poet focuses on the mystery of change rather than on the individual before him. Significantly, Dowson offers no physical affirmation or true psychological resolution to this encounter, but freezes the statement in a moment of wonder before it takes on more complicated significance or emotion. While one must not place the burden of an entire tradition on such a statement, one can see, through it, why Dowson's verse did not have lasting cultural value. Its delicacy insists upon its own ephemerality, offering little philosophical reward for the experience and dwelling intensely on personal or private (rather than generally communicable) concerns.

Dowson is less hesitant, however, to embrace or affirm reality when dealing with themes of madness, death or general withdrawal, but the distance between these unusual desires and his present state keep him in a condition of irresolution, making the yearning more compelling and ultimately thwarting all sense of social commitment or poetic mission. In "To One in Bedlam," he romanticizes the madman's dreams, longing to be released into that condition; in "Extreme Unction," he yearns for the perfection of death crowned by ritualistic absolution; in "The Garden of Shadow," he speaks of the decaying convention of Love, envisioning an unkempt garden where Love now walks forgotten and alone. In each of these poems, the tension between what is and what might be keeps the expression from nihilism and actually determines its success, but the pull away from the world and its values indicates the direction of Dowson's thought and the probable course of expression once that tension is released. In terms of the search for the new laureate, these offerings fall short of their goal. Ignoring obvious social imperatives, they do not confirm values or give viable answers to the questions they pose.

II. Lionel Johnson

Lionel Johnson's poems present a similar attitude of rejection and thus his unsuitability for the challenge. Of the six poems printed in the volume, the most powerful reflect his own illness and despair, offering only inadequate resolutions to the anxiety of the age. "Mystic and Cavalier," for example, opens with the poignant command, "Go from me: I am one of those, who fall," and "The Dark Angel" spins out in painful clarity the poet's internal conflict between his desire to sin and his less pressing desire to lead a pure life:

> Dark Angel, with thine aching lust
> To rid the world of penitence:
> Malicious Angel, who still dost

The Turning of the Gyre

My soul such subtile violence!

Because of thee, no thought, no thing,
Abides for me undesecrate:
Dark Angel, ever on the wing,
who never reachest me too late!

When music sounds, then changest thou
Its silvery to a sultry fire:
Nor will thine envious heart allow
Delight untortured by desire.

Through thee, the gracious Muses turn
To Furies, O mine Enemy!
And all the things of beauty burn
With flames of evil ecstacy.

Because of thee, the land of dreams
Becomes a gathering place of fears;
Until tormented slumber seems
One vehemence of useless tears.

When sunlight glows upon the flowers,
Or ripples down the dancing sea:
Thou, with thy troop of passionate powers,
Beleaguerest, bewilderest, me.

Within the breath of autumn woods,
Within the winter silences:
Thy venomous spirit stirs and broods,
O master of impieties!

The ardour of red flame is thine,
And thine the steely soul of ice:

Thou poisonest the fair design
Of nature, with unfair device.

Apples of ashes, golden bright;
Waters of bitterness, how sweet:
O banquet of a foul delight,
Prepared by thee, dark Paraclete!

Thou art the whisper in the gloom,
The hinting tone, the haunting laugh:
Thou art the adorner of my tomb,
The minstrel of mine epitaph.

I fight thee, in the Holy Name!
Yet, what thou dost, is what God saith:
Tempter! should I escape thy flame,
Thou wilt have helped my soul from death:

The second death, that never dies,
That cannot die, when time is dead:
Live death, wherefrom the lost soul cries,
Eternally uncomforted.

Dark Angel, with thine aching lust!
Of two defeats, of two despairs:
Less dread, a change to drifting dust,
Than thine eternity of cares.

Do what thou wilt, thou shalt not so,
Dark Angel! triumph over me:
Lonely, unto the Lone I go;
Divine, to the Divinity.

(BRC-2, 87-9)

A representative decadent expression, this poem succeeds in shocking the bourgeois reader, conveying as it does an essential doubleness of response between repulsion and delight. Confronting his Victorian audience with a newly-explored realm of sensuousness, Johnson describes not the glory of sanctified love but the serious attraction of evil. Desecrating all that the poet encounters, this so-called Dark Angel turns the Muses themselves to Furies and keeps the speaker from finding satisfaction in what he does. Thus, Pater's injunction to live life intensely, to seek new objects for art and new ways of expressing them, finds its unforeseen end. Alienated from the security or the stability of received values, the poet becomes a victim of his own unfulfillable desires.

But Johnson cannot rest with this depiction, and he turns from it as Caliban turns, seeing his face in the glass. His retrenchment in conventional religious thought in the final stanzas of the poem is a result of waning courage, an inability to face or remain secure with decadent amorality. The tension between evil and good, between the poet's baser appetites and his nobler aspirations thus culminates with a gesture towards divinity, but this gesture fails to provide the solace it intends. None of the implied criticisms of God and His system established in the initial ten stanzas of the poem are answered by the concluding four, and the imbalance itself, both in the time allotted each theme and the genuine emotional intensity of the opening statement, suggests the true leanings of the poet's mind. One cannot in the end reconcile the implied tardiness of God's angels with the punctuality of evil, the deliciousness of sin with the cold abstemiousness of purity or the usurping power of the poet's negative genius with the relative impotence of God. Indeed, the resolution of death offered in the closing stanzas depends upon the poet's ability to suppress such considerations, and the contemplation of death itself depicts a movement away from poetic engagement towards resignation and silence.

In terms of originality and passion—attributes important to harbingers of the new age—the achievement of Johnson's poem rests in sentiments he wished he did not have. Diction alone makes this fact apparent, where an intensity of language matches the poet's intensity of feeling. Thus, the Dark Angel displays an "aching lust," and beauty burns "with flames of evil ecstasy." Thus, an abundance of alliterative phrases underscores the attraction and dangers of evil, creating from these sounds a powerful music:

> *Th*ou with *th*y troop of *p*assionate *p*owers,
> *B*eleaguerest, *be*wilderest, me.
>
> *Th*y *v*enomous *s*pirit *s*tirs and *br*oods
> O *m*aster of *im*pieties!

The diction of the four concluding stanzas, however, offers fewer technical rewards and suggests the poet's lack of true philosophical commitment. Straying from his own principle of poetic purity, Johnson resorts to rhetorical spell-binding in order to convince us of his Christian solace. In so doing, he loses both the originality and the emotive power of his verse:

> The second death, that never dies,
> That cannot die, when time is dead:
> Live death ...

Ultimately, the poem does produce a necessary tension between opposites, but allows the wrong side of the oppostion to win out. Despite Johnson's resolution, the Dark Angel is more memorable and convincing than God, and one takes this caution away from the poem rather than any genuine sense of religious solace. Investing insufficient belief in his solution to make it work, Johnson retreats alone into the Divinity he has fashioned.

Other of Johnson's poems published in the books of the Rhymers' Club depict a similar fascination with death—from the idealization of another's demise in "The Last Music" and "Glories" to the creation of a mood indicative of death in "In Falmouth Harbour" and "To Morfydd." One does not find, as with Dowson, an increasing preoccupation with this theme, but an insistence, through repetition, which finds fulfillment as the poems become more personal. The first person narration of "Mystic and Cavalier" shocks because it offers, through a persona, a sense of self-doom which we have come to associate with Johnson ("Have you not read so, looking in these eyes? . . . The end is set:/Though the end be not yet."), and the elimination of the persona in "The Dark Angel" acknowledges the personal agony that lay behind many of his statements concerning death. Indeed, "The Dark Angel" may be seen as a touchstone in Johnson's career, the final point in an emotional trajectory that begins with his tribute to Oscar Wilde (*"In Honorem Doriani Creatorisque Eius"*), proceeds with his rejection of his mentor and his mentor's attitudes ("The Destroyer of a Soul") and ends with a rejection of his own native instincts, seemingly at the cost of life itself ("The Dark Angel"). Clearly, his moral sense disables him at this point, establishing a tension between fascination and guilt, between desire and disapproval, that can only be resolved in a turning away from life towards the comforts of death and the hereafter.[12] Johnson's artistic expression, thus, accurately reflects events occurring in his own life and reaffirms the pattern of withdrawal attested to by his friends.

III. Arthur Symons

Arthur Symons's contribution to the anthologies describes a movement away from worldly engagement towards a condition of simplicity and detachment. Poems such as "The Broken Tryst" and "Love and Art" locate the artist outside worldly experience, distancing him from love and the prospect of emotional fulfillment. "Music and Memory" and "Song" establish moods of nostalgia and yearning, again suspending the speaker in a moment of disengagement. These poems promote the same tension between alienation and belonging that Dowson's and Johnson's verse generated, and they remain true to the Paterian ideal of "soul, as opposed to mind, in style" ("Style," first printed in *Appreciations, with an Essay on Style*, 1889). De-emphasizing the cognitive aspect of language, they focus instead on musical or rhythmical apprehension, and thus create moods which depend only marginally on actual verbal significance. The tempo and repetitions of "Nora on the Pavement," for example, offer a simulation of Nora's movements and allow us to experience without rational intervention the mystery and immediacy of the dance:

> As Nora on the pavement
> Dances, and she entrances the grey hour
> Into the laughing circle of her power,
> The magic circle of her glances,
> As Nora dances on the midnight pavement;
>
> Petulant and bewildered,
> Thronging desires and longing looks recur,
> And memorably re-incarnate her.
> As I remember that old longing,
> A footlight fancy, petulant and bewildered;
>
> There where the ballet circles,
> See her, but ah, not free her from the race
> Of glittering lines that link and interlace;
> This colour now, now that, may be her,
> In the bright web of those harmonious circles.

> But what are these dance measures,
> Leaping and joyous, keeping time alone
> With life's capricious rhythm, and all her own,
> Life's rhythm and hers, long sleeping,
> That wakes, and knows not why, in these dance
>   measures?
>
> It is the very Nora;
> Child, and most blithe, and wild as any elf,
> And innocently spendthrift of herself,
> And guileless and most unbeguiled,
> Herself at last, leaps free the very Nora.
>
> It is the soul of Nora,
> Living at last, and giving forth to the night,
> Bird-like, the burden of its own delight,
> All its desire, and all the joy of living,
> In that blithe madness of the soul of Nora.
>   (BRC-2, 23-4)

With no other purpose than to catch the reader up in Nora's unconscious experience, Symons's lines trace the ritual of the dance. The girl's mysteriousness is enhanced by a counterpointing of rhyme ("Dances ... entrances ... glances"), and the central question of the poem (" ... what are these dance measures?") receives an answer of ultimate simplicity ("It is the very Nora."). This resolution, which dwells with some determination on essences, centers and stabilizes the multiple visual effects of the poem as well as its rhythmical progressions and makes of the whole an emotional entity rather than an intellectually apprehensible event.

But the method is intentionally limited and suffers the burden of Pater's psychological constraints. The move away from verbal expressivity is in effect a move away from the public sphere of poetry towards a more exclusive, essentially solipsistic art, and the mood that Symons creates tends to be the same with each application: vague excitement coupled with confusion or wonder. The syntactical repetitions of "Song," for example, produce the same headiness as "Nora on the Pavement," except that in this case the specificity of personality and event has been removed and with it a proportional amount of interest. One is left with a delicacy of statement that again almost insists upon its own ephemerality:

> What are lips, but to be kissed?
>   What are eyes, but to be praised?
> What the fineness of a wrist?
>   What the slimness of a waist?
> What the softness of her hair,
> If not that Love be tangled there?
>
> What are lips, not to be kissed?
>   What are eyes, not to be praised?
> What is she, that would resist
>   Love's desire to be embraced?
> What her heart that will not dare
> Suffer poor Love to linger there?
>
> These are lips, fond to be kissed,
>   These are eyes, fain to be praised:
> And I think, if Love has missed
>   Shelter in the wintry waste,
> That this heart may soon prepare
> Some nook for him to nestle there.
>
>   (BRC-2, 77)

Symbolical repetitions here are focussed around a single rhetorical question—essentially, what are lips, eyes and other parts of the woman for if not for love—and the declarative mode of the final stanza (*These* are lips, eyes, etc.) is not so much an answer to the question as it is a way of joining particular circumstances with general rules. Logically stated, if these are lips and eyes, then they deserve to be adored. This is not a particularly sophisticated argument for love-making, since it treats all physical attributes as having the same qualitative value. The woman remains well beyond the poem's reach, and the statement, so private (or so general) as to avoid significance. The repetitions, then, the anaphora of "What..." and the repeated end-rhymes, serve primarily to increase the light-headedness of the verse and convey the poet's mood. Furthered by such counters as "nook" and "nestle," the expression retreats into its own mysterious world of words.

Symons's adherence to Pater's notion of "purity" in art and the conviction that poetry should aspire to the condition of music imposed upon him a perspective that ultimately limited his expression. Like Dowson's and Johnson's preoccupations with death, Symons's rejection of intellect moved away from worldly engagement towards a condition where words became counters in a musical, or rhythmical, progression. The urge to greater simplicity (without interference of intellect or dependence upon the cognitive dimension of language) became in effect an urge for silence, an end that made poetry itself irrelevant. This urge may be seen behind much of Symons's verse at this time. "Javanese Dancers" and "Nora on the Pavement" invoke a state of semi-consciousness that supersedes language, and the hypnotic repetitions of "Song" implicitly comment on the limitations of words in rendering emotional truths.

Although Symons produced a significant number of poems during this era, he contributed only four (instead of the optimal six) to each of the Rhymers' Club anthologies, and these were almost exclusively light lyrics about love. The poems he collected for *Silhouettes* (1892) and for *London Nights* (1895) were not appreciably different, except that they dwelt more on the seamy aspects of urban sensuality, in keeping with the decadent desire to *épater le bourgeois*. The narrowness of his contribution helps us understand the limitations of Symons's expression and to anticipate the difficulties he would encounter as the decade progressed. A skilled craftsman in his particular vein, he could not expand or develop new facets of an essentially reductive art. Pater's prognostications concerning his career (See Chapter I) seem sound in view of this fact. His critical prose had intellectual content and was, thus, valuable to others. His verse was intellectually and philosophically stark and, thus, enjoyable only to those who shared his delight in music halls and ladies of the night.

Edgar Jepson claimed (MV, 288) that the poets of the nineties failed because they were tired by the end of the century, but the signs of strain were already apparent in Dowson's, Johnson's and Symons's verse by 1894, the year in which *The Second Book of the Rhymers' Club* was published. From this perspective in time, one can see that their failure was not so much a matter of technical or creative inability as it was of technical or creative narrowness, and their fatigue was manifested not so much by bad or inferior poems as by a pervasive attitude of self-destructiveness or defeatism, which contrasted with the contemporary social mood or need. Dowson turned away from the world to bask in adolescent fantasies and to celebrate the mysteries of madness and decay. Johnson withdrew into contemplations of death, where poetry would ultimately be unnecessary, and Symons moved progressively toward simplicity and silence. To them, Tennyson's death in 1892 was a reminder of a process of loss which they themselves—because of their commitment to failure and a lack of faith in art—could not hope to reverse.

IV. Victor Plarr

A final Rhymers' Club poet who should be mentioned in relation to Yeats and prospects of success or failure is Victor Plarr. Although Plarr is not greatly discussed either by contemporary reviewers or subsequent historians,[13] he nevertheless demonstrates many of the strengths and weaknesses that characterized the best aesthetic poets, and his influence on Yeats is probably more substantial than even Yeats would have had us believe. Plarr contributed five poems to the first anthology and a full budget of six to the second; his development within these volumes represents the path his career was taking during this era of rapid change.

His Gautier-like devotion to craftsmanship continues as strongly in the second anthology as in the first, but his thematic preoccupations move perceptibly deeper into the decadent mode. Whereas his early contemplations had centered on the mysteries of a Greek gem, his thoughts now focused on those of an unmarked funeral urn. The sound of children singing in a Norman church was supplanted by the importuning of a blind Breton beggar, and the figure of an old fisherman at twilight, suggestive of human pain, was succeeded by the nightingale's eerie call into the land of death. Like other poems of his canon, Plarr's "Deer in Greenwich Park" dwells in a contemplation of the past which can neither be fully understood nor fully abandoned:

> Pathetic in their rags, from far and near,
>   The children of the slum o'er-swarm the grass:
> Pathetic in their grace, the Greenwich deer
>   Leap up to let them pass.
>
> Where riot scares the gloom, and fevers burn,
>   These wizened babes were pent till morning
>   light:
> Slim shadows moving 'mong the moonlit fern
>   The shy deer strayed all night.

In the hot hours London's poor wastrels find
    Their paradise in this brown London park:
The lordlier brutes, in the scant shade reclin'd
    Pant for the hours of dark,

When some dim instinct from primaeval years
    Thrills, on a sudden, through each dappled
        breast,
And with untameable mysterious fears
    The herd is re-possessed!

Then the branch'd horns are tossed; the nostrils
  fine
    Respire the sleepy breath from London's
        heart,
And bucks, and does, and fawns, in spectral line,
    Forth from their bracken start.

An antlered watchman stamps a shapely hoof:
    —Is that a tartan'd Gael within the brake?
Did Luath bay below the heath-clad roof—
    Doth Fingal's son awake?

Hath a harp wailed in Tara? Did a bough
    Snap in Broceliande, where Merlin keeps
His drowsy magic vigil even now
    In the oakwood's sunlit deeps?

Was it a cry borne from Caerluda town,—
    A spell the Stag of Ages understands?
Or voices of old rivers raving down
    Through many heathery lands?

Or—since the red stag by wild mountain streams

> Is he whom such weird terrors most appal;
> Since these are fallow deer, and yonder dreams
>   The dom'd Stuart Hospital,—
>
> Was it the bugle echoing as of yore
>   In some vast chase, enwrapt in lake-side
>   mists?
> Swept Herne the Hunter by, or score on score
>   Of silken Royalists?
>
> Hunts captured Charles? or hath Cromwellian
>   shot
>   Laid some escaping war-spent gallant low
> In the far ride, where last year's leaf doth rot,
>   And, save the deer, none go?
>
> Who knows what stirs them? Nay, can any guess
>   That which their beautiful clear eyes
>   import
> When, at high noon, about your hand they press,
>   Begging in timid sort,
>
> Save haply the exile's doom, which is the same
>   Whether 'tis buried in the tragic eyes
> Of king discrowned, or wanderer without name,
>   Bondman, or brute that dies? (BRC-2, 57-9)

The contrast between the ragged boys and the timid deer establishes boundaries between the worlds of daylight and dreams, between present suffering and the nobility of past action. Retreating from its vision of the present, the poem moves into the ethereal world of the past, employing aesthetic vocabulary ("shadows," "moonlit," "dim," "mysterious") and rhetorical questioning to suggest the richness of this strange environment.

Plarr's historical sense materializes in the succeeding lines. As a stirring of conflict, anesthetized of pain, the Royalists' resistance to Cromwell's threat achieves the same mythical stature as stories of Merlin and Camelot. In the end, the reader is left with the image of exile, the communality of past and present in a condition of disinheritance. The discrowned Charles, the nameless ragged children, the hunter and the hunted, are all confused and reflected in the same mirror of the deer's eyes.

Not as self-destructive as many of his contemporaries, Plarr is equally fascinated with conditions of aesthetic withdrawal, and his nostalgia for the past draws him into a dream that can never be adequately answered or outdone by present circumstances. Looking into the books of the Rhymers' Club, one sees in Plarr a steady competence, a poetic talent, which, if it can be reproached for anything, it is for its late maturation. Significantly, his first and most valuable collection of poems, *In the Dorian Mood*, appeared in 1896, a year after the Wilde trials had made such moods obsolete. Failing to read the most obvious of cultural messages, Plarr moved deeper into the gloom of his own Celtic Twilight.

V. W. B. Yeats

Yeats's contributions to *The Second Book of the Rhymers' Club* are consistent in quality and subject matter with those of the first and stand in direct contrast to most of those expressions surrounding them in their continued focus on specifically Irish affairs. There seems also to be no marked development of mood from one volume to another, as with Dowson or Johnson, but a continued application of structural skills to Celtic subject matter—an indication that the poet remained committed to the importance and viability of his pursuit. Yeats writes about death, but not in a way that promotes its finality. In "An Epitaph" (BRC-1, 88. Later revised and retitled "A Dream of Death"), the death he commemorates is part of a dream, and in "The Folk of the Air" (BRC-2, 37-9), it becomes a mere transference of loyalties, symbolized by Bridget's abduction by the handsomest fairy. This situation is mysterious, but not (as with Johnson) violently self-destructive, or (as with Dowson) increasingly necrophiliac. He does not, indeed, portray himself as a victim of society so much as one who is set apart from that group and one who could, if called upon, speak for and redeem human inadequacies.

Yeats's instinct for withdrawal thus distinguishes itself from his contemporaries' insomuch as it is Orphic rather than purely escapist. If he descends into the underworld, it is with the intention of returning with new poetic power, and the source of this power lies in images that order as well as reinvoke basic human emotions. "The Man who Dreamed of Fairyland" is just such a descent, in which time-shifts and supernatural occurrences reinforce the dream-like atmosphere, and references to the dreamer's death transfer the poem into the domain of the hereafter:

I

He stood among a crowd at Drumahair,
   His heart hung all upon a silken dress,
   And he had known at last some tenderness
Before earth made of him her sleepy care;
But when a man poured fish into a pile,
   It seemed they raised their little silver heads
   And sang how day a Druid twilight sheds
Upon a dim, green, well-beloved isle,
Where people love beside star-laden seas;
   How Time may never mar their fairy vows
   Under the woven roofs of quicken boughs;—
The singing shook him out of his new ease.

II

As he went by the sands of Lisadill
 His mind ran all on money cares and fears,
 And he had known at last some prudent years
Before they heaped his grave under the hill;
But while he passed before a plashy place,
 A lug-worm with its gray and muddy mouth
 Sang how somewhere to north or east or south
There dwelt a gay, exulting, gentle race;
And how beneath those three times blessed skies
 A Danaan fruitage makes a shower of moons
 And as it falls awakens leafy tunes;—
And at that singing he was no more wise.

III

He mused beside the well of Scanavin,
 He mused upon his mockers. Without fail
 His sudden vengeance were a country tale
Now that deep earth has drunk his body in;
But one small knot-grass growing by the rim
 Told where—ah, little, all-unneeded voice!—
 Old Silence bids a lonely folk rejoice,
And chaplet their calm brows with leafage dim
And how, when fades the sea-strewn rose of day,
 A gentle feeling wraps them like a fleece,
 And all their trouble dies into its peace;—
The tale drove his fine angry mood away.

IV

He slept under the hill of Lugnagall,
   And might have known at last unhaunted sleep
   Under that cold and vapour-turbaned steep,
Now that old earth had taken man and all:
Were not the worms that spired about his bones
   A-telling with their low and reedy cry
   Of how God leans His hands out of the sky,
To bless that isle with honey in His tones.
That none may feel the power of squall and wave,
   And no one any leaf-crowned dances miss
   Until He burn up Nature with a kiss—;
The man has found no comfort in the grave.
                (BRC-1, 7-9)

The poem is narrated in the third person singular, but the narrator's internalized understanding of the dreamer, as well as the identifiability of the landmarks mentioned with Yeats's own native environment lead one to relate the dreamer to the poet himself. The narration progresses through three stages in which the dreamer's various achievements in life are undercut by suggestions from the supernatural world. Thus, his experience of "some tenderness" before death is undercut by the fish who sing of a land "Where people love by star-laden seas" and where "Time may never mar their fairy vows." Thus, his experience of "some prudent years" is surpassed by the lug-worm that sings of "a gay, exulting, gentle race" living in a land of abundance and happiness. Thus, his recourse to a country tale in silencing his would-be mockers is outdone by the knot-grass's report of a country where no tales are needed at all. The pull of the poem is, of course, towards death, where the imperfections of life are reputedly exceeded by realization of the ideal—but Yeats's statement does not allow such assumptions to stand for long. In the final stanza, the dreamer achieves that condition of perfection about which the spirits had spoken, and he finds it to be less than complete. On the other side of the grave, he is tormented by the worms that tell of the joys in the land of the living and of God's comfort for living men.

The poem resembles other decadent expressions of withdrawal, yet it is more successful in a social sense because it does not treat oblivion as a viable goal. Yeats moves away from waking reality into a realm where experiences can be and often are instructive, and he returns from them with a new sense of universal order. "The Man who Dreamed of Fairyland," like Blake's "The Sunflower," describes human yearning as a continuing and necessary phenomenon, familiar to all phases of existence. Knowledge of this drive and the elusiveness of contentment is realized in death, a phase which we can experience only through the simulating properties of art. The poet's creative energies, thus, are channelled into essential considerations, playing an active role in the processes of psychic and psychological discovery.

Yeats's contributions to *The Second Book of the Rhymers' Club* continue to exploit the richness of his Celtic mysticism and lore. Early versions of poems that would be included in *The Wind Among the Reeds*, these works convey similar concern for supernatural forces and their positive relation to art. In "The Rose in My Heart" (subsequently retitled "The Lover Tells of the Rose in his Heart") and "A Mystical Prayer to the Masters of the Elements" (revised and retitled "The Poet Pleads with the Elemental Powers"), he plays the role of bardic poet, invoking symbolic entities and implicitly reminding his readers of the religious roots of poetry. In "The Folk of the Air" ("The Host of the Air"), he tells of the seductive power of the Sidhe, while in "The Fiddler of Dooney" and "Song of the Old Mother" he refashions elements of the folk tradition, revealing both its celebratory joy and mournfulness, and infusing parochial tales with immediacy and life. "The Cap and Bells" too, although less clearly ethnic in orientation, speaks symbolically of the poet's power to overcome obstacles, the gift of his cap and bells ultimately curing the woman's indifference to him and winning her love.[14] While the poet does not directly proclaim himself Tennyson's successor in these lines, he reveals the appropriate social ambition, as well as a certain degree of achievement. More optimistic than his friends, he sought artistic control, believing it would give him spiritual power to influence events of this world.

Most of Yeats's contemporaries did not use their craft in this way, and their inability to credit the power of art to change or influence reality limited their capacity for growth. Yeats was capable of depression, withdrawal, mindlessness as were they, but he was also capable of change. Influenced by the decadents, he nevertheless integrated his craft with deeper religious feelings, making them central not only to his continuing existence but to his continuing spiritual enlightenment. He also invested his art with far-reaching practical value, finding in his study of Irish lore a prospect of defining and, thus, of controlling or ordering the culture from which he came. His intellectual adaptability and his belief in the power of images allowed him continuance while others of his generation failed. The cyclicality of his vision distinguished itself crucially from their essentially linear retreats, insomuch as he believed that present injustices and suffering constituted the axis on which the great historical gyre would turn.

NOTES FOR CHAPTER 3

[1] An important source for this aspect of Rhymers' Club history is James G. Nelson's *The Early Nineties: A View from the Bodley Head* (1971).

[2] Yeats's *The Wind Among the Reeds* is listed in PC (29 September 1894) and SJG (2 November 1894) as being in preparation for Mathews. But the book did not appear until April 1899, and, when it did, it bore both Lane's and Mathews's imprints. In a letter to Lady Gregory (10 February 1899, L, 313), Yeats alludes to a delay in the American printer's receiving and printing the galley sheets, but this problem hardly explains the five-year gap between announcement and actual publication. Yeats himself may have been slow in finishing the projected volume, or there may have been further complications with his publishers. We do know that several years after publication, Yeats tries to free himself from his commitments to Mathews, seemingly for economic reasons. See his letters to A. H. Bullen for 2 November 1905 and 13 February [?1906], in L, 464-5 and 469-71.

[3] Fifty titles listed for Lane and thirty-three for Mathews in the authors' circular (See illustration). See also DC (14 September 1894): 3, and DC (18 September 1894): 3. In the latter, Elkin Mathews protests the newspaper's treatment of the distribution of authors, saying it was misrepresentative of the actual situation and taken from a communication that was meant to be private.

[4] Wilde never contributed to *The Yellow Book*, and Beardsley never particularly liked Wilde, but both shared artistic stances which the public would have identified as "unhealthy."

[5] Mathews's and Lane's names both appear in the early publishing history of James Joyce and Ezra Pound. Through the recommendation of Arthur Symons, Mathews published Joyce's poetic lyrics (*Chamber Music*, 1906), and he brought out Pound's

first London publications (*Personae* and *Exultations*, 1909). Mathews, however, rejected the more controversial *Dubliners* in 1907 and felt uncomfortable with much of Pound's more experimental work. Urged by Pound to accept *A Portrait of the Artist as a Young Man*, John Lane did not, and, having accepted Pound's *Gaudier-Brzeska*, he was reluctant to pay him his percentage. Lane was the first English publisher of *Ulysses*, but did not bring the book out until 1936 and then only in a limited edition of 100 copies.

[6] Smithers was trained as a lawyer, but devoted most of his time to books and publishing. His dealings in literary erotica as well as his penchant for alcohol gave him a bad reputation among bookmen, but he was willing to print what others would not. He became responsible for Symons's and Dowson's work and would later publish Wilde's *The Ballad of Reading Gaol*.

[7] Oscar Wilde had supposedly wined, dined and bedded Charlie Parker, an unemployed valet, at the Savoy Hotel. Symons had been particularly anxious to include Beardsley in the project, not only because he valued his talent but because he wanted to make a strong political statement concerning the current situation in the arts. As Yeats recalls (Au, 323), "We knew that we must face an infuriated press and public, but being all young we delighted in enemies and everything that had an heroic air."

[8] Alfred Dowson died of an overdose of chloral in August 1894. Although the death certificate does not indicate as much, surrounding circumstances and subsequent silences indicate that the act was intentional. Dowson's mother hung herself six months later, feeling that she was a burden to her children.

[9] In a letter to Campbell Dodgson (December 1891), Johnson says that his doctor "says grim things about spinal paralysis." See LJL, 117.

[10] In August 1896, Yeats visited Ireland with Arthur Symons and made the acquaintance of Lady Gregory. In the following year, he discussed with Lady Gregory his ideas about founding

an Irish theatre, and by 1898 he, Lady Gregory and Edward Martyn had agreed to embark on "a three-year venture."

[11]Letter to John O'Leary (26 June [1894]) in L, 232: "Todhunter is of course skilful [sic] enough with more matter of fact themes and quite admits the dreadful burden of the TCD tradition." (TCD are the initials of Trinity College, Dublin, where Todhunter was educated.)

[12]Johnson's fascination with death and self-defeat began early in his life, and his attraction to the Catholic Church, paradoxically enough, was related to his urge to focus on human weaknesses. As early as 1884, he wrote to Edgar Jepson, outlining the terms of his belief: "The flowers of evil are more beautiful than the sensitive plants of purity—and tears and protestations have an ugliness about them. Baudelaire, the lonely gardener of what Whitman calls 'intoxicating exotics', was also not far from the kindgom of Catholic ritual—a fact worthy of remembrance. Exquisite emotions and desires and pangs—these are the spirit of the best life possible. I find pleasure in my personal discontent—the desire for new pleasures is what keeps the life of me from dullness" (LJLW, 7). In his later verse statements, however, the bravado has disappeared and a tired fatality has taken its place—a sense that all of these delicious urges must culminate in the ultimate experience of death and silence.

[13]He shows up as the all-but-forgotten M. Verog in Ezra Pound's *Hugh Selwyn Mauberley*, and in Peter Ackroyd's *T. S. Eliot: A Life* he is identified in one of the illustrations as "Victor Platt."

[14]This conclusion is also mixed with somber thoughts, as evidenced by the poet's comment that he will send her his cap and bells and die. The concluding stanzas, however, suggest continuance rather than death—the cap and bells demonstrating a vitality and happiness of their own.

THE MYTH OF FAILURE

In *Autobiographies, The Oxford Book of Modern Verse* and various other writings, Yeats depicted the Rhymers' Club as a group of youthful artists, victimized by social hostility and their own inordinate desires. This version of the group's identity has been generally accepted by scholars, coming as it does from Yeats himself and seemingly offering important information concerning his early career. Inconsistencies in the poet's account, however, indicate its possible historical shortcomings and point to the use of fact for mythical ends. While his debt to such Rhymers as Dowson, Johnson and Symons was genuine, one suspects that Yeats's motivation for speaking of them as part of an ideologically coherent unit was at least partially practical—at first, as a way of calling attention to an as yet unestablished group of poets and, later, of transforming that group into a genuine poetic movement, central to the modern tradition. As a founder of the Club and, eventually, its sole successful spokesman, Yeats was also calling attention to his own position in this literary development and locating himself at the source of modern poetic practice—demonstrating an instinct for historical definition that influenced, if not determined, the course of Ireland's cultural renaissance as well.

Yeats's vision of the Rhymers' Club, however, was not completely arbitrary or fanciful. Indeed, examination of the cultural situation in the early 1890s and the approach critics took to these poets' work indicates that he benefitted from existing notions and perpetuated imagery that others around him had used. The sense that the Victorian age was coming to an end, that one must look to the young poets for future developments, was both expressed and implied in contemporary journalistic accounts, and the Rhymers' Club anthologies, as collections of verse by new and aspiring writers, responded implicitly to the challenge for a new age. If some belittled the value of the cooperative venture, others pointed to its convenience and the courage of its supposed aims. If posterity left these poets virtually unacknowledged, then contemporary circumstance and the volatility of literary taste could be cited as primary causes.

The myth that Yeats created concerning the Rhymers' Club is based on two aspects of the historical development: first, on the sense of competition inherent in such a group; second, on the fact of failure and the swift deflation of the Rhymers' sense of promise. The dynamics of this situation are reflected in the format of the two Rhymers' Club anthologies and the contrasting reactions the two volumes produced. Appearing in February 1892, *The Book of the Rhymers' Club* (50 large paper copies; 450 small paper copies, 350 for sale) sold out almost immediately and generated a significant number of spirited responses. Appearing in June 1894, *The Second Book of the Rhymers' Club* (76 large paper copies; 718 small paper copies, distributed in U. S. and England) did not sell as well, and the reviews it produced lacked imaginative zeal. The sense of competition that had been suggested by the first anthology became with the second a means of self-protection, and the almost total absence of metaphor in the reviews of *The Second Book* indicated that the Rhymers' moment of poetic promise had passed. A year after publication, Elkin Mathews was still advertising fifty copies of the book on hand.

The present chapter examines the reviews of the two books of the Rhymers' Club to show how Yeats's myth evolved from images and ideas present in contemporary accounts. This perspective of the creative process calls attention to the practical side of the poet's mind and serves as a corrective to critical accounts that locate Yeats's influences strictly within the realm of the formal literary tradition. Yeats took inspiration from his environment, gaining from personal experience insights which he gradually worked into larger conceptual patterns. His notion of the poet as outcast grew from his experiences of London in the 1890s and gained scope as he was able to relate them to similar circumstances and identities throughout his career.

I. The Polarities of Response

The myth that grew up around the Rhymers' Club involved a coalition of two seemingly opposite notions. On the one hand, reviewers spoke of these poets as minor figures, whose work could not compete with the more recognized voices of the nineteenth century. On the other, they acknowledged the imminent end of the Victorian age and celebrated the courage of those who aspired to represent or speak for the new century. A survey of the kinds of statements made in the reviews shows the evolution of these themes and what they may have had to do with the developing myth.

Announcements concerning *The Book of the Rhymers' Club* appeared in such publications as the *Star*, the *Daily Chronicle*, the *Times* and *St. James's Gazette*.[1] These sources referred to the book as a new issue from the Bodley Head, identified its authors as little-known poets and provided a list of their names. In addition, reviewers spoke of the venture as a potentially rich object for imaginative speculation. The *Times* announced "a volume of somewhat original kind," and another source, focusing on its lack of literary pretentiousness billed it as "a modern 'Whistle-Binkie'":

> There is no link binding these twelve poets together apparently, save that they all suffer from the same disease of writing in rhyme. Each will be responsible for his own contributions, so far, at

least, as a poet can be responsible for anything. (EMC, MS 392/7/2)

The notion of the irresponsibility of poets—the feeling that writing is a kind of disease suffered by benign madmen—offered one perspective on how the volume would be treated. The reference to "whistle-binkie" itself (an anthology of light or humorous verse, taking its name from "bench-whistlers" at Scottish penny weddings) amounted to a trivialization of the Rhymers' endeavor, which was perpetuated in other accounts. Indeed, most reviewers dubbed these versifiers "minor" poets, disassociating them from the literary mainstream. Andrew Lang pointed out that the authors of the anthology were so insignificant that they were not even included in Traill's directory of minor poets in the *Nineteenth Century*. The *Saturday Review* concurred with both Traill and Lang, refusing to select its "immortals" from the twelve poets who had contributed to the volume. Richard Le Gallienne defended them blandly as "so-called though not *soi-disant* minor poets," and *Black and White* numbered them among the numerous then unknown writers competing (somewhat vainly) for the public's attention.

Many journalists also stressed the humbleness of the Rhymers' venture, taking poems by Ernest Rhys, T. W. Rolleston and others as evidence for their simple intentions of self-amusement. The *Daily Chronicle* stated that "they are in no hurry to be heard; they are not over-confident that they are worth hearing," and proclaimed that they wrote poems "for the same reason that the late Mr. Matthew Arnold drank wine, because they like it." Even Selwyn Image, who wrote to defend the Rhymers' right to be heard, cited the modest size, number of copies and price of the volume as evidence of its essentially unthreatening nature (CR, 65).

In keeping with the Whistle-Binkie concept, several reviewers pointed to the collective aspect of the venture as evidence of the book's diminutive import, but the tone of indulgence that accompanied such statements suggested a positive side to this primarily negative point of view. Recalling the tradition of the Elizabethan Miscellany, *Black and White* found in the collective format a solution to the modern dilemma. "When minor poets come upon us," the reviewer noted, "it certainly is best that they should come with their works sifted, as it were, by the votes of their brother authors." And Richard Le Gallienne offered a similar view in an attempt to defend the book's chances:

> When eleven heads collaborate to fill ninety pages, they must indeed be sheep's heads if they cannot do it respectably. And it might, at any rate, seem likely that a book into which eleven had put their best would be a better book than any one of them could do single-voiced. (St, 2)

While not denying the entertainment value of this volume, many of these critics played down its possible artistic import, either because they had been conditioned to expect little from new writers or because they felt that the public, out of sorts with versifiers in general, would be more receptive to an unassuming and quaint volume than to a high-powered literary manifesto. Andrew Lang, who had adopted the most hostile attitude toward *The Book of the Rhymers' Club*, later explained that evaluating new work was very difficult for him (See letter from W. B. Yeats to J. B. Yeats, 21 July 1906, L, 474-5), and one suspects that at least part of his critical stance stemmed both from this avowed uncertainty and a desire to write what he thought the public wanted to hear.

Yet many critics did notice the historical importance of such an undertaking, and, although they continued to nurture condescending attitudes toward it, were sufficiently inspired to translate their views into cosmic terms. *St. James's Gazette* anticipated future commentary when on 30 January 1892, it spoke of a contemporary Parnassus:

> An Anthology by a band of young living poets is always rather an interesting thing. The mere mention of the *Parnasse Contemporain* may remind us how much such a collection may contain in germ of what is to prove most destructive in the work of the new literary generation. To put such an effort at its lowest, it is at least wiser to club together to write poetry than to read it.

Alluding to the present reduced state of poetry, the author suggests both the need for accomplished verse and the impossibility of poets ever providing adequate examples of it. The notion of a collective anthology stimulates the imagination because it contains both the promise and the projected failure of the age. Inherent even in this attitude is a sense of challenge for writers and the feeling that those who attempt to overcome social indifference exercise courage rather than simple madness.

The reference to *Parnasse Contemporain* anticipates a number of journalistic comments and establishes a literary conceit periodically reinvoked in discussions of the Rhymers and their publishers. Edmund Gosse had used similar terminology in a letter to Ernest Rhys on 10 October 1891. "It seems to me," he said, "that it would be rather a good plan if four or five of the very best of you young poets would club together to produce a volume, a new Parnassus, and so give the reading public a chance of making your acquaintance..." (LFL, 71), and the ever-contemptuous Andrew Lang would substitute one sacred mountain for another when depicting their verse as "twitterings of an ignorant young bird on the sonorous Helicon of England" (DN,5). On the simplest level, the classical reference established an artistic parallel between these poets and the French *parnassiens*, whose verse many of the Rhymers had attempted to emulate, but, on a more clearly symbolic level, it indicated the literary ideal towards which these aspirants strained. A common metaphor throughout postclassical times, Parnassus played an especially important role in this era, when established poets were dying out and new voices were being sought. The inclusion of the Rhymers in this search for successors is evident both in the language and in the romantic speculations of the reviews. Speaking of the Rhymers' publishers, whose offices were in Vigo Street, one journal commented, "To many poets whose feet and fancies are set on the road to Parnassus, the way lies through Vigo-Street." Another dubbed it "the publishing house of Parnassus," and the *Athenaeum* continued the association by explaining, "Parnassus has two peaks and therefore the Bodley Head has two partners."[2] In their evaluations of the first anthology, the *Daily News* and the *Church Quarterly Review* spoke of a so-called "chosen one" who had yet to surface from the ranks of the unknown, and other critics pointed to an implicit challenge for younger poets to excel. Graham Tomson of the *Academy* intoned, "Out of the many that are called (and to young ears the Muse flutes ever with seductive note), who are the few that will be chosen?"(Ac, 295) And the *Speaker* added solemnly, "The future of these twelve writers, who have thus banded themselves together, will be watched with interest... What answers, if any, will they find for the questions with which their verses ache?" (Sp, 389)

By the time *The Second Book of the Rhymers' Club* appeared in June 1894, it had become evident that no answers were forthcoming. The Rhymers' failure to move beyond the realm of promise into actual achievement, to offer verse that was distinct from their earlier attempts, produced in critics a weariness that virtually eliminated metaphorical treatment. Although it was generally acknowledged that the second book was more substantial than the first, the tone with which this message was conveyed tended to obviate that assessment. As the *New Ireland Review* seemed to be pointing out, the romantic coupling of poetic insignificance with historical mission had evolved into a far less titillating paradox:

> I am afraid that there is some gnashing of teeth in the "Cheshire Cheese" in Fleet Street, London, over the reception accorded to the second book of the Rhymers' Club. True, it has been praised, but the modern young man considers himself a failure as a poet unless he either stuns or startles easy-going people. The first book of the club did something of both.

The Second Book's failure either to stun or startle had something to do with the fact that it was not a new or unique event, and the tendency to speak of it in terms of its predecessor altered the quality of even positive estimations. The *Pall Mall Gazette* pointed indirectly to the source of the problem, opening as it did with: "*The Second Book of the Rhymers' Club* presents no striking dissimilarity in kind to its predecessor." The *Speaker* announced, "The second book of the Rhymers' Club is quite equal to the first" (Sp, 193), and the *Globe* echoed with a positive though unexciting, "The Second Book of the Rhymers' Club (Mathews and Lane) is an improvement over the first." With the exception of a somewhat propagandistic statement in *United Ireland* concerning "the best collection of original poetry by Irishmen published in our time," none of these reviews suggested that one should hurry out and buy a copy or that it was the answer to the questions posed implicitly by the age. The romantic vision of the minor poet bravely defying the odds against success had disappeared from critical commentary, and evaluations proceeded with little recourse to rhetorical embellishment.

In addition, the cooperative aspect of the volume, which before had played a generally positive role in the "minor poet" motif, now drew criticism. This development stemmed also from a feeling of *déjà vu* and the resultant attitude of weariness. The *Nation* identified *The Second Book of the Rhymers' Club* as ". . . a book by a dozen or more minor poets. . .and giving a good view of the range of thought and art among a circle of the London men." But, more frequently, a suspicious attitude toward the genre emerged, denying both the advantages of the collective format and its possible symbolic import. Thus, the *National Observer* complained, "*The Second Book of the Rhymers' Club* is a characteristic product of the age in which we live, when art requires the stimulus of mutual admiration, and poetry becomes the business of a coterie." And the *Athenaeum*, while intending to express approval for various parts of the volume, issued a preferatory warning about the form in which it appeared: "We cannot profess to be in love with the tendency towards co-operative production which is displayed by [the Rhymers' Club], holding as we do that the strongest work is always done by those who stand apart from all such coteries, and shun the mutual admiration they are too apt to engender." *St. James's Gazette* further criticised the Rhymers' collective enterprise when it defined it as a barrier constructed against the outside world: "As the rhymers have a sturdy phalanx of admirers among themselves, what the *profanum vulgus* thinks about them will, no doubt, affect them not at all." Thus, the format that had once been taken as an interesting and unique vehicle for competition was now construed as a jaded means of protecting these poets from external reproach.

But even negative reactions failed to create much excitement in the press, and sporadic attempts to decide which one of the competing poets might be best were undermined by a broad lack of consensus. Partially, this problem was attributable to the backlash against decadence, which had begun to surface in the reviews but had not yet reached its full measure of influence.

Accordingly, the *Nation* qualified its approval of Yeats with a parenthetical barb concerning *The Countess Kathleen* ("disfigured and blighted in the publishing by one of Mr. Beardsley's ugliest and most meaningless frontispieces"), and the same journal identified Arthur Symons as "the low-water mark of the 'Rhymers' Club,'" a comment that was echoed by *St. James's Gazette* when it criticized Symons's poems for having "a faint smell of patchouli about them." Symons himself responded to the insult in his essay "Being a Word on Behalf of Patchouli," but no one else seemed particularly offended, and no critic arose to defend the minor poet from journalistic insensitivity. In terms of perceived quality, Yeats's name was mentioned most, but his preeminence was mitigated by comments from the *Times* ("The writer who appears to us to have the most genuine poetical fibre in him is Mr. Victor Plarr"), the *Globe* ("The contributors to the book are thirteen in number, and among them Mr. Richard Le Gallienne is easily first.") and the *Glasgow Herald* ("the best love-song is that by Arthur Symons, and the best spring-song is from the pen of Richard Le Gallienne."). The lack of critical consensus attests to the confusion of the time and to the Rhymers' failure (at this point at least) to produce from their midst a single outstanding talent.

II. The Lang Controversy

Yeats's vision of the Rhymers' Club stems primarily from the reviews of the first anthology, where metaphor and allusion combined to redeem these poets from their admittedly minor status and to suggest their symbolic potential as a group of dedicated though socially doomed writers. Ironically, the most important review in promoting both the book and the myth was the one that had sought to dismiss the Rhymers from consideration. Andrew Lang's negative response to *The Book of the Rhymers' Club* spurred the indignation of other reviewers, generating from them a number of spirited defenses. Both Lang's statement and the resulting commentary were central to the Club's image.

Lang's review appeared in the *Daily News* on 20 February 1892. Although largely unsympathetic, it dealt realistically with the problems confronting *fin-de-siècle* writers and attempted to find the proper place for such books as the Rhymers' anthology in the overall scheme. Lang affirmed that the times were not propitious for the poet, that a great deal of superfluous verse was then flooding publishers' offices. He then introduced the Rhymers' Club as a new set of literary aspirants who proposed not only to publish their work, but to make the public pay dearly for it. His statement that "a ransom of five shillings seems rather exorbitant for their combined efforts" may well have been the phrase that rang in Yeats's ears when, years later, he reported to his father that Lang had been "very uncivil indeed" in his review of the first book of the Rhymers' Club (L, 474-5).

But Lang's comments were based on a practical understanding of what the public wanted, and the faults he found with this predominantly youthful group were precisely those of their youth and *naïveté*. Thus, while noting that the volume was intended as a manifesto, he claimed that the limited number of available copies could hardly qualify it as a far-reaching or potentially successful assault on the public imagination. And, while including these poets among the ranks of minor versifiers, he also made it clear that even this classification was an exaggeration of their actual status: "A glance at Mr. Traill's Directory of Minor Poets in *The Nineteenth Century* will show that his sixty have received some additions to their numbers."

Familiar issues of youth and lack of pretentiousness brought Lang to different conclusions concerning the advisability of these poets' attempt. After regretting aspects of their individual verses, he ended with a lengthy rebuttal to G. A. Greene's proclamation that the Rhymers will "Hammer the ringing rhyme, /Till the mad world hears":

It is natural to wish him every success, but the mad world is very much engaged with the plainest and least artistic prose. Poets keep on hammering, but nobody attends to the summons. Even if a great poet appeared, it would be difficult to get the mad world persuaded into buying a comfortable number of copies. Yet we can hardly say that poetry is out of fashion, when such vast quantities of poetry are written. It is the malady of not marking that we suffer from. Nobody can catch the public ear.

Estimating that no one wants to listen to the kind of verse then being written, Lang translates Greene's sense of craftsmanship (conveyed in his poem by the word "hammering") into a senseless and unmelodious badgering of metal. He closes with a call for a more sympathetic artist—one whose ear is attuned to what the public wants—and in his estimation, the public wants the straightforward sagaciousness of prose. "How thin, how imitative, how superfluous they seem," chimes the middle-aged critic on the poetic effusions of youth, "twitterings of an ignorant young bird on the sonorous Helicon of England."

Among those articles written in reaction to Lang's statements was that of Lionel Johnson's friend and mentor, Selwyn Image. Published in the *Church Reformer*, March 1892, this piece offered less an appraisal of the anthology than an attack of Lang's critical methods and attitudes. "I am not in a position to review the book," said Image, "But a copy of it has come into my hands, and it has given me, and for many a day will give me, a great deal of pleasure." Image's statement focused on issues and concepts that had dominated discussions of the Rhymers' Club so far: the modesty of the Club's undertaking, the precedent to be found in the native tradition, the situation of the mi-

The Myth of Failure

nor poet and of poetry itself at the end of the nineteenth century. It also reinvoked the bird conceit perpetuated by Lang, to depict how these innocent young men were maligned by the affected and ill-tempered critic of the *Daily News*:

> This guide and chastener of our taste never tires of assuring us, that ours is not an age of poetry; that these minor poets do not write poems, but only verses; that at best they are but little mockingbirds, chirping on England's Helicon: and then he catches up a note or two of their poor little song, and shows to our admiration what a smart fellow he is by making game of it.

For Image, the modesty of the Rhymers' endeavor underscored its rarity and attractiveness. Pointing to the book's small size, number of copies and price, he demonstrated both the unpretentiousness of the operation and the transience of the opportunity. "Three hundred and fifty copies will not go far amongst us," he claims, "and then we will call on these Rhymers to issue a second edition." He also refuted Lang's comments concerning the Rhymers' obscurity, stating that they were "for the most part well-known amongst the younger generation of journalists and critics." The remark elevated these poets in prestige, while failing to point out that they themselves constituted a large percentage of that younger generation of journalists and critics.

Another of Image's correctives to Lang's position came in the form of an appeal to tradition. Describing the Rhymers' habitual meeting place and activities, he invoked the shades of Johnson and Goldsmith as writers who would have approved these poets' endeavor. Image also disagreed that the age had turned away from verse and that minor poets merely flood the market with unwanted rhapsodies. "There are plenty of ridiculous, incapable, ones amongst them," he explained, "but . . . you know, as well as I do, that there are plenty of charming, and quite singularly capable, ones too." The problem, in Image's mind, was Lang's inability to offer a balanced view of surrounding circumstances. This inability was reflected in Lang's claim that all of the major Victorian writers were dead and that the age not only demanded miracles from its young poets but attempted to ignore their efforts to provide such miracles. In pointing out that Tennyson, Morris, Christina Rossetti and Swinburne were still alive, Image not only de-emphasized the burden placed upon these young writers, but suggested that the public had not completely turned its back on poetry and poets in general.

The *Daily Chronicle* review, published 26 February of the same year (1892), refuted Lang's attack by saying that the major problem with the Rhymers' anthology was its overmeasure of good sense. It also used Lang's statement of condemnation to develop a new and historically potent parallel for the socially maligned and alienated artist, one that would add an important dimension to later interpretations of the Club's significance.

Entitled "A Round Table of Rhymers," this review anticipated an analogy Yeats would make between the poets of the Rhymers' Club and King Arthur's court. A few lines into the text, the motif was recast to include the bird imagery of earlier criticsm with an allusion to a poetical "round-robin." But the epigraph presented a new and suggestive historical parallel in the form of John Keats. The lines quoted ("Sweet are the pleasures that to verse belong,/ And doubly sweet a brotherhood in song") are from "To George Felton Mathew," in which the young Keats complains of his present disfavor with the Muse and desires more time in the company of his friend, "Where we may soft humanity put on, And sit and rhyme and think on Chatterton." In addition to extolling the advantages of artistic association, the poem develops the conceit of the poet as bird, straining to reach the heights of poetry, and the *Daily Chronicle* reviewer uses this notion and Keats's own poetical history to develop his comments on the difficulties besetting innocent poets:

> A volume by twelve young rhymers is promising food for the middle-aged cynic. It was evidently too great a temptation for Mr. Lang the other day. All seems fish that comes to Mr. Lang's net—a serious charge against an angler. "*The Quarterly* savage and tarterly," has the reputation of killing a certain poetical cock-robin. Ah, but that's a very different matter! A poet with twelve heads, as this Rhymers' Club may be described, is a hydra which needs some killing. Besides, the cynic must be very determined who could find many chinks for his arrows in "The Book of the Rhymers' Club," which twelve Fleet-street nightingales have sung together with their breasts against a quill.

Meant presumably to detract interest from the Rhymers' publication, Lang's review had obviously had the opposite effect, leading the *Daily Chronicle* reviewer and others to draw historical parallels that elevated these poets in terms of courage and potential achievement. The allusion in this passage to *The Quarterly* reminds us that an earlier, more famous songbird (Keats) had once been victimized by a similarly insensitive man of letters, and knowledge of what had happened on that occasion speaks almost prophetically of the Rhymers' supposed future.[3] Depicting man's senseless drive to prey on less aggressive creatures, this reviewer set himself up as a defender of misprized youth. The object of his defense, however, had grown to twelve rather than one maligned artist, and the product of their combined efforts was virtually without flaws. The image of the incompetent angler, as well, offered a realized portrait of the critic as enemy, and the notion of artistic association became in this light the poet's only defense, offering the Rhymers a better chance of reaching poetic heights than had their predecessor, Keats.

A final report with bearing on the myth appeared in October 1892, in the *Church Quarterly Review.* Published relatively late in the year, it indicates that Lang was not alone in his doubts concerning the Rhymers' Club and that the disaffection suggested in the reviews of their second anthology started somewhat earlier than what might otherwise have been believed. It also rehearses the themes of cultural confusion and loss that had occupied many critics' minds and offers a source for the ideas of challenge and defeat that would surface in Yeats's work. "We may now think of the Victorian age," says this unnamed critic, "no longer as that in which we live, and of which it is consequently difficult to form a dispassionate judgement, but as one of which the work is done and may be estimated, which stands on its achievements to be praised or to be condemned; and, finally, we may look forward to another age which shall succeed it in the near or distant future" (201).

Written only slightly before Tennyson's death,[4] this piece identifies him as the primary representative of the Victorian age and sees his individual falling off as the mark of a larger trend of decay. The critic contends that the younger generation has refined the Tennysonian style while ignoring its spirit, and in this group he includes the poets of the Rhymers' Club:

> The lessons of past literature have been learned; there is much earnestness, probably much real pains, but the note of distinction, of originality, is wanting. The scale, moreover, is very small; it is cameo-carving, not sculpture, and in a great work of art, as Aristotle taught long ago, the element of size must not be absent. It may be said

that these are but preludings, specimens of the self-training in composition by which the poet, however great his natural genius, must learn his trade. But we doubt very much whether these writers are below the age at which great poets have generally shown some real and decisive promise of great work. (211-12)

Like Lang, this reviewer translates the Rhymers' humble ambitions and espousal of *parnassien* values into distinct stylistic liabilities and in so doing drains them of whatever romantic aura they had once had. He also points to the issue of youthfulness, suggesting that these poets were too old in terms of what they had achieved. This pessimistic note seemingly deprives the Rhymers of their mythical promise, but, while the reviewer shares Lang's doubts, he lacks his sarcasm and dismissive attitude. Expressing his concern for the future of poetry, he extends a gesture of hope even for those who have not yet progressed beyond the level of learning their trade. Thus, he alludes to the unpredictability of the future as a reminder of continuing possibility, and he reinvokes the notion of challenge in the speculative nature of his closing remarks:

When the new age of poetry will come, or which of us will be alive to see it, it is impossible to say. It may be on the threshold now; it may be barely on the horizon. The new poet may be sending his manuscript to the printers, or he may be playing with his coral in his cradle. (216)

Sober and realistic, this statement nevertheless attempts speculation. If it denies the Rhymers a probability of success, it does not ultimately eliminate them from the competition and creates a vision both of the nobility and the necessity of the challenge. This quality of hopefulness, contrasted with the negative reception afforded by Lang and, eventually, the disappointing fate of *The Second Book* created an image for the Club which rested upon the uncertainties and injustices of the cultural moment. Yeats himself contributed to that reputation, writing contemporaneous critical statements and also drawing on notions expressed in the reviews for his retrospective myth.

III. YEATS

Yeats's first article on the Rhymers' Club appeared in the *Boston Pilot* on 23 April 1892 (LNI, 142-8). His approach was both serious and sensational, differing little from those reports that spoke of these poets in terms of poetic mission. Opening with a consideration of the clubbing mentality, Yeats claimed that the instinct for artists to form groups or movements belonged to the French or Celts and was essentially foreign to the English mind. "All this," he says, "makes the existence of the Rhymers' Club the more remarkable thing"(143). His sense of the remarkable was underscored by the metaphor he chose, linking the Rhymers' Club with the Arthurian Court and depicting its challenge in terms of medieval notions of quest and trial. Like Selwyn Image, Yeats stresssed the humbleness of the group, but redeemed it from total obscurity with reference to an earlier, comparable tradition:

> Into this little body, as about a round table of rhyme, have gathered well nigh all the poets of the new generation who have public enough to get their works printed at the cost of the publisher, and some not less excellent, who cannot yet mount that first step of the ladder famewards. (143)

The Arthurian allusion suggests a series of provocative parallels—not the least of which is the concept that the success or failure of the Round Table, according to Malory at least, was predetermined by the limitations of its human membership.[5] Yeats, however, focused on an early stage of the myth, promoting his artistic brothers as a band of literary Lancelots and Percevals, naturally gifted but dependent upon an opportunity to prove their worth in the public sphere. The potency of this statement lies in the consideration that, while the group is small, it includes nearly all of those figures who could hope to bring vitality and interest back to verse. Despite the sense of fraternity and purpose conveyed by the metaphor, Yeats denied that these poets shared a unified ideological commitment, repeating simply that they conscientiously avoided tricks of style:

> Not that the Rhymers' Club is a school of poets in the French sense, for the writers who belong to it resemble each other in but one thing: they all believe that the deluge of triolets and rondeaus has passed away, and that we must look once more upon the world with serious eyes and set to music—each according to his lights—the deep soul of humanity. (143)

The musical motif fostered by Le Gallienne and others through a metaphor of singing birds is herein perpetuated, and the announced goal of the Club—to capture in music "the deep soul of humanity"—remains sufficiently free of prescriptions to include any of the various poetical approaches practiced by individual members. Yet Yeats moved away from a concern for accuracy when he indicated that the Rhymers shared a universal aversion to traditional poetic forms. Indeed, several poems in their anthology bore titles that demonstrated allegiance to such forms (T. W. Rolleston's *"Ballade* of the 'Cheshire Cheese,'" Ernest Dowson's *"Villanelle* of Sunset," G. A. Greene's "The *Son-*

net"), and virtually all of the poems included in the anthology functioned normally with regard to established patterns of stanza and rhyme.⁶ One suspects that Yeats altered the truth to fit more securely into his poetic vision, and his sense of the "purity" of the Rhymers' poems—the "absence of affectation, tricks of style or mere eccentricity of fancy" as Le Gallienne had expressed it in the *Star*—relies upon this supposed independence from established literary conventions. Such an interpretation is given support somewhat later in the text when Yeats speaks of John Davidson and Arthur Symons as artists who distinguish themselves from the outgoing generation "that search for new forms merely." Rejecting the narrowness of their forebears, these poets search "for new subject matter, new emotions" as well. Thus, Yeats's purportedly neutral characterization does, indeed, offer a sense of ideology, a translation into intellectual terms of these poets' very rejection of unified poetic belief.⁷ The rejection becomes in Yeats's presentation an acceptance of the challenge of experience, a willingness to deal with new subjects in new ways, free of preconceived ideas of structure. He relates this willingness, in turn, to the open-mindedness and vigor of youth, poetic voices to whom song comes as naturally as breath:

> "What is the good of writing poetry at all now?" said the other day a noted verse writer whose fame was at its height ten years ago. "Sonnets are played out and ballades and rondeaus are no longer novel, and nobody has invented a new form." All despairing, cry of the departing age, but the world still goes on, and the soul of man is ever young, and its song shall never come to an end. (143)

Yeats, like Image, contends that poetry is neither dead nor dying, and the despair he notes in older writers stems from their inability to adapt to inevitable poetic change. His appeal to renewal and the claim that the Rhymers constitute "well nigh all the poets of the new generation" allow him to speak of their book in terms of a "poetic manifesto," elevating that term far beyond the ironic implications of Lang's usage. The poets of the Rhymers' Club find in this appraisal both the vigor and sobriety, the promise and likelihood, attested to in other reviews; and these polarities are combined into a vision of purpose—a future as inevitable in both its promise and failure as the flow of time itself.

In adapting his present reality to the Arthurian example, Yeats moved away from the literal truth into a conceptual apprehension of the group, as had other critics who had spoken of the Club in metaphorical terms. The rich literary and visual associations latent even in these trite formulations prepared the way for an historical interpretation which was based more on what these writers wanted or needed to believe than on strict critical observation and analysis, and they established in Yeats's mind an image that was to occupy his imagination from that moment onward—a sense of their nobility, their uncompromising devotion to beauty and craftsmanship that would lead them to confront evils they could not possibly overcome.

As early as October 1892, in an article entitled "Hopes and Fears for Irish Literature" (*United Ireland*), Yeats was speaking of his aesthetic brothers as products of a doomed generation. Yet he claimed that their poetic aspirations were worthy of much praise and defended them against the imagined hostility of the masses.[8] "Never before," he said, " ... were men so anxious to write their best—as they conceive that best—and so entirely loth to bow to the prejudices of the multitude" (UP1, 248). In July 1893, while reviewing a new collection of Arthur Hallam's work ("A Bundle of Poets," UP1, 276-9), Yeats once again noted the prejudices of the multitude and their consequent antipathy toward his contemporaries' brand of art. "Writing long before the days of Rossetti and Swinburne," he said, "Arthur Hallam explained the principles of the aesthetic movement"(277). Quoting Hallam's statements concerning the common reader's unwillingness to raise his ability of emotional perception to the level of the poem, Yeats pinpoints the reason for the public's hostility towards aesthetic verse. "Whatever is mixed up with art, and appears under its semblance," Hallam had said, "is always more favourably regarded than art free and unalloyed"(277). This statement Yeats found to be the best explanation of the popularity of didactic poets and anecdotists of all ages, with the implication that the true poets—those who were dedicated to perpetuating purity in art—would always be publicly reviled.[9]

By 1910, Ernest Dowson, Lionel Johnson, John Davidson and Arthur Symons had completed the Keatsian parallel, tragically dying before reaching full poetic maturity, or in Symons's case, suffering a severe and more-or-less permanent mental breakdown. Yeats took these individual failures as evidence of a greater end, and spoke of the Rhymers' Club as a movement that now belonged irrecoverably to the past. Writing to T. Sturge Moore on February 9th concerning his intentions to prepare a lecture on Modern Poetry, he stated, "I am taking you as the typical poet of the movement immediately after the Rhymers' Club."[10]

Yeats's ability to treat the Rhymers' Club as an actual "movement" demonstrates the completion in his mind of a process of conceptualization that had begun with a denial of coherent structure, and his depiction of this "movement" continues to capitalize on images and ideas made familiar through the reviews of the first Rhymers' Club anthology. Writing to his father concerning the lecture he was preparing, Yeats explained the humble intentions of these poets in terms of an ideal of self-expression: "The doctrine of the group or rather of the majority of it was that lyric poetry should be personal. That a man should express his life and do this without shame or fear" (IY, 128). The idea that a poet could experience "shame" or "fear" in expressing an honest subject honestly seems to have come from Yeats's experience of the reviews, where notions of humbleness and lack of pretentiousness anticipated accusations that the Rhymers were attempting to outperform the great masters. The true courage of such a gesture is evident in Yeats's tone when he speaks of the false yet more fashionable alternatives: "In poetry the antithesis to personality is not so much will as an ever growing burden of noble attitudes and literary words. The noble attitudes are imposed upon the poet by papers like the 'Spectator'" (128).

The relation of these statements to a concept of poetic purity and the possible parallel to be drawn between "papers like the 'Spectator'" and Andrew Lang's popularist blast in the *Daily News* is made clear through the position Yeats takes in the presentation itself. He carefully maintains the double nature of these individuals' characters as well as his own ambivalence of response, but he states without reservation the necessity for honesty in art and the fatuousness of all but the most humble undertakings:

> If you express yourself sincerely I don't think your moral philosophy matters at all. The expression of the joy or sorrow in the depth of a spiritual nature will always be the highest art. Everything that can be reduced to popular morality, everything put in books and taught in schools can be imitated. The noblest art will be always pure experience—the art that insists on nothing, commands nothing—an art that is persuasive because it is almost silent, and is overheard rather than heard. And when I think of that doomed generation I am not sure whether it was sin or sanctity which was found in their brief lives. (128)

Thus, Yeats disposes of "popular morality" by promoting the inimitable purity of Experience and suggesting that those who had dared face it unarmed may have transcended common notions of sin. The joining of opposite values—of persuasiveness and silence, of sanctity and sinfulness—imitates the paradoxical quality of the reviews, creating a mysterious sense of wholeness for these figures. The bird imagery has disappeared, but the same sense of alienation and danger lurks in these lines as had lurked in the critical commentary of Le Gallienne and others. The same key notions of intensity and brevity inform this vision as had informed earlier notions of the Club's mission—the difficulty of the quest, the sense that many would have to die in service to the cause before the race or the art could be won.

Yeats's desire to believe in the artistic quality and literary impact of his poetic brothers led him to speak again of the inevitable succession of generations in his B. B. C. broadcast "Modern Poetry" (1936). "When the Rhymers' Club was breaking up," he said, "I read enthusiastic reviews of the first book of T. Sturge Moore and grew jealous. He did not belong to the Rhymers' Club and I wanted to believe that we had all the good poets"(E&I, 491-508). Yeats resolved his dilemma by placing Moore at the vanguard of a new poetic generation, and he continued to speak of the Rhymers as a movement that had been dedicated to the cause of poetic renewal. Their verse, he claimed, had generated an essential departure from Victorian values of science, morality and rhetoric in art, and its apparent humbleness only served to underscore its actual worth:

> Their poems seemed to say: "You will remember us the longer because we are very small, very unambitious." But my friends were most ambitious men; they wished to express life at its intense moments, that are brief because of their intensity, and at those moments alone. (494)

Again, the double notion of the humbleness of their venture and the seriousness of their intent may be traced back to the earliest comments concerning the Rhymers' Club anthologies—traced, indeed, to the physical presentation of the books themselves, which had been a point of interest for Lang, Image and others. That Yeats had actually transformed his colleagues' lack of pretentiousness into an event of literary value speaks for the power of the book as gesture and the importance, to him, of being able to hold these volumes in his hand. The limited edition spoke implicitly of the rarity of the occasion; the simple binding, of the simplicity of their aims.

Yeats admitted never having found sufficient reason for the tragedy of his generation, but in *The Trembling of the Veil* (1922) he attempts explanation. In the first chapter ("Four Years"), he speaks of youth's inherent quarrel with the present, which his elders control and which he must strive to overcome. This natural opposition between youth and age, between unestablished and established voices, offers an archetypal view of history and reflects the preoccupation with youthfulness, idealism and unlikelihood of success expressed both in the reviews of the Rhymers' anthologies and Yeats's own commentary. Although the poet does not connect this opposition directly with the failure of the Rhymers' Club, he presents it at the onset of his treatment of the nineties and purposefully comments that "in a few months I was to discover others of my own age, who thought as I did" (Au, 115). The suggestion that his fellow Rhymers had "thought as he did" lends cosmic proportions to the actual and creates a situation wherein mythical associations can be drawn. As Cuchulain had inspired the wrath of his father, so other young men would confront their fathers; so indeed would the young members of the Rhymers' Club, losing their lives in attempts to overthrow the established order.

The motif of life as theatre, also developed in this volume, supports associative connections and offers indication of the power of socially-derived metaphors. Yeats sees the major mode of his generation as Tragedy and claims with respect to the Rhymers' Club that "we shared nothing but the artistic life" (Au, 303). Living one's life as if it were art called for intensity and closure in experience—interpretations imposed upon nature by one's aesthetic values. The attempt to live up to this idea of performance created an uneasy balance between the imaginative and the actual worlds, a problem with which the young Hamlet had struggled and which Yeats himself knew from his experiences of the nineties. Citing Pater's *Marius the Epicurean* as a potent influence, Yeats suggests the dangers he and his friends had faced. "It taught us to walk upon a rope," he explained, "tightly stretched through serene air, and we were left to keep our feet upon a swaying rope in a storm"(Au, 302-3). Adopting Pater's aestheticism, poets took on the outsider's role, living intense but uncertain lives. That they performed on this high wire increased their heroic potential; that they sometimes fell indicates the extent to which they were willing to take on the images others had devised for them.

Yeats comes closest to directly identifying the cause for Dowson's and Johnson's downfalls when he quotes from "Ego Dominus Tuus" and speaks of artistic alienation. "What portion in the world can the artist have," he asks, "Who has awakened from the common dream, But dissipation and despair?" The question is rhetorical, containing the answer to its own musing: the artist who rejects the world inherits disappointment as reward. In the poem as well as the text, Yeats reinvokes Keats, whose *Endymion* inspired controversy and whose passion for perfect beauty alienated him from others. This pattern, as the *Daily Chronicle* pointed out, resembles that of the Rhymers, whose quarrel with the common dream drew critical hostility. The "purity" of their verse, its refusal to engage in science, morality or argument, not only made it more beautiful, but made it proportionately less a product of the real world, and this tendency to lyric abstraction alienated them from the public that would ultimately be their judge. Alluding to the Romantic tradition as a whole, Yeats traced a pattern of failure and suffering in the lives of those who had so dedicated themselves to poetic purity:

> But Coleridge of the *Ancient Mariner*, and *Kubla Khan*, and Rossetti in all his writing made what Arnold has called that "morbid effort," that search for "perfection of thought and feeling," and to unite this "perfection of form" sought this new, pure beauty, and suffered in their lives because of it. (313)

Projected into the historical sphere, this tendency to withdrawal is ultimately related to Yeats's theory of antithesis, offering new significance to the doubleness motif that had occurred in earlier accounts ("Was it that we lived in 'an age of transition,' and so lacked coherence, or did we but pursue antithesis?" [304]). Dowson and Johnson found temptation and despair in their Christian beliefs, presaging for Yeats a more general shift in cultural mood. Speaking of the inevitably short span allowed for any movement or idea, he questioned the sufficiency of Christianity for the aesthetic mind and indicated a dissatisfaction that led these poets away from established values into the mystical unknown. Again, he returned to Pater's notions of youth and youthful undertakings, precious because of their vigor and beauty, and the extreme brevity of their duration:

> Our love letters wear out our love; no school of painting outlasts its founders, every stroke of the brush exhausts the impulse, pre-Raphaelitism had some twenty years; impressionism thirty perhaps. Why should we believe that religion can never bring round its antithesis? Is it true that our air is

disturbed, as Mallarmé said, by "the trembling of the veil of the temple," or "that our whole age is seeking to bring forth a sacred book"? Some of us thought that book near towards the end of the last century, but the tide sank again. (315)

In his introduction to *The Oxford Book of Modern Verse* (1936), Yeats again alluded to Pater and related the Rhymers' poetic activities directly to a sense of sacredness. "Poetry was a tradition like religion," he said, "and liable to corruption, and it seemed that they could best restore it by writing lyrics technically perfect, their emotion pitched high"(ix). But the human frailties of these poets, as well as the imperfections of those around them, foretold a tragedy that by then had been played out. The ominousness expressed in the reviews had been realized; the artistic scrupulousness of these poets had found its unjust reward:

> Some of these Hamlets went mad, some drank, drinking not as happy men drink but in solitude, all had courage, all suffered public opprobrium—generally for their virtues or for sins they did not commit—all had good manners. (x)

Andrew Lang's abusive comments have here been transformed into public opprobrium itself, and the immoderacy of his position with regard to the Rhymers' poetic venture has acquired the virulence first suggested in the *Daily Chronicle*'s allusion to Keats. The poetic energy of these youths, their bacchanalian vigor, has been turned inward upon themselves, but behind this attitude of self-destruction lies the image of a critic and a public who could not grasp the nobility of the Rhymers' mission and denied them the opportunity even to approach their goal. Choosing Hamlet as a metaphor, Yeats was responding to the parallels implicit in the drama: a young prince who meditated on the corruption of his elders, who himself sought out the deeper truths of life through play-acting, who was called upon to sacrifice both life and love to expiate others' sins. This conceptualization remains consistent with the Rhymers' Club reviews and with Yeats's own role-playing during the nineties. Focusing on concepts of nobility and mission, youthfulness and historical moment, it acknowledges the personal qualities that Yeats and his aesthetic contemporaries brought to their profession and suggests a pattern (tragedy) for otherwise formless or meaningless behavior. Elevating their experiences to the level of metaphor, Yeats justifies his friends' personal failures and thus establishes a context for art.

In 1914, after many of these poets had died or settled into obscurity, Yeats began another stage of his ascent of the sacred mountain. In the introductory poem of *Responsibilities*, he offered an apology to his ancestors for having nothing but a book to carry on his name. And in the first poem proper of the same collection, he re-created a scene of divine story-telling, dedicated to his former companions at the Cheshire Cheese. Although Yeats acknowledges the difference between himself and his former friends who had felt that passion necessarily leads to death, he counterpoints their story with a story of the Irish gods and so elevates them to mythical status. The assembly at the top of Slievenamon bears an unmistakable resemblance to its earthly counterpart—that association of all-too-mortal celebrants from whom Yeats, as he claims in his poem, had learned his trade. The "wine-drenched eyes" of these beings, their goblets painstakingly "hammered out" to hold the brew of poetic inspiration, the story of faithless and unsuited love recounted by the frantic Aoife creates on a divine scale a situation that had once been true in strictly mortal terms. The Rhymers themselves, whose tragedies long ago had ceased to entertain these figures, achieve in Yeats's mind a solidity of purpose—and in some sense achievement—as constant as the Grey Rock itself:

> *Since, tavern comrades, you have died,*
> *Maybe your images have stood,*
> *Mere bone and muscle thrown aside,*
> *Before that roomful or as good.*
> *You had to face your ends when young—*
> *'Twas wine or women, or some curse—*
> *But never made a poorer song*
> *That you might have a heavier purse,*
> *Nor gave loud service to a cause*
> *That you might have a troop of friends.*
> *You kept the Muses' sterner laws,*
> *And unrepenting faced your ends,*
> *And therefore earned the right—and yet*
> *Dowson and Johnson most I praise—*
> *To troop with those the world's forgot,*
> *And copy their proud steady gaze.*
>
> (273)

Implicit in these lines are notions that had dominated the reviews: allusions to the Rhymers' bacchanalian spirit, their youthfulness and bravery in the face of overwhelming odds, their humbleness and dedication to art. Although these traits undid them in a worldly sense, they also made this group worthy of praise, and Yeats's monument to them suggests the power of language to transform and transcend the triteness of death.

The story Aoife tells within the frame of Yeats's poem suggests further associations and reasons why the poet has fashioned his tribute in just the way he has. Aoife's unnamed lover throws off her protection in favor of his country, having witnessed the suffering of the king's son at the hands of the Danes. His death in the struggle parallels the deaths of certain Rhymers who had dedicated themselves to art—events that by the time of the poem's writing had been accomplished, as had the

The Myth of Failure

anonymity presaged by such a choice. Aoife goes in anger to the gods and asks them to dig her lover up and harry him, complaining of the disloyalty and fickleness of humankind. The complaint is one that Yeats himself as a survivor or the Rhymers as steadfast lovers would certainly understand:

> Why should the faithfullest heart most love
> The bitter sweetness of false faces?
> Why must the lasting love what passes,
> Why are the gods by men betrayed?[11]

At the center of these questions lies a sense of abandonment and confusion over how to deal with the memory of those who choose other loyalties than our own. Aoife in this context becomes an agent of life, perhaps even the guarantor of fame which poets like Dowson and Johnson have rejected, and her anger echoes the resentment of reviewers who felt that the Rhymers had turned their backs on accepted values of life and art. As one whose choices (and fate) had been different, Yeats, along with Aoife, seeks an answer to his confusion and finds in the gods' wordless response the value of tragic gaiety. Dowsed with Goban's wine of immortality, Aoife forgets her complaint and stares back at the gods "with laughing lip." This laughter in the face of suffering and defeat is possible only in a divine context, removed from the dimension of time, and, insomuch as the Rhymers demonstrated similar detachment from critical hostility and imminent failure, helps explain the mythical quality they have achieved in Yeats's mind.

On this level, the text is a meditative self-questioning, focusing on loyalty and the nature of the poet's choices. In the intervening sections, one discovers the answers Yeats has devised: Maud Gonne's dream of the immortals made her dissatisfied with the imperfections of life; the Rhymers' adherence to the Muse's "sterner laws" was in itself a dream of perfection which left them vulnerable to bitterness and defeat; Yeats's loyalty to art was similar to theirs, but less self-destructive, having "more life in it than death." Unlike Aoife's lover, he embraced music rather than war, ignoring the unpopularity of such commitments. Thus, he found hardship not in death but survival; kinship, in suffering for a cause.

Several years afterwards in "In Memory of Major Robert Gregory," Yeats connected his vision of the Rhymers' Club with the fate of other artistic friends. A representative of the Club as a whole, Lionel Johnson takes his place among the shades with whom Yeats cannot sup and who, through memory, occupy his symbolic household. Johnson's juxtaposition to Gregory and John Synge underlines the similarity between his fate and that of all truly talented artists, disvalued or ignored by society because of their talent. Yeats also expands the image of the artist as outcast in this poem to include an acknowledgement of the artist's own instinct to turn away from the world. His depiction of Johnson's withdrawal reflects the claim advanced in "Hopes and Fears for Irish Literature" and other writings that aesthetic poetry finds beauty insomuch as it distances itself from the world:

> Lionel Johnson comes the first to mind,
> That loved his learning better than mankind,
> Though courteous to the worst; much falling he
> Brooded upon sanctity
> Till all his Greek and Latin learning seemed
> A long blast upon the horn that brought
> A little nearer to his thought
> A measureless consummation that he dreamed.
> (VP, 324)

Here, the conflict between the artist and the world is depicted as a choice between learning and mankind, polarities that suggest on the one hand spiritual and on the other hand common concerns. That Johnson had to choose between these two polarities recalls Yeats's arguments on poetic purity and the corrupt values of those who judge but do not create art. Johnson's nobility rests in his unwillingness to mix the mundane with the sublime, as well as his ability to accept or ignore those who do not understand him. Like his fellow Rhymers, he was "courteous to the worst," not bitter or outspoken against those who maligned his attempts at refashioning art. That Yeats juxtaposes Johnson's "falling" with the contemplation of sanctity, however, indicates his human imperfection and the inevitability, because of it, of worldly failure. His perseverance despite this certainty again recalls the spirit of the Rhymers' Club: young artists who defied failure in their pursuit of impossible goals. As the Rhymers' passion for poetry generated both their nobility and their strength as symbol, so Johnson's passion for learning prepares the transition from the human to the mythical plane. His dream of "a measureless consummation" makes release into pure art possible, a perfection that supersedes worldly concerns and renders the poet free of organic constraints.

The myth of the Rhymers' Club and the myth surrounding its anthologies is one of failure. Well-received within the range of their limited readership, these volumes neither spoke nor attempted to speak to the public's demands, and they produced no poetic statement whereby their authors could move beyond their acknowledged status of "minor" versifiers. Yet these books and the individuals who contributed to them did achieve historical significance, producing from their midst "the chosen one" about whom Lang and others had spoken and providing continuing literary examples for him on whose career the gyre of the next century was to turn. The ideal of organic form, the integrity of experience in art, the notion of poetry as a religion from which universal secrets could be derived—these ideas Yeats adopted from his contemporaries who had been more fortunate than he in terms of formal education, but who would never progress beyond that first step of the ladder famewards.

NOTES ON CHAPTER 4

¹For complete bibliographical information on these and other reviews in this chapter, see the Journals section of the Works Cited list.

²The first two references are to unidentified newspaper clippings. All three come from the Elkin Mathews Collection. See MS 392/7/2 & 3.

³In April 1818, *The Quarterly Review* printed a devastating review of Keats's *Endymion* by John Wilson Croker. The article triggered a host of complaints, including a letter from Shelley that claimed the review had brought on the illness and distress from which Keats was soon to die.

⁴Tennyson died in the same month that the article appeared.

⁵In Malory's historical account, the break-up of Arthur's court is traceable to Uther Pendragon, whose adulterous union with Igraine occasioned Arthur's birth. In terms of the Rhymers' Club, their untimely ends are sometimes attributed to illicit desires which the principals could not control. The notion that the sins of the fathers are visited upon the sons is strong in the case of Ernest Dowson, whose parents were both suicides and whose own life was purportedly reckless and dissolute, tempting self-destruction.

⁶The *Globe* complains of the quality of the Rhymers' rhymes ("depart"/"part", "science"/"lions") and calls attention to Rolleston's freedom with the ballad form in his "Ballade of the Cheshire Cheese," but generally these poems present no challenge to conventional notions of structure.

[7] See Au, 165-6, where Yeats admits his guilt for such a transformation: "I sometimes say when I speak of the Club, 'We had such and such ideas, such and such a quarrel with the great Victorians, we set before us such and such aims,' as though we had many philosophical ideas. I say this because I am ashamed to admit that I had these ideas and that whenever I began to talk of them a gloomy silence fell upon the room."

[8] The similarities between this piece and the article in the *Church Quarterly Review*, along with the style of the review and its comments concerning Browning and the importance of critical prose, lead one to believe that the article may have been written by Pater and that Yeats, a friend of Pater's *protégés* Arthur Symons and Lionel Johnson, may have benefitted from his ideas in creating his own essay.

[9] Yeats's attitude towards aesthetic verse was somewhat ambivalent and very likely influenced by his perceived audience. In this instance, he treats it as a cause to which he himself belongs. In "Hopes and Fears for Irish Literature," he dubs it a sterile outgrowth of an aging culture, devoid of the social conviction necessary to make it truly valuable.

[10] From LTSM, 16. Yeats's lecture "Friends of My Youth" has been included in Robert O'Driscoll and Lorna Reynolds's *Yeats and the Theatre*, 21-41.

[11] VP, 275. The Rhymers' sense of love and commitment is as strong as but more self-destructive than Yeats's. Compare, for example, the sentiment of this passage with Dowson's "Cynara," another poem that deals with misprized love.

VISIONS AND RESPONSIBILITIES

In his introduction to *The Oxford Book of Modern Verse* (1936), Yeats mentions 1900 as the year in which decadence came to an end. "Henceforth," he says, "nobody drank absinthe with his black coffee; nobody went mad; nobody committed suicide; nobody joined the Catholic Church; or if they did I have forgotten" (OBMV, xi-xii). In truth, Yeats had forgotten, or, at least had allowed convenience to take precedence over fact. Dowson and Wilde had indeed died in 1900, but the majority of these poets faced their ends after the turn of the century. Johnson died in 1902. Symons suffered a mental collapse in 1908; John Davidson committed suicide in the following year, ending his own madness, fears of professional failure and disease. Whether these artists continued to drink absinthe, joined or participated in the Catholic Church is immaterial to the larger concern. They survived beyond the turn of the century, unable to reconcile their artistic habits with the subsequent changes in taste.

Yeats's decision to link these poets' personal ends with the end of the century was not so much a factual oversight as it was an attempt to organize and make sense of experience—in typical aesthetic fashion, to make better sense of it than actuality had allowed. His eventual position as spokesman for his age left him with the responsibility of evaluating such contemporaries as Dowson, Johnson and Symons, and gave him the privilege of embellishing those facts which others had little knowledge of. Understanding the importance of these figures to him and realizing that claims for their importance were in many ways advertisements of his own centrality to the tradition, Yeats incorporated their fates into a sweeping vision of history. In such *exposés* as his B.B.C. broadcast "Modern Poetry" and his introduction to *The Oxford Book of Modern Verse*, he stated that their dedication to artistic purity had successfully brought about the end of Victorian corruptions in art. "We tried to write like the poets of the Greek Anthology," he said, "or like the Jacobean lyrists, men who wrote while poetry was still pure" (E&I, 495). This impulse had made possible the changes that would occur after the turn of the century and, thus, had made the poets of the Rhymers' Club important figures in the scheme of literary history. If they themselves had not brought about the new age, they had at least created a situation from which the new age could evolve.

But Yeats did survive these poets artistically, and his understanding of the reasons for having done so was at least partially accurate. As early as 1892, in "Hopes and Fears for Irish Literature," he had spoken of the expressive limitations and jadedness of the aesthetic school of writing and had called upon his countrymen to create a literature based upon belief—not in traditional religious institutions, but in the social, political and spiritual consequence of art. This notion that poetry could bring about changes in the world distinguished him from his contemporaries and gave his work a substantiality that they had lacked. Unlike Johnson and Dowson, he had retreated from society in order to gain a better understanding of it; unlike Symons, he had used his symbols to organize and thereby control basic emotional experience. His belief in art and the magic of art made it an act that could not be superseded or improved upon by silence, and this commitment, in turn, had kept him from ultimate despair.

Yeats's dream (outlined in *Autobiographies*) of providing Ireland with a unity of culture was prepared for on both the entrepreneurial and creative levels. Not only did he continue to use traditional themes and figures in his work, but he created a situation by which these interests could be fully realized. While Dowson and Johnson were becoming increasingly isolated in their private griefs and Symons was persevering with an unpopular art, Yeats was establishing educational and cultural programs for Ireland and preparing for the realization of his dramatic interests in the Irish Literary Theatre. Although he occasionally sensed that his efforts were largely ineffectual, he generally acknowledged the influence his verse had had on political events in his country. Writing to William Rothenstein in December 1938, he noted that "Some of the best known of the young men who got themselves killed in 1916 had the Irish legendary hero Cuchulain so much in their minds that the government has celebrated the event with a bad statue" (NLI). And in his contemplative poem, "The Man and the Echo," he brooded over the possible ill effects his words may have had on others:

> Did that play of mine send out
> Certain men the English shot?
> Did words of mine put too great strain
> On that woman's reeling brain?
> Could my spoken words have checked
> That whereby a house lay wrecked?
> And all seems evil until I
> Sleepless would lie down and die. (VP, 632)

Yeats may have violated aesthetic rules of "purity," but he never reduced his expression to mere propaganda or promoted the sentimentality often associated with Victorian verse. He saw in Ireland and her political situation the opportunity for creative advancement and was sufficiently dedicated to artistic success not to be constrained by theoretical scruples. However self-reproachful he may have felt concerning the choices he had made, he clearly believed in the power of art to bring about intellectual and emotional changes, and this belief had made poetry more central to him than to those who had adhered strictly to the doctrine of "Art for Art's Sake." For Yeats, poetry had offered a means of ordering and controlling experience, of interpreting events that otherwise would have remained essentially meaningless.

Although he gradually distinguished himself in purpose and degree of success from his nineties contemporaries, Yeats understood his debt to them and expressed his obligation in various ways. In the same essay of 1892 in which he spoke of the jaded nature of aesthetic art, he also pointed to the potential benefits of an aesthetic influence on Irish verse. "Can we but learn," he said, "a little of their skill and a little of their hatred of the commonplace and the banal, we may make all these restless energies of ours alike the inspiration and the theme of a new and wonderful literature" (UP1, 250). He had voiced the same notions in "To Ireland in the Coming Times," calling for a new rhythm that would loosen the pace at which his countrymen, sensitive to cultural and political drumbeats, consumed themselves in hatred and war. In *The Trembling of the Veil*, Yeats identified Johnson, Symons, Dowson and Horne as examples for such changes—poets with the ability to exercise "conscious, deliberate craft" in their work. The relationship between English and Classical meters, between poetry and songs to accompany the lute *à la Dolmetsch*, between speech as one hears it and the new form of chanted delivery which Yeats and Florence Farr subsequently developed for the theatre, were all concerns that grew out of conversations at the Rhymers' Club and which ultimately found expression in their poetry.[1] The slow-moving cadences of Yeats's "Innisfree":

I will aRISE and GO NOW ...

The supple dance rhythms of Symons's "Javanese Dancers":

SMILing/beTWEEN/ her PAIN/ted LIDS/a
    SMILE
MO/tionless, /UN/inTEL/Ligi/BLE/she TWINES

The rhythms of vague regret that power Dowson's "Cynara":

LAST NIGHT, ah, YES/terNIGHT,// beTWIXT
   /her LIPS/ and MINE

all stem from a common source of interest: the desire to control experience rhythmically rather than let the experience drive and control the verse. Yeats's contemporaries could not associate such technical achievements with problems and solutions in the real world, but they nevertheless provided examples whereby the principle could be fulfilled. Beginning, as he claims, after the publication of *The Wanderings of Oisin*, Yeats restructured the rhythmical (and, thus, syntactical) underpinning of his poetry, and this restructuring continued to exert an influence on future expressions. He learned from these early experiments the expressive possibilities of form, how it could isolate and control complexities of his psychological universe.

Interestingly, the verse form he adopted in "To Ireland in the Coming Times" began to appear regularly in his later work, and his concern with artistic craftsmanship, clearly associated with metrical strategies among other things, remained a potent cultural argument to the end of his career. In his vatic farewell to Ireland, "Under Ben Bulben," the poet exhorts his countrymen to respect the values of craft, expressing this point of view via the same metrical arrangement he had made familiar in "To Ireland in the Coming Times":

/   /   /   /
Irish poets, // learn   your   trade,

```
        /         /         /       /
    Sing   whatever //   is well made,
        /      /    (/------/)      /
    Scorn the sort // now growing up
        /       /              /      /
    All out of shape // from toe to top,
        /     /             /          /
    Their unremembering // hearts and heads
       /       /           /       /
    Base-born products // of base beds. (VP, 639)
```

Yeats adapted the form of this poem from William Blake, who had used it in such poems as "A Poison Tree," "To Tirzah" and "For the Sexes: the Gates of Paradise" and whom he had studied with the Rhymer Edwin J. Ellis from 1889-93. He also very likely was influenced by William Morris, who employed it in "The Haystack in the Floods" and whose Pre-Raphaelite values Yeats had sought to emulate early in his career. Both Blake and Morris had used this pattern of four isochronic stresses per line, arranged in rhymed couplets, to produce an energy and mysteriousness reminiscent of a very old tradition of verse and to support the mythical distance of their subject matter.[2] Wanting to distance his own expression from conventional accentual-syllabics, Yeats re-employed this meter, achieving an energy and balance which complemented his verbal expression. The metrical underpinning of the passage supports the oracular intentions of the poem by suggesting a measured tympany, and the reproductive concerns of the metaphor are furthered by a line that expands or contracts with respect to the number of syllables it includes. While Yeats in this statement criticizes contemporary artistic products for their formlessness and lack of traditional sense, he offers an example of the opposite condition in his own meter and suggests the ritualistic roots of his statement in the choices he has made. As in the earliest use of the form, the rhythm of the poem is meant to suggest a rhythm for life and, in these lines, life is equated with a process of regeneration. Thus, as he teaches his countrymen how to write, he is also teaching them how to make love.

The identification of artistic energy with sexual energy is pervasive in Yeats's work and is also strongly associated in his mind with the aesthetic movement of the 1890s, specifically with poets like Ernest Dowson whose unrequited passions were channelled into poetry. One recalls "Pardon, Old Fathers," in which the poet identifies his only progeny as a book, and such poems as "The Scholars" and "The Tower," where he relates the sexual energy of youth with the ability to create a vibrant art. One also recalls the thirteenth phase of *A Vision*, the phase of the "sensuous man" in which he locates Dowson, Beardsley and Baudelaire and speaks of the polarities of self-expression and self-absorption, subjective truth and morbidity. "Phase 13 is a phase of great importance," Yeats explains, "because the most intellectually subjective phase, and because only here can be achieved in perfection that in the *antithetical* life which corresponds to sanctity in the *primary*: not self-denial but expression for expression's sake" (AV-A, 64-5). The duality inherent in Yeats's system is echoed in other statements dealing with the same subject. In "Hopes and Fears for Irish Literature," he warns his countrymen of the artistic sterility implicit in the aesthetic code, and in "Pardon, Old Fathers," he asks forgiveness for actual, biological sterility brought on by an adherence to this code. On the other hand, he recognizes the necessity of commitment and emotional intensity in art, and comes to identify this level of vitality with the poets of his youth. In "The Tower," for instance, Yeats measures himself against this early example, attempting to preserve that sexual potency which helps justify his art. A survivor of an age in which poets had "burned with a hard, gem-like flame," the mature Yeats looks back longingly on the past, leaving behind its freshness and vitality only to the degree that his present condition requires him to do so. Like Wordsworth or Tennyson, he has become a victim of longevity, an intellectual reduction of an earlier romantic self:

> It seems that I must bid the Muse go pack,
> Choose Plato and Plotinus for a friend
> Until imagination, ear and eye,
> Can be content with argument and deal
> In abstract things; or be derided by
> A sort of battered kettle at the heel. (VP, 409)

Although limited by his present physical condition, the poet remembers the lessons of his youth and the value of youthful vitality. In the succeeding years, he would even attempt to overcome the effects of time—first, by actual, physical rejuvenation and then by joining sensual themes with a recognition of aging. As Morton Seiden points out in *The Poet as Mythmaker* (179 ff.), Yeats's Steinach operation in 1934 directly influenced his work: poems written after it find a union of body and soul, a tragic joy dependent upon the seeming paradox of wild sexuality and old age.

In addition to loosening and experimenting with rhythms in the period following *The Wanderings of Oisin*, Yeats also, as he claimed, worked on eliminating traditional metaphors from his verse.[3] His ability to do so without at once sacrificing the essential poetic quality of his lines had to do with notions that had evolved in relation to his rhythmical experimentation as well as to concepts of symbolism that had been made available to him through his occult studies and through the example of his aesthetic contemporaries. In the 1908 version of his *Collected Poems*, he explained the process whereby he eliminated metaphors and moved steadily into a realm of more mystical intensity:

> When I wrote these poems I had so meditated over the images that came to me in writing 'Ballads and Lyrics', 'The Rose', and 'The Wanderings of Oisin', and other images from Irish folklore, that they had become true symbols. I had sometimes when awake, but more often in sleep, moments of vision, a state very unlike dreaming, when these images took upon themselves what seemed an independent life and became a part of a mystic language, which seemed always as if it would bring me some strange revelation. Being troubled at what was thought a reckless obscurity, I tried to explain myself in lengthy notes, into which I put all the little learning I had, and more wilful phantasy than I now think admirable, though what is most mystical still seems to me the most true. (quoted from VP, 800)

The objects about which the poet wrote had been elevated to mystical importance as he continued to concentrate upon them: repetition of the visual image without entertaining the meaning of that images and repetition of the accompanying rhythm or phrase had produced a condition similar to trance in which sense was always partially deferred and expectation heightened. The tension implicit in this situation matched the tension produced by the aesthetic poets in their use of opaque terminology, in their juxtapositioning of opposing values (positive with negative, attraction with repulsion), in their concentration on the emotional surface of an object rather than on the internalized, intellectual apprehension of it. Yeats benefitted from these notions, as his verse of the period shows, but he ultimately distinguished himself from others who exercised similar techniques in his ability to apply them to new situations when the old ones had ceased to be of interest.

The Mask, for example, is a concept he adopted from Oscar Wilde, but which takes on new depth and significance in Yeats's visionary system. As he came to depict it, the Mask was an image of desire towards which the individual (poet or actor) strained, and through which he would penetrate at the moment of greatest violence or sympathy. It was, as he explained "a being in all things the opposite to [one's] natural state"(Au, 247). The original or simplest use of this term, as a barrier which heightens the tension between the object perceived and the object imagined, is at work in his poem "The Mask" (1910) and recalls the early development of this concept in Wilde's *The Picture of Dorian Gray* (1891). In Yeats's poem, one lover asks another to "Put off that mask of burning gold/With emerald eyes" and is refused because "It was the mask engaged your mind . . . /Not what's behind"(VP, 263). In *The Picture of Dorian Gray*, Dorian abandons Sybil when she puts aside the Mask of her acting career for love. "You used to stir my imagination," Dorian complains, "Now you don't even stir my curiosity" (OWW, 75). The significance of this comment with regard to art is underscored by Wilde's own alleged comments on the Mask, as well as by Lord Henry Wotton's attitude in the book, generally considered to be a reflection of the author's own point of view. According to Yeats, Wilde claimed that he lived in the fashionable West End of London because "nothing in life interests me but the mask" (Au, 165). Lord Henry points out the essence of this interest in a conversation with the Duchess in Chapter Eighteen:

> "What are you looking for?" she inquired.
> "The button from your foil," he answered.
> "You have dropped it."
> She laughed. "I have still the mask."
> "It makes your eyes lovelier," was his reply.
> (OWW, 155)

In both writers' minds, the Mask, as an analogue for art, creates a tension between what is seen and what is imagined and, thus, heightens the beauty or the power of the natural object. The distinction to be made between the two points of view is in the attitude each writer assumes concerning the *value* of this concept. Wilde obviously sees no moral responsibility in art and emphasizes this point by creating a situation wherein the protagonist is protected from culpability and reproach to the degree that he immerses himself in art. Yeats, on the other hand, discerns in this structure a positive, cohesive power, whereby two antagonistic spirits may find mutual attraction and stability in a volatile universe. Wilde's notion necessitates failure insomuch as truth must eventually annihilate artistic deception. Yeats's notion is more hopeful and complete, since it suggests how destruction may be waylaid in a joining of opposite values.

In other poetic writings, Yeats develops our understanding of the concept of the Mask, offering a sense of tragedy and redemption which goes beyond Wilde's merely gothic attempts or the unresolved tensions of Dowson's and Johnson's verse. The apotheosis of the heroes in "Easter 1916" offers just such an example, where man becomes his Mask at the moment of greatest intensity. The heroes in this poem have so identified with their artistic images that they have given up their lives to achieve that ideal, and "a terrible beauty" has been born from the violence of the sacrifice. The permanence of this image, like the permanence of the stone, offers a crucial consideration for Yeats's later vision of artistic fulfillment. In "Sailing to Byzantium" and "Under Ben Bulben," for example, artifice is valued precisely because it endures above and beyond considerations of organic decay. Yeats's transformation of Maud Gonne from strident revolutionary to a vision of Helen of Troy also benefits from this concept. In "The Circus Animals' Desertion," the poet depicts the process whereby desire transforms the individual into her artistic counterpart and, thus, creates an image which controls and resolves unfulfilled emotions:

> I thought my dear must her own soul destroy,
> So did fanaticism and hate enslave it,
> And this brought forth a dream and soon enough
> This dream itself had all my thought and love.
> (VP, 630)

The process depicted in this passage is similar to that described as the second stage of Art in Wilde's "The Decay of Lying," but it improves upon Wilde's notion insomuch as it provides a means whereby one's life can be lived, irrespective of organic shortcomings and disappointments. The relationship Wilde establishes between Art and Life has as its end a separation between the two dimensions of experience and requires that one or the other dimension ultimately be renounced:

> Art begins with abstract decoration, with purely imaginative and pleasurable work dealing with what is unreal and non-existent. This is the first stage. Then Life becomes fascinated with this new wonder, and asks to be admitted into the charmed circle. Art takes life as part of her rough material, recreates it, and refashions it in fresh forms, is absolutely indifferent to fact, invents, imagines, dreams, and keeps between herself and reality the impenetrable barrier of beautiful style, of decorative or ideal treatment. The third stage is when Life gets the upper hand, and drives Art out into the wilderness. This is the true decadence, and it is from this that we are now suffering.
> (OWC, 176)

This perception of Wilde's system is reflected in *A Vision*, where the individual's abilities and inabilities play an important role in classification. Yeats places Wilde in the 19th phase of *A Vision*, where "Unity of Being is no longer possible." The individual of this phase "is compelled to live in a fragment of itself," his strength of conviction "temperamentally formed to fit some crisis of personal life" (AV-A, 82-3). Wilde's inability to use his dualistic system for more than a personal or private preoccupation with social inversion shares in this typification, since neither polarity (socially acceptable behavior vs. privately intoxicating behavior) may be successfully integrated with or enriched by the other. Yeats's celebration of artifice depends on and in many ways results from organic experience, in the same way that his organic experience takes inspiration and meaning from art. He is capable of seeing the Mask as a negative extension of the self, but also enriches that notion by insisting upon a larger, more inclusive, perspective. As is true in Eastern mysticism, the cycles of creation move toward universal apprehension, including rather than eliminating all phases and aspects. The resignation of self implied in such processes is not one of giving up but of giving over to the experience, of appreciating the moment for what it renders of the whole:

> *My Self.* A living man is blind and drinks his drop.
> What matter if the ditches are impure?
> What matter if I live it all once more?
> Endure that toil of growing up;
> The ignominy of boyhood; the distress
> Of boyhood changing into man;
> The unfinished man and his pain
> Brought face to face with his own clumsiness;
>
> The finished man among his enemies?—
> How in the name of Heaven can he escape
> That defiling and disfigured shape

> The mirror of malicious eyes
> Casts upon his eyes until at last
> He thinks that shape must be his shape?
> And what's the good of an escape
> If honour find him in the wintry blast?
>
> I am content to live it all again. (VP, 478-9)

Yeats's Self recognizes and embraces the processes of becoming, hardship offering a foil whereby true identity can be revealed. Unlike Dorian Gray, who himself determined the corruption of his portrait, the Self is shaped by external forces, and his image is registered in his own eyes rather than placed at a safe and objective distance. Both depictions depend upon a tension between opposites, but one sees the individual as an inherent victim, the other as an inherent victimizer.

Yeats's poem "The Statues," published March 1939, goes further to indicate the relationship to be drawn between reality and art. According to the poem, passion inspires a dream which then requires form: so Pythagoras' numbers were translated into a statue which youths "Pale from the imagined love of solitary beds" could recognize and understand. Seeing through the object to the perfection that inspired it, they treated the symbol as the thing itself and so "pressed at midnight . . . Live lips upon a plummet-measured face" (VP, 610). But Yeats goes on to insist that the possibilities of art are greater: that Phidias' creations actually gave to European culture their archetype for physical beauty, against which all specific representations would be measured. In both cases, Life imitates Art, a Platonic reversal commonly accepted by the decadents, but which for them brought on unusual suffering. The oppositions, too, between intellectual apprehension and sensual immediacy are placed in a modern context as Yeats recalls Watts's portrait of William Morris (See Au, 141-2; also CP, 415): he was not a Hamlet (or thinker) grown thin from eating flies, but a fat (sensual) dreamer of the Middle Ages. Morris, and presumably other Pre-Raphaelites, had learned from the Renaissance the potentially disturbing nature of thought—that knowledge increases irreality, that "Mirror on mirror mirrored is all the show" (VP, 610). Thus, they had turned their attention to the Middle Ages, a sensuous dream world that depended more on emotion than thought. Finally, Yeats relates the Irish to the Greeks, who saw God as measure or intellect, but he depicts them as being out of place in the violent sensuousness of modern times. The image of Cuchulain, thus, offers an example of heroism, a symbol whereby these modern Platonists could move through the present violence to structural essences and so create a new order.

The influence of Arthur Symons's notions of symbolism on Yeats has been adequately explained by Frank Kermode and others (See RI). One need only point out that Yeats revised his early poems to fulfill their inherent conceptual possibilities as he gained the skill to employ these techniques and that, although his methods changed as his career progressed, these notions continued to have bearing upon his expression. Symons's image of the dancer, for example, which he had gleaned from the French *symbolistes* (specifically Mallarmé) and his own experiences as Music Hall critic for the *Star*, appears in Yeats as a cosmic energy most often related to the affairs and activities of the fairy world. The first occurrence of this concept in Yeats's poems, however, is in "The Song of the Happy Shepherd," where he alludes to the eternal pattern of flux that governs the world ("Of all the many changing things /In dreary dancing past us whirled"). This expression (1885) predates any possible influence by Symons and suggests that the germ of that idea was present in Yeats's mind before aesthetic methods and interests were readily available to him. Such is generally the impression given by those poems that appeared in the books of the Rhymers' Club, although the connotative sphere of the term broadens slightly in his various uses of it: "A Man who Dreamed of Fairyland" mentions "leaf-crowned *dances*," Bridget of "The Folk of the Air" joins in the fairies' mysterious and exciting *dance*, and "The Fiddler of Dooney" proclaims the fiddler's blessings in heaven because he makes others "*dance* like a wave of the sea." Unlike Symons's image, Yeats's dance is a rural or mythical experience with only tangential relation to the civilized world, but like his, it depicts a perfection of movement or abandon that sustains itself beyond rational comprehension. Perhaps because of Symons's growing influence on him, Yeats returns to these poems at the end of the century to reinforce in them the importance of the dance. Thus, in "A Man who Dreamed of Fairyland" (retitled "The Man who Dreamed of Faeryland"), the dreamer is now identified as a "*dancer*," and in "A Mystical Prayer to the Masters of the Elements," the Seven Lights "bowed in their *dance* and wept." At this point, the identification of the performer as a "dancer" begins to acquire importance, and the possible feminine quality of the the Seven Lights suggests the role that a female dancer might play.

Yeats continued to expand his concept of dancing and the dance as the new century progressed and generally took the notion beyond Symons's somewhat narrow range of the music hall and the solitary woman dancing. Yet one can see in his later poems echoes of that early influence. In "Nineteen Hundred and Nineteen," he captures the ethereality and mystery of Loie Fuller's dancers as they perform:

> When Loie Fuller's Chinese dancers enwound
> A shining web, a floating ribbon of cloth,
> It seemed that a dragon of air
> Had fallen among dancers. (VP, 430)

In "Her Vision in the Wood," women move forgetfully to sombre music, suggestive of Symons's fascination with the

Visions and Responsibilities

purely emotive, nonintellectual aspect of the dance:

> All stately women moving to a song
> With loosened hair or foreheads grief-distraught,
> It seemed a Quattrocento painter's throng,
> A thoughtless image of Mantegna's thought—
> Why should they think that are for ever young?
> (VP, 537)

And in various other expressions, such as "To a Child Dancing in the Wind" and "A Crazed Girl," he focuses on an individual child who dances and unconsciously celebrates her own innocent joy. Notable in this respect is the memorable young figure in "Long-Legged Fly," who seems a direct descendant of Symons's "Nora on the Pavement":

> She thinks, part woman, three parts a child,
> That nobody looks; her feet
> Practice a tinker shuffle
> Picked up on a street.
> *Like a long-legged fly upon the stream*
> *Her mind moves upon silence.* (VP, 617)

> [As Nora on the pavement
> Dances, and she entrances the grey hour
> Into the laughing circle of her power,
> The magic circle of her glances,
> As Nora dances on the midnight pavement.
> (BRC-2, 23)]

Yeats ultimately associated his notion of the dance with his concept of the Mask—thus offering a fitting tribute to those figures who had provided him with important directives for his experiments in drama. As with the Mask, the dichotomy between performer and performance disappears as the individual identifies with his or her role. In Paterian terms, the expression perfects itself insomuch as what is to be communicated is complemented by and dependent upon the way it is communicated—that is, insomuch as it approaches a so-called "organic" ideal. Thus, in "Among School Children," Yeats presents his image of perfection in organic terms, joining the image of the tree with an allusion to the dancer:

> O chestnut-tree, great-rooted blossomer,
> Are you the leaf, the blossom or the bole?
> O body swayed to music, O brightening glance,
> How can we know the dancer from the dance?
>   (VP, 446)

Classicists such as Lionel Johnson and Victor Plarr suggested an orientation that related Yeats's Irish interests to more universal concerns. The example of Johnson's Platonic idealism and the architectural (structural) balances that Plarr adopted from the French *parnassiens* offered Yeats a means whereby his expression could move beyond mere provincialism and reaffirm the real similarities to be found between different cultures and eras. The Mask theory itself remains consistent with Plato's implied dualism—that incarnate forms are limited versions of the ideal pattern—and Yeats's use of this theory to transform Maud Gonne into Helen of Troy indicates to what extent native images must be associated with non-native ones.

In his autobiography, Yeats spoke of Arthur Symons having returned from Europe with stories of Maeterlinck and Verhaeren and how these reports suggested to him "a poetry like that of the Sufis." Not wishing to turn his expression into "an international art," he focused on Ireland alone, believing that his expression would find correlation with other forms of national art. "Perhaps even these images," he said, ". . . might move of themselves and with some powerful, even turbulent life, like those painted horses that trampled the rice-fields of Japan" (Au, 193-4).

In his later work, he sometimes denied the usefulness of Plato, but primarily as an intellectual rather than a sensual approach to art. In so doing, he was remaining loyal to his aesthetic past that saw sexual energy as superior to intellectual passivity and considered art the *primum mobile* of all creation.[4] Even at this stage, however, there remains an appreciation for the dramatic possibilities provided by Platonic philosophy—in the presence of a ghost that urges the poet to ever greater achievements:

> 'What then?' sang Plato's ghost. 'What then?'
> (VP, 576)

And in the figure "like Milton's Platonist" who toils to discover the nature of his world:

> A winding stair, a chamber arched with stone,
> A grey stone fireplace with an open hearth,
> A candle and written page.
> *Il Penseroso*'s Platonist toiled on
> In some like chamber, shadowing forth
> How the daemonic rage
> Imagined everything. (VP, 419)

In "The Phases of the Moon," Yeats continues with this motif. The ethereality of this scene invokes a sense of communion between living and dead, present and past, and generates a numinousness reminiscent of Johnson's "Plato in London":

> He has found, after the manner of his kind,
> Mere images; chosen this place to live in

> Because, it may be, of the candle-light
> From the far tower where Milton's Platonist
> Sat late, or Shelley's visionary prince:
> The lonely light that Samuel Palmer engraved,
> An image of mysterious wisdom won by toil.
> (VP, 373)

> [The hours pass; and the fire burns low;
> The clear flame dwindles into death:
> Shut then the book with care; and so,
> Take leave of Plato, with hushed breath,
> A little, by the falling gleams,
>   Tarry the gracious dreams:
>   And they too go. (BRC-1, 90-91)]

Victor Plarr's classicism benefits from the concerns and teachings of the French *parnassiens*, and, although Yeats never spoke effusively of Plarr's artistic talents,[5] he seems to have derived a certain amount from his example. Yeats's attention to the details of craftsmanship, evident in such later poems as "Lapis Lazuli," "Sailing to Byzantium" and "The Statues," has much in common with Plarr's celebration of classical artifacts in "To a Greek Gem" and "Ad Cinerarium." The basically Keatsian understanding that man-made creations outlast and so give meaning to organic reality lies behind both Yeats's and Plarr's expressions and suggest—at least to Yeats—how artifice might be an improvement over the real. There is also in Plarr an indication of how organic reality may be transformed into art. In "Twilight Piece," for example, Plarr offers a verbal sketch of the scene before him, fixing as he does the geometric and tonal relations in artistic permanence. While Plarr denies the artist's ability to reproduce the full significance of the moment, his image possesses the same palpability as that of a finely cut intaglio:

> And here on the slim arch that spans
> The rippling stream, in dark outline,
> You see the poor old fisherman's
> Bowed form and patient rod and line.
> (BRC-1, 86)

Yeats's own fisherman was summoned, as he claims, from the imagination alone, but there is ample evidence in his work of similar organic transformations. The physical properties of "Beautiful Lofty Things," for example, do not suggest flesh and bone. Rather, they promote the poses and textures of sculpture—an artistic refiguring which the poet fulfills in such poems as "A Bronze Head" and "The Municipal Gallery Revisited." Yeats's own transformation from an elderly man into a perpetually singing mechanical bird in "Sailing to Byzantium" shares its identity with such precedents as Keats's "Nightingale," Andrew Lang's "twittering young bird on the sonorous Helicon of England" (DC) and Victor Plarr's "Night-Jar" (BRC-2, 124), calling the human spirit into the land of death. The classical source for such a transformation seems to be Ovid's *Metamorphoses*, a text which points, again, to the superiority of art over nature, and which produces those shapes or emblems that render human suffering meaningful:

> Once out of nature I shall never take
> My bodily form from any natural thing,
> But such a form as Grecian goldsmiths make
> Of hammered gold and gold enamelling
> To keep a drowsy Emperor awake;
> Or set upon a golden bough to sing
> To lords and ladies of Byzantium
> Of what is past, or passing, or to come. (VP, 408)

As the previous pages have shown, Yeats realized the importance that the Rhymers' Club held for him, and he expressed his debt to its members in many ways. In such critical enterprises as his introduction to *The Oxford Book of Modern Verse* (1936) and his B. B. C. broadcast "Modern Poetry" (1936), he identifies the Rhymers as important precursers to the modern period, and in *Autobiographies* he offers one of the most extensive treatments available of that period and the individuals who had characterized it. Yeats also demonstrated these poets' influence on him in his verse—developing techniques and themes that the aesthetic school had made available to him and continuing to refer to these figures as examples of artistic integrity. In his early verse (specifically, in poems ultimately collected in "The Rose" and "The Wind Among the Reeds"), he manipulated syntax and verbal expectations to enforce an emotional rather than a rational apprehension of his subject, and, as his career progressed, he developed the concerns of symbolism and artifice that had always played an important role in aesthetic expression. If Yeats's memory of these poets was not always factually precise, it remained consistent with a poetic ideal that stressed the value of their principles and demanded fulfillment by those who had survived them. Envisioning an historical role for the Rhymers' Club, Yeats subsequently sensed the responsibility of making that vision come true.

There remains for this chapter the necessity of tracing Yeats's poetic treatment of these figures—the process whereby they were transformed into archetypal representations and, thus, were given meaning beyond mere individuality. The transformation of Maud Gonne into the mythopoetic Helen is a well-known example of this phenomenon, but it was not the only instance in which Yeats resolved personal difficulties by submitting them to the depersonalizing and universalizing tendencies of poetry. To approach this event from the point of view of the Rhymers' Club not only shows the evolution of his attitude toward the group but gives a new perspective on the mystical beliefs that sustained him personally and artistically throughout his career. Yeats's ability to make these poets "live" in the present, to continue to learn from their example long after he had lost touch with them helped him emotionally, and this practice created a case for the psychological efficacy of magic if not for its factual soundness.

The most extensive poetic tribute to the Rhymers' Club that Yeats made may be found in "The Grey Rock" (1914), the first poem proper of the volume *Responsibilities*. The title of that volume as well as the epigraphs with which the poet introduces it indicate the perspective he has adopted concerning the poems that follow: that these expressions are "responsibilities," originally associated with a dream or ideal; that the poet in reaffirming his allegiance to the past helps fulfill his own sense of identity. Thus:

"In dreams begins responsibility"

Thus:

*"How am I fallen from myself, for a long time
   now
I have not seen the Prince of Chang in my
   dreams."*

(VP, 269)

This notion that dreams beget responsibility departs from Pater's belief that art exists for its own sake, with no other end but beauty and pleasure, and indicates the lesson that Yeats has learned from his aesthetic contemporaries. Having moved away from the affairs of this world into a world of increasing abstraction, they found images that were beautiful but sterile and, so, had failed to produce a lasting and meaningful art.[6] That Yeats sees himself as having taken part in this process is evident in his dedicatory poem to his ancestors ("Pardon, Old Fathers"), where he asks their forgiveness for his own sterility and states that he has exchanged the progeny of this world for a book. Significantly, however, Yeats's failure to produce is strictly biolological, and his artistic product is an offering which he hopes "will prove your blood and mine." Thus, he both identifies with and distinguishes himself from the dilemma of his past—recognizing the price one must pay for a life of art and yet expressing the determination to make that sacrifice count.

The placement of "The Grey Rock" at the opening of *Responsibilities* thus suggests the importance of the Rhymers' Club as an influence on Yeats's early career and as a starting point for his implied new beginning. The poem combines two levels of experience—the personal and the mythological—to underscore the relationship between his earthly cenacle and the assembly of gods on Slievenamon, as well as to point to the essential irreality, *qua* artistic fabrication, of both levels. His resolution of this dream-like experience, however, is not to dismiss it as useless (as the gods and ultimately Aoife do) but to express continuing commitment (as does the legendary hero Cuchulain).[7] Although speaking as a survivor, Yeats sees himself as a kindred spirit to the former members of the Rhymers' Club, one whose value of love has made him an exile in his present world:

> *I have kept my faith, though faith was tried,*
> *To that rock-born, rock-wandering foot,*
> *And the world's altered since you died,*
> *And I am in no good repute*
> *With the loud host before the sea,*
> *That think sword-strokes were better meant*
> *Than lover's music—let that be,*
> *So that the wandering foot's content.* (VP, 276)

Visions and Responsibilities

The image of the rock, which Jeffares identifies with Aoife and Maud Gonne (CP, 104-5), captures a sense not only of Ireland's terrain but the solidity of purpose that has caused the poet to resist public expectations and demands. In this respect, the image shares its identity with future uses of the rock and the stone in Yeats's poems: the sense that suffering is at the heart of transformations from organic flux to inorganic permanence. There follows from this example the stone in "Easter 1916," born out of too much love; the figure of Old Rocky Face looking forth in "The Gyres" (a visionary permanence in the midst of flux); and the stone monument that marks the poet's grave in "Under Ben Bulben." We recall then that "The Grey Rock" itself is a kind of monument, commemorating a bygone age and marking new departures. Consistent with Yeats's desire, it is a poetic statement at once emotional and cold.[8]

Yeats's commemoration of the past acquires magical potency in the concluding poem to *Responsibilities*. "While I, from that reed-throated whisperer" speaks of the poet's muse as a presence "who comes at need," and of those figures who populate his poems as "companions" which he "inwardly surmises." The suggestion of corporeality implicit in these terms is strengthened by their ability to protect the dreamer from external circumstances, where Notoriety has supplanted Fame and the poet is a victim of misrepresentation and critical scorn. Yeats's conceptual position as that of a Survivor (first expressed in "A Dream of Death") has here been realized, and the techniques learned from early experiments have acquired direct practical value. The deaths of those who had influence on his art left him lonely and vulnerable, but his ability to bring these figures back through the strength of his imagination allows him continuance in the world. Like Orpheus, he has the power to animate the inanimate, his music having taught the very stones to dance.

The process of reconciliation continues in the next volume of Yeats's canon, in which Lionel Johnson comes to represent the tragic generation and, through his supposed Irishness, is related to other, more indigenous losses. The title poem of *The Wild Swans at Coole* reestablishes Yeats's sense of vulnerability, and the succeeding poem, "In Memory of Major Robert Gregory," commemorates those figures who have died. Significantly, this poem also marks the beginning of Yeats's residence at Thoor Ballylee, a domicile that commemorates the poet's past values and a symbol of his present intellectual life. In dedicating his house, Yeats names those friends who could not be with him, recalling first Lionel Johnson: "Though courteous to the worst; much falling he/Brooded upon sanctity . . ." (VP, 324). It is easy in his statement to mistake "falling" for "failing," the allusion to Johnson's physical infirmity finding a relation, through sound association, to his intellectual dissatisfaction with the affairs of this world. Needless to say, Johnson's classical interests— specifically, his Platonic idealism—makes him a fit frequenter of the house where Yeats contends with his own relationship to external reality and where intellectual acuity vies with physical decay. The Hamlet metaphor—identifying these former artists as tragic figures—finds further application here insomuch as Johnson, like Hamlet, brooded on basic issues of right and wrong and found in the imperfections of life his undoing. Although representative of a general pattern of behavior, Johnson's passion seems to go beyond Dowson's or Symons's, including intellect, with which Yeats in his old age must come to terms.

Yeats mentions three other figures in his litany of spiritual guests, all of whom had been essentially misprized by the world[9] Yeats's account of Synge's career, however, bears the closest resemblance to Johnson's, and his juxtaposition of it to that of Johnson suggests how the two were associated in the poet's mind:

> And that enquiring man John Synge comes next,
> That dying chose the living world for text

> And never could have rested in the tomb
> But that, long travelling, he had come
> Towards nightfall upon certain set apart
> In a most desolate stony place,
> Towards nightfall upon a race
> Passionate and simple like his heart. (VP, 325)

Although Yeats typifies Synge as one who made his art from earthly rather than otherworldly materials, he implicitly establishes a connection between him and his predecessor with the continuing rock/stone motif. Elsewhere identified as "that meditative man" ("Coole Park, 1929") and "that rooted man" ("The Municipal Gallery Revisited"), Synge is here an "enquiring man," a figure like Hamlet's ghost who stalks the countryside for resolution to an unspoken need. The use of "desolate stony place" to indicate the focus of his art (to be sure, an accurate description of the Aran Islands where Synge stayed) recalls the desolate landscape which serves as Yeats's backdrop for "The Grey Rock," if not the barren environment where Hamlet's ghost encountered the young Hamlet. This geographical "rooting" reminds us that Yeats valued his aesthetic contemporaries partially because they had taught him the attractiveness of an art based upon personal experience, or, by extension, natural or native themes.[10] The joining of passion with simplicity—in Synge's case, of a cultural nature; in Johnson's, of an intellectual or philosophical nature—and the added understanding that this aesthetic position contributed to both artists' tragic ends, further draws a correlation between them. Indeed, when Yeats alludes to Synge in future poetic expressions, he seems to be referring to the literary archetype of artistic martyrdom itself, a category that includes Lionel Johnson and, insomuch as Johnson is representative of the group as a whole, the Rhymers' Club as well. Thus, in "Coole Park and Ballylee, 1931," the poet suppresses the precise identity of the "last romantics" to whom he refers and thereby broadens the scope of his historical comment:

> We were the last romantics—chose for theme
> Traditional sanctity and loveliness;
> Whatever's written in what poets name
> The book of the people; whatever most can bless
> The mind of man or elevate a rhyme;
> But all is changed, that high horse riderless,
> Though mounted in that saddle Homer rode
> Where the swan drifts upon a darkening flood.
>
> (VP, 491-2)

While the juxtapositioning of this poem with "Coole Park, 1929" and the title itself suggest identities, omission of names gives rise to association. Most directly a reference to those organizers of the Irish theatre who gathered at Lady Gregory's house, "the last romantics" could also refer to the Rhymers' Club, with whom Yeats conflated his Monday night meetings at Woburn Buildings and from whom his association with Lady Gregory evolved.[11] This connection is supported by the theme of "traditional sanctity and loveliness"—values which the nineties' aesthetes promoted and for which Yeats congratulated them in his prose. The reference to "the book of the people," although perpetuating the familiar humbleness motif, relates more closely to Synge, who returned to the Irish peasantry for his artistic inspiration, but as Jeffares points out in his commentary (CP, 291), it originates with the Irish poet Raftery and, thus, includes him in its scope. The closing allusion to the riderless horse recalls Robert Gregory ("Soldier, scholar, horseman, he") and even George Pollexfen ("In muscular Youth well known to Mayo men for horsemanship") because of their purported nobility, and thus remains consistent with Yeats's image of Johnson, who was "courteous to the worst" and whose Irish constablary father qualified him for honorary Irishness. The process of integration whereby all these figures come to share identities is similar to the transformation of Maud Gonne in Yeats's poems—from the Irish activist with whom he fell in love to the mythically potent figure of Helen of Troy, a symbol which, in "Among School Children," he realizes has many possible earthly representations. They also resemble the characters of "Easter 1916," who became their Masks at the moment of greatest intensity. Through a process which Pater has called "intensely realized memory," Yeats gives these figures new life—and that newness implies a change from organic imperfections to actualization of the ideal.[12] While they sacrifice strict individuality in the process, they gain archetypal significance, and the poet is able to reconcile his sense of personal loss with a greater vision of the universal plan.

The strategy of "intensely realized memory" and of fusing individual identities is nowhere more explicitly rendered than in "The Results of Thought," a poem of Yeats's later career. Herein, the Rhymers take their place among other half-perceived ghosts, figures whose youthful passion has determined their tragic ends. The poet's intense need to justify their fates had dictated a life of art, culminating in his ability not only to recall these figures but to give them life within the poetic context. If their message is not completely clear to him, their presence guarantees continuing inquiry and attests to the magical powers Yeats has claimed almost from the beginning of his career:

> Acquaintance; companion;
> One dear brilliant woman;
> The best-endowed, the elect,
> All by their youth undone,
> All, all, by that inhuman
> Bitter glory wrecked.

> But I have straightened out
> Ruin, wreck and wrack;
> I toiled long years and at length
> Came to so deep a thought
> I can summon back
> All their wholesome strength.
>
> What images are these,
> That turn dull-eyed away,
> Or shift time's filthy load,
> Straighten aged knees,
> Hesitate or stay?
> What heads shake or nod? (VP, 504-5)

One can see in these fragile images features of Johnson, Dowson and others who had given up their lives to art, and one can see the value of Yeats's own commitment in his demonstrated ability to bring these figures back to life. Although the present invocation offers little direct reward in terms of information or spiritual wisdom, it points to an essential feature of Yeats's work: its ability to move beyond barriers of time, to transcend mortal limitations.

This practice—which is actually a mystical rendering of a traditional artistic concept—comes to full fruition in "Under Ben Bulben," where the poet speaks from beyond the grave and where the poem itself provides the body or medium for spiritual voice. Life and Death are herein devalued because they no longer define or limit one's experience, and the poem, with its powers of penetration and influence, thus gains in authority and prestige. The image of the stone reinforces the implied value of artifice as a means of preserving love, commitment, communication, even after organic existence has ended, and the inscription on the stone teaches the final lesson: that the tragedies of life are meaningless if we cannot apprehend their full scope, if we cannot find in them further impulse to continue with the work:

> *Cast a cold eye*
> *On life, on death.*
> *Horseman, pass by!* (VP, 640)

Thus, Yeats's vision of cyclicality, first expressed in "The Man who Dreamed of Faeryland," finds fulfillment in his valedictory statement, and the fact of death (in this case, his own death) provides a center around which the rest of creation turns. Beyond the simple escapism of his former associates, the poet finds voice and authority. His words attest to the influence of art on life: the unmoving stone in the midst of a turbulent stream.

In the end, we see that the Rhymers' importance to Yeats was both practical and aesthetic. The Club provided an environment for sharing ideas and aspirations. It brought him into contact with individuals who could teach him current trends, and it made available to him outlets for publishing and publicizing his work. Although the principal members of this group died relatively young and much of their direct influence—that of conscious verbal distortion and complicated syntactical arrangements—had disappeared from his work by the time he began to involve himself seriously with the drama, he continued to hold these poets in esteem and to benefit from the broader example of their lives. Yeats's historical and critical statements indicated that he thought of the Rhymers' Club as a movement crucial in bringing the corruptions of the Victorian age to an end, and his poetry remembered these figures as youthful devotees whose dedication to art had brought about their own martyrdom at the hands of an indifferent and insensitive world. He outlasted them poetically because he had a practical sense of what art could do—because it was not, for him, an isolated experience, but a starting point for moral and intellectual responsibility. If he was not concerned with factual precision, he was at least conscious of the choices he had made and the reasons he had made those choices. In response to a letter Rhys had written him concerning the present whereabouts of various members (Yeats had stated that "only two or three were still alive"), he acknowledged his inaccuracy and revealed as he did so the fanciful nature of his thought. As always, the Keatsian equation held true for him, that beauty and truth were one and the same thing, at least in the domain of art:

> For the moment I forgot both Plarr & you in my pleasure at the thought that Greene had showed so much genius—a sort of fat weed on Lethe's wharf; then re-wrote the sentence to bring in Plarr who had done a little beautiful work—nature is so miserably incomplete and so little respects our sentences. Neither you nor Rolleston came into my head at the moment. One begins to think of 'The Rhymers' as those who sang of wine and women—I no more than you am typical. (LFL, 158-9)

Critics have overlooked the Rhymers' Club in their analyses of Yeats's work, either because they did not know enough about these enigmatic poets or because they saw no relation between their poetry and the kind of expression Yeats ultimately produced. But familiarity with these figures and Yeats's relationship to them gives us a new perspective on his art and helps clarify concepts that have not yet been adequately explained. Specifically, the notion of myth as it relates to survival, an idea that grows increasingly important to Yeats as he matures, benefits from this point of view, giving us insights concerning the instincts of mythmaking that a strictly esoteric approach could not do. Similarly, this focus acts as a necessary corrective to literary studies that speak of Yeats in terms of the larger Romantic tradition while ignoring the personal nature of his work. A poet who "learned his trade" from his contemporaries, he necessarily combined formal knowledge with personal reminiscences, and, in his poetry, images from the tradition exist alongside of, and often intersect with, images from his own life. This pairing of the personal with the universal offers a solution to the crises of the moment: removing experience to the artistic plane and, by identifying it with the timeless, achieving dramatic catharsis. Yeats's use of Hamlet and similar theatrical metaphors to speak of his friends not only captures the self-dramatizing tendencies of the age but points to the larger concept of life's unreality and the necessity of giving structure to the dream. If his associates at the Rhymers' Club did not fully recognize the redemptive qualities of art, they at least provided a need and an example whereby those qualities could be achieved.

The difference between the aesthetes of the nineties—which Yeats commonly spoke of in terms of the Rhymers' Club—and those at the vanguard of modern expression had to do with the extremely personal aspect of their art. Through Pater and his sometimes misinterpreter Wilde, followers of aestheticism learned to experience life with such intensity that it gained the status of artistic expression. When, as with Wilde, this expression wandered into self-destructiveness or forbidden fruit, the true ephemerality of the movement became clear. Poets who had defied social norms were in turn rejected by society, and the passion with which they pursued the unique or unattainable found apotheosis in early death or destruction. Poets of the succeeding generation took this eventuality as a caution and sought to exempt themselves from the hardship these "pure poets" underwent. Yeats was the first to deal with the issue, finding in myth not only personal solace but the key to a more sophisticated, objective art.

Symons and Dowson experimented with French meters, an

interest that had distinguished their verse from mainstream Victorian practice and which may have suggested to Pound that breaking the pentameter would be the first true achievement of modernism. But the daemonic energy with which these poets lived became more artistically important than the art itself. For this reason, perhaps, critics like Ellmann have dismissed the Rhymers as "dissolute and confused when alive" (IY, 114), and Daiches has claimed that the Club's aim "was that of a rather tired sensationalism" (PMW, 139). These statements, like others, miss the larger historical and critical points, ones of which Yeats was at pains to inform his audience. "Each age unwinds the thread another age had wound," he explains in *A Vision*, "all things dying each other's life, living each other's death" (AV-A, 183). The nineties provided a mirror or Mask of what was to come; in order to get a proper image of ourselves we had to look in the glass and see.

NOTES FOR CHAPTER 5

[1] Although it is generally assumed that nothing of substance was ever discussed at Rhymers' Club meetings, C. Lewis Hind reports otherwise: "Most of the poets talked most of the time with articulated precision about quantitative equivalents, and with the exception of courteous Dr. Todhunter, no one seemed to notice the guest of the evening—Francis Thompson"(N, 97).

[2] Isochronic (alliterative) meter was common in the Anglo-Saxon period and was carried over to a certain degree into the Middle Ages, usually with the addition of rhyme and a corresponding slackening of alliteration. Chaucer, for example, had used this specific verse form for his long poem *The House of Fame*. The substitution of rhymed couplets for alliteration was a way of maintaining rhythmic tightness.

[3] "I cast off traditional metaphors and loosened my rhythm, and recognizing that all the criticism of life known to me was alien and English, became as emotional as possible but with an emotion which I described to myself as cold"(Au, 74).

[4] See "The Tower": "I mock Plotinus' thought/And cry in Plato's teeth, /Death and life were not/Till man made up the whole, /Made lock, stock and barrel/Out of his bitter soul"(VP, 415).

[5] See LFL, 158-9, where Yeats says in a letter to Rhys that Plarr had written "a little beautiful work."

[6] In *Autobiographies*, Yeats speaks of Dowson's and Johnson's dissipation: "I think that the movement of our thought has more and more so separated certain images and regions of the mind,

and that these images grow in beauty as they grow in sterility"(Au, 313).

[7]Jeffares disassociates Aoife from Cuchulain in "The Grey Rock"(CP, 104), but the imagery of the concluding passage suggests that Yeats is thinking of Cuchulain's fight with the sea. The "you" who has died becomes in this context Cuchulain's predecessor, and his faith that of fate: having engendered by her a son, he has had to live out and suffer the repercussions of that act.

[8]See note 2. Also "The Fisherman": "Before I am old/I shall have written him one/Poem maybe as cold/And passionate as the dawn"(VP 348).

[9]John Synge, George Pollexfen and Robert Gregory. George Pollexfen's world, that of the environs of Sligo, was somewhat smaller than the others', yet it offered the same opposition. As William Murphy points out (PF, 79), the Pollexfens as a family demonstrated a striving for property, a worship of class and a tendency to depressive melancholia—qualities which did not endear them to the locals. Obviously, W. B. Yeats did not agree with the prevailing attitude toward his uncle and preferred to consider him a misunderstood man of culture.

[10]See letter to his father quoted in IY, 128: "The doctrine of the group or rather of the majority of it was that lyric poetry should be personal. That man should express his life and do this without shame or fear."

[11]Yeats met Lady Gregory for the first time while touring Ireland with Arthur Symons.

[12]"... the peculiar sanctuary of [Marius's] mother, who, still in real widowhood, provided the deceased Marius the elder with that secondary sort of life which we can give to the dead, in our intensely realized memory of them"(ME, 20).

WORKS CITED

BOOKS:

                                                     Abbreviations

Allt and Alspach, eds.   VP
The Variorium Edition of the Poems of W. B. Yeats.
NY: Macmillan, 1957.

Beckson, Karl, ed.   MAS
The Memoirs of Arthur Symons.
University Park: Penn State Press, 1977.

Bloom, Harold.   Y
Yeats.
NY: Oxford U. Press, 1972.

Bridge, Ursula.   LTSM
W. B. Yeats and T. Sturge Moore: Their Correspondence 1901-1937.
NY: Oxford U. Press, 1953.

Croft-Cooke, Rupert.   ULOW
The Unrecorded Life of Oscar Wilde.
NY: David McKay, Inc., 1972.

Daiches, David.   PMW
Poetry and the Modern World.
Chicago: U. of Chicago Press, 1940.

Donoghue, Denis, ed.
Memoirs of W. B. Yeats.
London: Macmillan,
1972.

Ellmann, Richard.   IY
The Identity of Yeats.
NY: Oxford University Press,
1964.

Evans, Lawrence, ed.   LWP
Letters of Walter Pater.
Oxford: Clarendon Press,
1970.

Finneran, Richard, ed.
The Poems of W. B. Yeats.
New York: Macmillan,
1983.

Fletcher, Ian, ed.   LJP
The Complete Poems of Lionel Johnson.
New York: Garland,
1982.

Elkin Mathews--Poet's Publisher.   EMPP
Reading, Berks.: U. of Reading Library,
1966.

Flower, Desmond and Maas, Henry, eds.   EDL
The Letters of Ernest Dowson.
Rutherford: Farleigh Dickinson U. Press,
1967.

Frayne, John P., ed.   UP1
Uncollected Prose of W. B. Yeats
(vol. 1).
NY: Columbia University Press,
1970.

Works Cited

Grosskurth, Phyllis.   HE
    Havelock Ellis: A Biography.
    NY: Knopf,
    1980.

Gwynn, Stephen.   GELM
    Experiences of a Literary Man.
    London: Thornton Butterworth, Ltd.,
    1926.

Gwynn, Stephen, ed.   GET
    William Butler Yeats: Essays in Tribute.
    Port Washington: Kennikat Press,
    1965.

Harper, George Mills and Hood, Walter K., eds.   AV-A
    A Critical Edition of Yeats's A Vision (1925).
    London: Macmillan,
    1978.

Hart-Davis, Rupert, ed.   OWL
    The Letters of Oscar Wilde.
    NY: Harcourt, Brace and World,
    1962.

Hind, C. Lewis.   N
    Napthali.
    London: John Lane, Bodley Head,
    1926.

Holland, Vivian, ed.   OWW
    The Complete Works of Oscar Wilde.
    London and Glasgow: Collins,
    1967.

Hyde, Harford Montgomery.   OWB
    Oscar Wilde, a Biography.
    London: Methuen,
    1976.

Jeffares, A. Norman. CP
A New Commentary on the Poems of W. B. Yeats.
London: Macmillan,
1984.

Jepson, Edgar. MV
Memories of a Victorian.
London: Victor Gollancz,
1933.

Johnson, Lionel. LJLW
Some Winchester Letters of Lionel Johnson.
London: G. Allen & Unwin,
1919.

Joyce, Stanislaus. MBK
My Brother's Keeper.
London: Faber & Faber,
1958.

Kelly, John and Domville, Eric, eds. L-K
The Collected Letters of W. B. Yeats (vol. I).
Oxford: Clarendon Press,
1986.

Kenner, Hugh. CE
A Colder Eye.
NY: Knopf,
1983.

Kermode, Frank. RI
Romantic Image.
New York: Vintage,
1957.

Le Gallienne, Richard. RN
The Romantic Nineties.
NY: Doubleday and Page,
1925.

Lhombreaud, Roger.   AS
   Arthur Symons, a Critical Biography.
   London: Unicorn Press,
   1963.

Longaker, Mark.   LED
   Ernest Dowson.
   Philadelphia: U. Penn Press,
   1944.

Longaker, Mark, ed.   EDP
   The Poems of Ernest Dowson.
   Philadelphia: U. Penn Press,
   1962.

Mackmurdo, Arthur, ed.   SIL
   Selwyn Image Letters.
   London: Grant Richards,
   1977.

May, James Lewis.   PTW
   The Path Through the Wood.
   London: G. Bles,
   1930.

Murphy, William.   PF
   Prodigal Father.
   Ithaca: Cornell University Press,
   1978.

Nelson, James G.   EN
   The Early Nineties: A View from the
   Bodley Head.
   Cambridge: Harvard U. Press,
   1971.

Nowell-Smith, Simon.   HC
   The House of Cassell 1848-1958.
   London: Cassell,
   1958.

Pater, Walter. ME
  Marius the Epicurean.
  London: Macmillan,
  1909.

  The Renaissance. PR
  Donald L. Hill, ed.
  Berkeley: U. California Press,
  1980.

Plarr, Victor. PED
  Ernest Dowson.
  NY: Laurence J. Gomme,
  1914.

Pound, Ezra. EPC
  The Cantos of Ezra Pound.
  London: Faber & Faber,
  1968.

Rhymers' Club, The. BRC-1
  The Book of the Rhymers' Club.
  London: Bodley Head (Elkin Mathews),
  1892.

  The Second Book of the Rhymers' Club. BRC-2
  London: Bodley Head (Elkin Mathews
  and John Lane),
  1894.

Rhys, Ernest. ER
  Everyman Remembers.
  London: J. M. Dent,
  1931.

  Wales England Wed. WEW
  London: J. M. Dent,
  1940.

Rhys, Ernest, ed.   LFL
  Letters from Limbo.
  London: J. M. Dent,
  1936.

Roseliep, Raymond, ed.   LJL
  Some Letters of Lionel Johnson.
  Ann Arbor: University Microfilms,
  1955.

Seiden, Morton.
  The Poet as Mythmaker.
  New York: Cooper Square,
  1975.

Sturge-Moore, Thomas and D. C., eds.   WD
  Works and Days from the Journal of
  Michael Field.
  London,
  1933.

Symons, Arthur.   SML
  The Symbolist Movement in Literature.
  London: W. Heinemann,
  1899.

  Silhouettes.   S
  London: Smithers,
  1896.

Townsend, James Benjamin.   JD
  John Davidson: Poet of Armageddon.
  New Haven: Yale U. Press,
  1961.

Tynan, Katherine.   TFY
  Twenty-Five Years.
  London: Smith & Elder,
  1913.

Wade, Allan.   B
   A Bibliography of the Writings of W. B.
   Yeats.
   London: Rupert Hart-Davis,
   1968.

Wade, Allan, ed.   L
   The Letters of W. B. Yeats.
   NY: Macmillan,
   1955.

Yeats, W. B.   Au
   The Autobiography of William Butler Yeats.
   London: Macmillan,
   1955.

   Essays and Introductions.   E & I
   London: Macmillan,
   1961.

   Letters to the New Island.   LNI
   Cambridge: Harvard U. Press,
   1934.

Yeats, W. B., ed.   OBMV
   The Oxford Book of Modern Verse.
   Oxford: Clarendon,
   1936.

REVIEWS:

Anon.   Ath
   "Recent Verse."
   Athenaeum
   25 August 1894: 252.

Anon.   B&W
   "A Nest of Singing Birds."
   Black and White
   27 February 1892: 284.

Anon. CQR
    "The Poetry of To-day and To-morrow."
    Church Quarterly Review
    October 1892: 201-4.

Anon. DC
    "A Round Table of Rhymers."
    Daily Chronicle
    26 February 1892: 3.

Anon. DN
    "Poetry's Chances."
    Daily News
    20 February 1892: 5.
    (Written by Andrew Lang.)

Anon. GH
    "Poetry, Verse, and Drama."
    Glasgow Herald
    28 June 1892.

Anon. Gl
    Globe
    2 July 1894: 6.

Anon. Na
    "Recent English Poetry."
    Nation
    22 November 1894: 388.

Anon. NO
    "Some Recent Verse."
    National Observer
    21 July 1894: 257.

Anon. NIR
    New Ireland Review
    August 1894: 392.

Anon. PMG
"A Batch of Verse."
Pall Mall Gazette
13 July 1894: 5.

Anon. SJG
St. James's Gazette
30 January 1892: 12.

"The Second Book of the Rhymers' Club."
16 August 1894: 5.

Anon. SR
Saturday Review (London)
19 March 1892: 342.

Anon. Sp
"Rhymes in the Range of the Times."
Speaker
26 March 1892: 388-9.

"Verse in Translation."
18 August 1894: 193-4.

Anon. St
"Logroller."
Star
11 February 1892: 2.
(Written by Richard Le Gallienne.)

Anon. T
"Literary Notes."
The Times (London)
23 January 1892: 9.

"Books of the Week."
6 July 1894: 14.

Anon. UI
"North and South."
United Ireland
21 July 1894: 1.

Image, Selwyn.   CR
    "The Book of the Rhymers' Club."
    Church Reformer
    March 1892.

Tomson, Graham.   Ac
    "The Book of the Rhymers' Club."
    Academy
    26 March 1892: 294-5.

ARTICLES:

Beckson, Karl.   ELT 13.1
    "New Dates for the Rhymers' Club."
    English Literature in Transition
    13.1 (1970): 37-8.

Jepson, Edgar.
    "The Real Ernest Dowson."
    Academy
    November 1907

Roberts, Morely.   JOL
    "The Rhymers' Club."
    John O'London's Weekly
    30 September 1933: 901-2, 908.

Rutenberg, Daniel.   ELT 12.3
    "A New Date for the Rhymers' Club."
    English Literature in Transition
    12.3 (1969): 155-6.

Thornton, R. K. R.   ELT 14.1
    "Dates for the Rhymers' Club."
    English Literature in Transition
    14.1 (1971): 49-53.

Yeats, W. B.
  "Friends of My Youth."
  Yeats and the Theatre.
  O'Driscoll, Robert and Reynolds, Lorna, eds.
  Toronto: Macmillan of Canada,
  1975: 21-41.

COLLECTIONS:

John Lane Collection.   JLC
  Westfield College,
  London.

Elkin Mathews Collection.   EMC
  University of Reading Library,
  Reading, Berks., England.

E. C. Stedman Collection.   CUS
  Columbia University Library,
  New York.

British Museum Library.   BM
  British Museum,
  London.

National Library of Ireland.   NLI
  Dublin.

MISCELLANEOUS JOURNALS:

Fortnightly Review.   FR

Daily Chronicle.   DC

Irish Times.   IT

Publishers' Circular.   PC

Savoy.   SA

Scots Observer.   SO

St. James's Gazette.   SJG

Times Literary Supplement.   TLS

Yeats Studies.   YS

The Bodley Head,
6a Vigo Street, London.
September 1894.

Dear Sir,

On the 29th instant the partnership between us will be dissolved by mutual consent.

Mr. Mathews will continue his business as a Publisher and Bookseller at the old premises, No. 6a Vigo Street. He has registered the telegraphic address: "Elegraion."

Mr. Lane will carry on business as a Publisher at new premises which he has acquired opposite, and in future he will use the sign: "The Bodley Head," Vigo Street, and the telegraphic address: "Bodleian."

The books hitherto published or announced as in preparation by the firm have been apportioned between us according to the understanding, and in future all communications whatsoever concerning any of these books must be addressed to the partner under whose name it appears in these Lists.

Yours faithfully,

Elkin Mathews & John Lane.

[O.T.O.

ELKIN MATHEWS
6a VIGO ST., LONDON, W.

Abbott's Travels in a Tree Top.
Bozman's Lyric Poems.
Bouillier's Last God.
Chapman's Little Child's Wreath.
Coleridge's Sancity of Confession.
Coming's Ancient Greece.
De Gruchy's Under the Hawthorn.
The Dorset Colours Series, viz.:
  Herne's Dorset Colours.
  Image's Carols and Poems.
  Galton's Matthew Arnold.
  Dowson's Poems.
  Letters of Adam Legendre.
Field's Sight and Song.
"   Stephania.
"   Question of Memory.
Hickey's Verse Tales, Lyrics
    and Translations.
Hallam's Poems.
E. Johnson's In the Fire.
Lionel Johnson's Poems.
Murray's Last Harvest.
Martin's Quatrains.
Noel's Poor People's Xmas.
Pinkerton's Galeazzo.
Mrs. Radford's new volume of
    "Songs."
The Book of the Rhymers' Club.
Scull's Literature and Poetry.
Scaunda's In the Key of Blue.
Todhunter's Sicilian Idyll.

JOHN LANE
"THE BODLEY HEAD"
VIGO ST., LONDON, W.

Adam's Essays in Modernity.
Allen's Lower Slopes.
Davidson's Plays.
"   Fleet Street Eclogues.
"   Random Itinerary.
"   North Wall.
Dr. Tatler's Poems.
Gale's Orchard Songs.
Garnett's Poems.
Gosse's Letters of Boulden.
Graham's Pagan Papers.
Greene's Italian Lyrics.
Hake's Poems.
Hamilton's Ballad of Hadji.
James's Romantic Professions.
L. Johnson's Art of Thomas Hardy.
Keynote Series, viz.:
  Keynotes.
  Dancing Faun.
  Poor Folk.
  Child of the Age.
  Great God Pan.
Leather's Verses.
Le Gallienne's Prose Fancies.
"   Book Bills of Narcissus.
"   English Poems.
"   George Meredith.
"   Religion of a Literary Man.

[O.T.O.

ELKIN MATHEWS—continued
Van Dyke's Tennyson.
Watson's Pastoral—Renunciations.
Wicksteed's Dante.
Wynne's Whisper.
The Hobby Horse.

JOHN LANE—continued
Meynell's Gallery of Pigeons.
"   Rhythm of Life.
Monkhouse's Books and Plays.
Nettleship's Robert Browning.
Noble's Sonnet in England.
Oxford Character.
Rhys's A London Rose.
Rolleston and Shannon's Hero and Leander.
Streete's Autobiography of a Boy.
Francis Thompson's Poems.
Tree's Imaginative Faculty.
Tynan's Cuckoo Songs.
Theodore Watts' Poems.
Watson's Eloping Angels.
"   Excursions in Criticism.
"   Prince's Quest.
Wilde's Salomé.
"   The Sphinx.
"   A Woman of No Importance.
"   Duchess of Padua.
"   Mr. W. H.
The Yellow Book.

APPENDIX I: BIOGRAPHICAL SKETCHES

JOHN DAVIDSON (1857-1909)

Born in Barrhead, Renfrewshire. From 1876-77, an arts student at Edinburgh University. Thereafter taught in various public schools. In 1885, married Annie Smith and, at the end of 1889, came with her and his two sons to settle in the London suburb of Hornsey. Attempted to make a living writing articles for various London journals. Was the editor of the ephemeral *Weekly Review* to which W. B. Yeats and Ernest Rhys contributed articles. Later became editor of a literary column in the *Speaker* called "The Week." Davidson wrote plays (*Bruce*, 1886; *Scaramouch in Naxos*, 1889) and fiction (*Perfervid*, 1890), but was best known for his urban balladry (*In a Music Hall and Other Poems*, 1891; *Fleet Street Ecologues*, 1893). Was considered at one time for the poet laureateship, but it was given to Alfred Austin instead. Suffered continually from financial problems. Haunted by professional failure and fears of cancer, jumped to his death from the cliffs at Penzance, Wales.

ERNEST DOWSON (1867-1900)

Born in Kent, partially educated in France and Italy, where his parents would go winters for their health. Spent five terms at Queens College, Oxford, where he met Lionel Johnson, but left without his degree in March 1888. Went home to live with his parents in Woodford (Essex) and worked as a clerk in his father's Thames drydock. That same year, he met Victor Plarr and renewed his friendship with Johnson. By November 1889, had met Adelaide Foltinowitz, the daughter of a Polish restaurant keeper. Although "Missie" was barely thirteen at the time, Dowson conceived a deep and enduring love for her, a fruitless devotion that continued to affect his life even after she married Carl Frederick A. Noelte in 1897. Was received into the Catholic Church in 1891, shortly after Lionel Johnson. In 1894 and 1895, his parents died—his father, of an overdose of chloral; his mother, by hanging herself. The same year, Dowson left London to live in France, returning periodically to earn money. His book of stories, *Dilemmas*, was published in 1895 and was dedicated to "Missie." His *Verses* were published 1896. Homeless and forgotten by most of his friends, Dowson died of consumption in the house of Robert Sherard.

EDWIN J. ELLIS (1848-1918)

The son of Dr. Alexander Sharp Ellis, a Scottish linguist and natural scientist. Met J. B. Yeats at Heatherley's art school when he (Ellis) was nineteen. With J. B. Yeats, J. T. Nettleship and Sidney Hall, formed "The Brotherhood," an informal group of artists whose spiritual leader was Blake. At one time shared a studio with J. B. Yeats and was a frequent visitor to the Yeats's home. An article in *Bookman* (February 1893) reports that he lived for awhile in Perugia, Italy, where he farmed, then married and settled in London. An illustrator of books and a writer of poetry, edited with W. B. Yeats a three-volume editon of Blake's work. Also published *Poetical Works of William Blake* (two volumes, 1906) and *The Real Blake* (1907). Volumes of verse are *Fate in Arcadia* (1892) and *Seen in Three Days* (1893). His verse drama *Sancan the Bard* (1895) furnished the plot for Yeats's *The King's Threshhold*.

Appendix I

GEORGE ARTHUR GREENE (1853-1921)

Nicknamed by Victor Plarr "Il Greno." Born in Florence, Italy. Educated in Italy and at Trinity College Dublin, from which he received his B. A. in 1876 and his M. A. in 1879. Contributor to *Kottabos* and *A Treasury of Irish Poetry* (edited by Stopford Brooke and T. W. Rolleston, 1900). Published *Italian Lyricists of Today* with John Lane and Elkin Mathews in 1893 and again with Lane in 1898. Worked with A. C. Hillier and Ernest Dowson on a translation of Muther's *History of Modern Painting* (1895-6). Served as vice-chairman of the Irish Literary Society and secretary of the Rhymers' Club. Was also a practicing physician.

ARTHUR CECIL HILLIER (1857-?)

Born at Calais in 1857, son of the Inspector General of the Royal Irish Constabulary. Entered Trinity College Dublin 1874, receiving his B. A. degree in 1878. Went to Oxford and matriculated at Worcester College, January 26, 1892. Received his B. A. in 1885. After Oxford, became London correspondent to the *New York Herald*. Contributed to *Kottabos* and *Dublin University Review* (T. W. Rolleston, ed.). Contributed to *The Second Book of the Rhymers' Club*. Has poems in *Dublin Verses* (H. A. Hinkson, ed.)

HERBERT HORNE (1864-1916)

Born in Chelsea section of London. An early acquaintance of Ernest Rhys, who settled in the area. Decided to study architecture and entered the office of Robert Vigers in Old Jewry, 1880. Became apprenticed to Arthur Mackmurdo in 1883 and entered into partnership with him (The Century Guild of

Artists) in 1885. Helped with the designs for the Guild and their periodical the *Hobby Horse*. Served as the sole editor for that journal from 1886-1892 and published in it some of his poems. With Arthur Symons, edited *Nero and Other Plays* for Havelock Ellis's Mermaid Series. His volume of verse, *Diversi Colores* was published by the Bodley Head in 1891. Retired to Florence in 1900. Wrote a biography of Botticelli, 1908. Willed his house and its contents (Museo Horne) to the city of Florence.

LIONEL JOHNSON (1867-1902)

Born at Broadstairs, Kent, youngest son of Irish army officer, Captain William Victor Johnson and Catherine Delicia Walters, his wife. Entered Winchester College at age thirteen, where he served as editor of the school magazine *Wykehamist*. Became involved in a homosexual circle of boys. Met Alfred Douglas. In 1885, won Winchester scholarship to New College, Oxford, and in his second year came into contact with the Century Guild of Artists (Arthur Mackmurdo, Herbert Horne and Selwyn Image). Upon leaving Oxford, moved into their lodgings at 20 Fitzroy Street, London. Received into Catholic Church on St. Alban's Day, 1891, and in the same year introduced Alfred Douglas to Oscar Wilde, whom he had met through Pater. When Wilde's homosexual activities came to light, Johnson turned violently against him. Joined the Irish Literary Society in 1892, and thereafter his work began to reflect his new-found Irishness. Had begun drinking to excess and had suffered several collapses, which had resulted in his removal from the Fitzroy Establishment. On 29 September, 1902, suffered another such collapse when entering the Green Dragon pub. Died October 4. Autopsy found death due to a ruptured blood vessel in the brain. *The Art of Thomas Hardy*, published 1894. *Poems*, 1895.

Appendix I

RICHARD LE GALLIENNE (1866-1947)

From Birkenhead (Liverpool), son of a Channel Island family. His father, in business. Studied to become an accountant, but failed his exams. Published privately *My Lady's Sonnets* in 1887. Obtained volumes to review for the *Academy*. His own poems also were reviewed in that periodical. John Lane read about him and wrote him soon after. Met the actor Wilson Barrett, whose secretary he became February-October 1889. That same year, Lane published his *Volumes in Folio* at the Bodley Head. Settled in London, 1891, taking the post of literary critic for the *Star* (pseudonym "Logroller"). Became first reader for the Bodley Head, January 1892. Wife Mildred died of typhoid, 1894. Married twice after that, residing in U. S. and France. Among his many publications are a study of Meredith (*George Meredith, Some Characteristics, with a Bibliography by John Lane*) and a memoir of his experiences of the '90s (*The Romantic Nineties*).

VICTOR PLARR (1863-1929)

Born at Le Kapferhammer near Strassbourg. Left Alsace after Franco-Prussian War (1871). Went to Scotland, then Oxford. Graduated from Worcester College, Oxford, in 1886 in Modern History and came to London. Met Ernest Dowson in 1888 in Charles Sayles's rooms and began to associate with members of the Fitzroy Establishment. In 1890, became Librarian of King's College, London. Married two years later to Helen Marion Shaw and took a house in Blackheath. In 1897, became Librarian of the Royal College of Surgeons, where he remained for the rest of his career. Translated Zola's *Nana*. Also wrote a *Lives of the Fellows of the Royal College of Surgeons* and compiled a dictionary of contemporaries called *Men and Women of the Time*. His first mature collection of poems was published a year after the Oscar Wilde debacle and was entitled *In the Dorian Mood*. In 1905, he published his most ambitious work, *The Tragedy of Asgard*; in 1914, his biography of Dowson (*Ernest Dowson, 1888-1897*) in which he speaks of his memories of the '90s.

ERNEST RADFORD (1857-1919)

A London lawyer and poet, married to another poet, Dollie (Maitland) Radford, whose volume of verse *A Light Load* was published by the Bodley Head in 1891. Educated at Cambridge, Radford was a member of William Morris's socialist group and secretary to the Arts and Crafts Society (circa 1890). Also wrote for the *Pall Mall Gazette.* Became one of Mathews's most ardent supporters when the Bodley Head partnership (Mathews/Lane) broke up. Wrote a book on Rossetti (*Dante Gabriel Rossetti*) and edited the poems of Walter Savage Landor. His own verse includes *Measured Steps* (1884), *Chambers Twain* (1890) and *Songs in the Whirlwind* (1918). Apparently suffered a mental breakdown in 1892.

ERNEST RHYS (1859-1946)

Of Welsh nationality. A mining engineer by training. Came to London, January 1886. Became editor of the Camelot Classics series, for which he prepared a volume of Malory's *Morte d'Arthur.* Frequented William Morris's socialist gatherings at Kelmscott House, where he met W. B. Yeats. With Yeats and T. W. Rolleston, founded the Rhymers' Club in 1890. Le Gallienne was instrumental in getting his *A London Rose* (verses) published in 1894 by the Bodley Head. Became first editor of J. M. Dent's Everyman series, begun 1906.

T. W. ROLLESTON (1857-1920)

Educated at Trinity College Dublin. In 1885, came under the influence of John O'Leary and Thomas Davis. Joined Charles Hubert Oldham's Contemporary Club, where he met Yeats. Editor of the *Dublin University Review* (from August 1885) to which Yeats had contributed and would continue to contribute poems. In London, Yeats brought him first into the Rhymers' Club, then into the Irish Literary Society. Rolleston, who was elected first secretary to the society, supported Gavan Duffy for the leadership, and Yeats never forgave him. Wrote a biography of Gotthold Lessing, 1889; edited books on Irish myth (*The High Deeds of Finn*, 1910; *Myths and Legends of the Celtic Race*, 1911). His own volume of verse, *Sea Spray*, published 1909.

ARTHUR SYMONS (1865-1945)

Born in Wales, son of a Cornish parson. Parents moved to Nuneaton in Coventry 1885, where Symons began his writing career. Had no formal higher education, but studied and read a great deal at home. In 1886, published two important critical works, *An Introduction to the Study of Browning* and an article published in the *National Review* on the provençal poet Frederei Mistral. These achievements attracted the attention of such notables as Walter Pater and Havelock Ellis. In 1889, Symons made his first trip to France with Havelock Ellis, meeting Mallarmé, Huysmans, Remy de Gourmont and others. In 1890, met Verlaine. Thereafter, the French influence was strongly marked in his work. Sponsored Verlaine's visit to England in 1893 and housed him at his rooms in Fountain Court. Also housed Yeats (1896) preparatory to the latter's move to Woburn Buildings. In 1896, Symons edited the *Savoy*. His most influential critical work, *The Symbolist Movement in Literature*, was published in 1899 and was dedicated to Yeats. Married Rhoda Bowser, January 1901. In 1908, in Ferrara, Italy, suffered a severe mental breakdown from which he never fully recovered. Volumes of verse include *Days and Nights* (1890), *Silhouettes* (1892) and *London Nights* (1895).

JOHN TODHUNTER (1839-1916)

From a Quaker family. A friend of J. B. Yeats, with whom he had become acquainted while Yeats was in law school. Received his B. A. from Trinity College Dublin 1866 and took up medical studies after college. He also taught English literature at Alexandria College for four years. His first volume of poems, *Laurella and Other Poems*, was published 1876. In approximately 1877, he abandoned medicine and moved to London. Married (for the second time) Dora Louise Digby and settled in Bedford Park near the Yeats's. May 5, 1890, his play *A Sicilian Idyll* was performed at the Bedford Park Social Club, and in 1894 his *A Comedy of Sighs* appeared alongside W. B. Yeats's *The Land of Heart's Desire* at the Avenue Theatre. He was playwright to the literary club "Ye Sette of Old Volumes," and was instrumental in founding the Irish Literary Society.

APPENDIX II: CHRONOLOGY

YEATS'S PRE-LONDON YEARS

1883 -The Century Guild founded.
-Le Gallienne attends lecture by Wilde in Birkenhead (December).

1885 -Contemporary Club founded in Dublin.
-Yeats's poems in *Dublin University Review* (from March onward).
-T. W. Rolleston becomes editor of *Dublin University Review* (August).
-Symons's family moves to Nuneaton, Coventry (September).
-Rhys publishes *The Poems of George Herbert* with Canterbury Poets series.
-Herbert Horne enters into partnership with Arthur Mackmurdo.

1886 -First issue of the *Century Guild Hobby Horse*; Ernest Rhys moves to London; Symons's article on Frederei Mistral appears in *National Review* (January).
-William Morris goes on lecture tour in Ireland, meets Yeats at Contemporary Club (April).
-Yeats publishes *Mosada*.
-Rhys is named general editor of the Camelot Classics series, publishes *Malory's King Arthur and the Quest of the Holy Grail* as its first book.

-Symons's *An Introduction to the Study of Browning* appears; Symons working on Shakespeare quartos and *Venus and Adonis.*
-Symons begins project of editing Massinger's plays for Havelock Ellis; Victor Plarr graduates from Oxford and comes to London; Wilde's essay "Keats' Sonnet on Blue" appears in the *Hobby Horse* (July).
-Wilde and Horne collaborate to establish a plaque to Thomas Chatterton (August).
-Rhys meets Symons; Symons begins work on Leigh Hunt for Rhys's Camelot Classics.

YEATS'S LONDON YEARS

1887   -Yeats comes to London (spring).
-Rhys writes introduction for Horne's edition of Herrick's poems.
-Johnson meets Pater in Arthur Galton's rooms (April).
-Dowson meets Johnson at Oxford (spring or early autumn).
-Yeats meets Rhys (May).
-Symons's *Essays of Leigh Hunt* appears with Camelot Classics.
-Yeats meets Herbert Halliday Sparling (June 25).
-Rhys lectures at Kelmscott House Socialist League on "The New Poetry" (July 24).
-Le Gallienne's *My Lady's Sonnets* published privately in Liverpool (August).
-Le Gallienne and Jimmy Welsh talk to Wilson Barrett as he is leaving Royal Court Theatre, Liverpool; Le Gallienne visits London and gets books to review for the *Academy*, also visits Wilde (September).

Appendix II

-Bodley Head established in Vigo Street (October).
-Pater reviews Symons's *Introduction to the Study of Browning* in the *Guardian* (November 9).

1888 -Lionel Johnson meets the *Hobby Horse* associates.
-Yeats has sent *The Wanderings of Oisin* to Kegan Paul (14th); has been introduced to Francis Fahy, founder of the Southwark Irish Literary Club (21st); writes to Katherine Tynan from Herbert Horne's office (22nd); Dowson leaves Oxford without degree and comes to London (March).
-The Yeatses move to 3 Blenheim Road; W. B. Yeats begins French lessons with the Socialist League (April).
-*Poems and Ballads of Young Ireland* appears with poems by Yeats, Rolleston, Todhunter and others (May).
-Le Gallienne visits London, meeting John Lane and spending three days with Wilde (June).
-Ernest Dowson meets Victor Plarr in Charles Sayles's rooms, Gray's Inn.
-Yeats attends reception by Lady Wilde (July 25).
-Yeats meets W. E. Henley (summer).
-Oscar Wilde put up for the Saville Club by W. E. Henley (13th); Johnson's "In Falmouth Harbour" published in the *Hobby Horse*; Le Gallienne sends Wilde a manuscript collection of *Volumes in Folio* (October).
-Camelot Classics publishes Yeats's *Fairy and Folk Tales of the Irish Peasantry* (autumn).
-Le Gallienne in London for final accountancy exam (fails), stays with John Lane; Symons meets Pater at Oxford; Yeats meets Wilde at Henley's, has Christmas dinner at Tite Street (December).
-The Century Guild disbands.
-Yeats proposes to Katherine Tynan.

1889 -*Wanderings of Oisin* published; Wilde's "The Decay of Lying" in *Nineteenth Century*; Morris says he will review *Oisin* for *Commonweal* (January).
-Richard Le Gallienne becomes Wilson Barrett's secretary, comes to London (February).
-Arthur Symons's *Days and Nights* published.
-Yeats's "Scots and Irish Fairies" in *Scots Observer* (2nd); Wilde reviews Yeats's *Fairy and Folk Tales of the Irish Peasantry* in *Woman's World*; Le Gallienne's *Volumes in Folio* published by the Bodley Head (March).
-W. E. Henley's review of Yeats's poems, "A New Irish Poet," in *Scots Observer* (February/March).
-Wilde reviews Yeats's *Wanderings of Oisin* in *Woman's World*; Lionel Johnson visits London with parents and sister--sees Kegan Pauls, Herbert Horne, Selwyn Image, Walter Pater and Edmund Gosse (April).
-Yeats's "Village Ghosts" in *Scots Observer* (May 11).
-Wilde reviews Yeats's *Wanderings of Oisin* in *Pall Mall Gazette* (July).
-Symons's first trip to Paris with Havelock Ellis (September).
-Yeats mentions "Le Gallienne's publisher" and "Le Gallienne's publisher's reader" in letter to Katherine Tynan; Le Gallienne ceases to serve as Barrett's secretary; returns to Liverpool (October).
-Captain and Mrs. O'Shea divorce case.
-John Davidson moves to London.

1890 -Victor Plarr becomes Librarian at King's College, London.
-Ernest Radford publishes *Chambers Twain* with the Bodley Head.
-Horne speaks of Rhymers' meeting at his house and of

Appendix II

>
> Wilde arriving late (9th); Wilde meets Johnson at Oxford (February).
>
> -The *Critic*, with Ernest Dowson as assistant editor, folds after five issues (March 8).
>
> -Johnson's review of *Strafford* in the *Hobby Horse* (April).
>
> -Symons and Havelock Ellis on a three-month trip to Paris, meeting Verlaine and others (spring).
>
> -Todhunter's *A Sicilian Idyll* performed at the Bedford Park Social Club (May 5).
>
> -Oscar Wilde's *The Picture of Dorian Gray* published in *Lippincott's*; John Davidson and Ernest Rhys meet at a party at William Sharp's house (June).
>
> -Lionel Johnson moves to London, installing himself at the Fitzroy Establishment; Davidson mentioned as having been at the Rhymers' Club (9th); Dispute between Wilde and Henley's men in the *Scots Observer* over the relative merits of *The Picture of Dorian Gray* (July).
>
> -Le Gallienne's *George Meredith, Some Characteristics* published; Yeats's "The Old Pensioner" in *Scots Observer* (15); Yeats contributing work to Davidson's *Weekly Review*; *Scots Observer* renamed *National Observer* (22nd) (November).
>
> -Yeats's "The Lake Isle of Innisfree" in *National Observer* (December 15).

1891
>
> -Lionel Johnson introduces Lord Alfred Douglas to Oscar Wilde (circa January).
>
> -Kelmscott Press founded.
>
> -Wilde's *Intentions* published.
>
> -Davidson's *Weekly Review* folds.
>
> -Ernest Rhys marries Grace Little (5th). Davidson's column "The Week" begins in the *Speaker* (January).

-*The Picture of Dorian Gray* published in book form; Le Gallienne moves to London; Dowson publishes *"Non sum qualis eram bonae sub regno Cynarae"* in *Hobby Horse* (April).
-Symons returns from trip to Provence and Spain; Dowson writes to Arthur Moore, says he has just met Symons and is to meet Le Gallienne next week (29th) (May).
-Lionel Johnson received into Roman Catholic Church (St. Alban's Day).
-Le Gallienne becomes book critic for the *Star* under the pseudonym "Logroller"; Yeats sends Katherine Tynan notes on Henley and speaks of Rhymers' intentions to put out a book (week ending 27th) (July).
-Symons in Germany with Josiah Flint; Yeats writes to Katherine Tynan saying, "Owing to the Rhymers' Club I have a certain amount of influence with reviewers." (July).
-Johnson's father dies (15 September).
-Dowson publishes "*Amor Umbratilis*," "Carmelite Nuns" and "Fleur de la lune" in *Hobby Horse*; Le Gallienne marries Mildred (October).
-Yeats, Johnson and Greene meet with Elkin Mathews concerning Rhymers' Club anthology (November).
-Symons taken on regular staff of *Athenaeum*.
-Death of Charles Stewart Parnell.
-Davidson publishes *In a Music Hall*.

1892   -John Lane becomes Elkin Mathews's partner at the Bodley Head, with Le Gallienne as their first reader (January).
-Le Gallienne and wife attend first night of Wilde's *Lady Windermere's Fan* at St. James Theatre; *The Book of the Rhymers' Club* published (February).

Appendix II

- Lionel Johnson agrees to join Irish Literary Society (April 29).
- The Irish Literary Society officially founded at the Caledonian Hotel in the Adelphi, London (May 12).
- Adverse criticism of Yeats's *The Countess Cathleen* in the *Daily Chronicle* which J. B. Yeats thinks may be Davidson's ("as a tit for your tat?"); Le Gallienne's *English Poems* published (27th) (September).
- Tennyson dies (October 6).
- Victor Plarr marries.

1893
- Horne becomes sole editor of the *Hobby Horse*.
- Yeats and Ellis's edition of Blake's work published.
- Davidson's *Fleet Street Ecologues* published with Lane and Mathews.
- Yeats sends Henley "Celtic Twilight" for *The National Observer*.
- Joseph Foltinowicz, "Missie's" father, dies (April 24).
- Johnson's first visit to Dublin (September).
- Symons arranges to have Verlaine come and lecture at Barnard's Inn, High Holborn (November).

1894
- Yeats's first visit to Paris, stays with Mathers, visiting Maud Gonne and Verlaine, and attending a performance of *Axel* (February).
- Yeats's *Land of Heart's Desire* performed with Todhunter's *A Comedy of Sighs* at the Avenue Theatre (March).
- First issue of the *Yellow Book* (16th); Johnson in Ireland lecturing on "Poetry and Patriotism" (April).
- *The Second Book of the Rhymers' Club* published (June 20).
- Walter Pater dies (July).
- Yeats meets Olivia Shakespear (by August).
- Alfred Dowson dies of overdose of chloral (August 15).

-Mathews writes to Horne, attempting to acquire a third Rhymers' Club anthology for his firm (20th); Mathews and Lane's partnership dissolved (29th) (September).
-Yeats meets the Gore-Booths (autumn).

1895 -Dowson's mother hangs herself; Wilde receives Queensberry's accusation of "posing as a somdomite" (28th), sees solicitor to obtain warrant for Queensberry's arrest (29th) (February).
-Le Gallienne visits U. S. with John Lane; Queensberry arrested and given hearing (2nd) (March).
-Libel trial opened against Queensberry (3rd); Wilde loses litigation and is arrested (5th); press begins its campaign of abuse against decadence; Beardsley dismissed from *Yellow Book* and his drawings eliminated from April issue; Mathews testifies at Old Bailey that he dismissed Shelley after learning of his association with Wilde, and trial ends in hung jury (26) (April).
-Alfred Douglas leaves England.
-Le Gallienne begins his affair with Julie Norregard; Dowson visits Wilde while he's out on bail (7th); Greene sends post card to Mathews postponing Rhymers' Club dinner (13th); Wilde's second trial begins (22nd); Wilde sentenced to two years imprisonment and hard labor (25th) (May).
-Smithers publishes Symons's *London Nights*, having opened his book business in Arundel Street (June).
-Dowson experiencing severe troubles with "Missie," makes several trips to Dieppe to plan the *Savoy* (summer).
-Beardsley, Symons and Smithers in Dieppe to plan the *Savoy* (summer).
-Yeats moves to Fountain Court (late summer/early autumn).

Appendix II 239

       -Johnson moves to 7 Gray's Inn Square; Dowson moves to 6 Featherstone Buildings (September).
       -Dowson tours Belgium with Conal O'Riordan (October), then stays in Paris (through January 1896).
       -Wilde transferred from Wandsworth to Reading Gaol; flare-up of dispute between Mathews and Lane over the use of Beardsley drawings (November).
       -*A Book of Irish Verse* published, edited by Yeats.
       -Mathews publishes Ernest Dowson's *Dilemmas* and Lionel Johnson's *Poems*.

1896   -Alfred Austin named Poet Laureate; Verlaine dies (8th); first issue of the *Savoy* (11th) (January).
       -Dowson moves from Paris to Brittany (February).
       -Yeats moves to 18 Woburn Buildings; Symons's mother dies (14th).
       -Beardsley suffers severe tubercular attack at Brussels (April).
       -Beardsley returns to England from Brussels (4th); Symons goes to Guernsey (May).
       -Dowson's *Verses* published; Symons in Dieppe and Paris (June).
       -The *Savoy* changes to a monthly publication (July).
       -Yeats visits Ireland with Symons, meets Lady Gregory and visits the tower at Ballylee (August).
       -Post card from Yeats to Greene revealing that Yeats convened a Rhymers' Club meeting (November 2).
       -Last issue of the *Savoy*; Yeats in Paris with Symons, sees performance of Jarry's *Ubu Roi* and meets Synge; Wilde's petition for release refused; Beardsley suffers another breakdown; Symons goes from Paris on to Italy for 5 1/2 months (December).
       -Alfred Douglas's *Poems* published.

1897 -Victor Plarr becomes Librarian of the Royal College of Surgeons.
-Dowson moves to apartment above the Poland Restaurant.
-Dowson's *Pierrot of the Minute* published by Smithers; Very ill with tuberculosis, Beardsley is received into the Roman Catholic Church (31st) (March).
-Last issue of the *Yellow Book*; Dowson travels with Charles Condor to Britany (April).
-Wilde released from prison (19th); Wilde in Dieppe, renews friendship with Dowson (May).
-Yeats spends summer at Lady Gregory's Coole Park.
-Beardsley's and Wilde's paths cross in Dieppe (July).
-Dowson returns to England, having borrowed money from Wilde; Dowson travels to Ireland with J. de Courcey MacDonnell, staying until October; Symons and Havelock Ellis tour Munich, Beirut, Warsaw and Moscow (August).
-Adelaide ("Missie") Foltinowicz marries the German waiter (September 30).
-Dowson returns to Paris (October).
-Havelock Ellis's *Sexual Inversion* published, starting a controversy that would culminate in successful prosecution for obscene libel in the following year.

INDEX

Academy, 44, 79, 143
Adam, Villiers de l'Isle, 5
Aoife, 166-167, 197
Arnold, Matthew, 17, 140
Athenaeum, 143, 145
Bale, Edwin, 35
Barrett, Wilson, 42, 43
Baudelaire, Charles, 179
Beardsley, Aubrey, 3, 6, 101, 146, 179; *Under the Hill*, 6; effect of Wilde trials on, 98-99
Beardsley, Mabel, 3
Beckson, Karl, 54, 93
Beerbohm, Max, 5, 32
Binyon, Lawrence, 59
Black and White, 140, 141
Blake, William, 6-7, 22, 130; "The Sunflower," 130; rhythmical influence on Yeats, 178
Bloom, Harold, 3, 105
Bodley Head, the, 9, 94, 139, 143; effect of Wilde trials on reputation of, 98-99
Book of the Rhymers' Club, The, 57, 59, 61, 93-94, 138, 158, 161, 187; analysis of poems in, 104ff; reviews of, 139ff; Lang controversy, 146ff
Bornstein, George, 3-4
Boston Pilot, 15, 154
Bradley, Catherine. *See* Field, Michael
Brotherhood, the, 22
Browning, Robert: Arthur Symons's study of, 30; Oxford production of *Strafford*, 38
Brushfield, T. N., 94

Calumet, the, 21
Camelot Classics series, the, 22, 24, 25, 29
Canterbury Poets series, the, 25
Century Guild, 27, 53
Century Guild Hobby Horse. See Hobby Horse
Chambers's Encyclopedia, 34
Cheshire Cheese pub, 9, 61, 68, 74, 96, 144, 155, 165
Chubb, Percival, 22
Church Quarterly Review, 143; review of *The Book of the Rhymers' Club*, 152-154
Church Reformer, 148
Commonweal, 19, 20
Contemporary Club, the, 20, 21; precursor to Rhymers' Club, 13ff; William Morris's visit to, 18-19
Cooper, Edith. *See* Field, Michael
Crane, Walter, 60, 62-63
Cripps, Arthur S., 59
Croft-Cooke, Rupert, 99
Cuchulain, 161, 187, 196
Daiches, David, 7, 206
Daily Chronicle, 139, 140, 150-151, 162, 164
Daily News, 143, 147, 149, 159
Davidson, John, 9, 12, 21, 30, 53, 57, 61, 87, 96, 99, 104, 156, 158; *Scaramouch in Naxos*, 55; at Rhymesters' Club meeting, 55-56; incident with the four Scotsmen, 72ff
Dictionary of National Biography, 34
Dodgson, Campbell, 62

Dolmetch, Eugene, 176
Douglas, Lord Alfred, 38, 39
Douglas, Lord, the Marquess of Queensberry, 98
Douglas, George, 59
Dowson, Ernest, 3, 4, 9, 10, 11, 15, 27, 28, 30, 36-37, 54, 56, 59, 60, 61, 72-73, 74, 87, 104, 105, 107-108, 118, 121, 122, 126, 127, 137, 155, 158, 173, 174, 175, 176, 177, 179, 183, 198, 202, 205-206; letter on early Rhymers' Club meeting, 62-63; analysis of "Cynara," 64ff; influence on Yeats, 75-77; Symons's portrait of, 79ff; personal dissolution, 102-103; poems in Rhymers' Club anthologies, 108ff; Yeats speaks about his downfall, 162-163; mentioned in "The Grey Rock," 166-167; works: "*Ah, dans ces mornes séjours*," 109; "Amor Umbratilis," 71; "Carmelite Nuns," 71; "Extreme Unction," 109, 112; "The Garden of Shadow," 109, 112; "Growth," 109-111; "*Non sum qualis eram bonae sub regno Cynarae*," 64ff, 78, 109, 110, 177; "To One in Bedlam," 109, 112
Dublin University Review, 17
Duffy, Charles Gavan, 18
Eliot, Thomas Stearns, 1, 31
Ellis, Edwin J., 6-7, 107, 178; context for acquaintance with W. B. Yeats, 21ff
Ellis, Havelock, 23, 29, 30
Ellmann, Richard, 3, 206
Fabian Society, 23
Fahy, Frances, 20
Farr, Florence, 104, 176
Fellowship of the New Life, 22, 29
Field, Michael, 80

Fitzroy Establishment, 27, 30, 36, 37, 43, 53, 55, 56, 60, 62, 103
Fortnightly Review, 23
Foltinowicz, Adelaide ("Missie"), 65, 69, 102, 109
Fuller, Loie, 188
Gael, 15
Galton, Arthur, 38
Gannon, Patricio, 72
Gautier, Théophile, 123
Ghose, Manmohan, 59
Glasgow Herald, 146
Globe, 144, 146
Goldsmith, Oliver, 9, 149
Gonne, Maud, 9, 167, 190, 194, 197, 201; Yeats's association with, 15-17; conceptual similarity to "Missie," 69-71; in "The Circus Animals' Desertion," 183-184
Gosse, Edmund, 100, 142
Grahame, Kenneth, 32
Gray, John ("Dorian"), 62-63
Greene, George Arthur, 17, 56, 95, 107, 155-156, 204; Lang's comment on his verse: 147-148
Gregory, Lady Augusta, 68, 104, 200
Gregory, Major Robert, 168, 200
Gwynn, Stephen, 18, 42
Guardian, 30
Hallam, Arthur, 157-158
Hamlet, 13-14, 15, 21, 22, 45, 164-165, 186, 198, 199, 205
Harland, Henry, 59
Harper, George Mills, 3
Heffernan, William, 34
Heinemann, William, 99
Henley, W. E., 21, 37; Yeats's association with, 32ff; *A Book of Verses*, 32-33
Herbert, George, 25
Herrick, Robert: referred to in "At the Rhymers' Club: The Toast," 57-58

Index

Hillier, Arthur Cecil, 17
Hobby Horse, 27-28, 38, 62, 64; Le Gallienne's review of, 66-67
Horne, Herbert, 9, 30, 36, 56, 58, 176; association with Rhys and Yeats, 26ff; host of early Rhymers' Club meeting, 60-62; influence on Yeats, 176
Hunt, Leigh, 29
Huysmans, Joris-Karl, 30
Hyde, Douglas, 17
Ibsen, Henrik, 1
Image, Selwyn, 27, 28, 61, 100, 140, 154, 156-157, 161; rebuttal to Lang, 148-150
Irish Literary Society, 17, 56
Jeffares, A. Norman, 3, 200
Jepson, Edgar, 65, 79, 84, 86, 103, 122
John O'London's Weekly, 73
Johnson, Lionel, 3, 4, 5, 9, 10, 11, 27, 28, 30, 42, 56, 58, 61, 62, 63, 64, 67, 72, 74, 78, 87, 97, 104, 105, 107-108, 118, 121, 122, 126, 127, 137, 148, 158, 173, 174, 175, 176, 183, 202; Yeats speaks about his downfall, 162-163; mentioned in "The Grey Rock," 166-167; mentioned in "In Memory of Major Robert Gregory," 168-169; his Platonism influenced Yeats, 190, 191-192; symbolic figure in Yeats's poems, 197ff; works: "The Dark Angel," 112ff, 117; "The Destroyer of a Soul," 103, 117; "Glories," 117; "In Falmouth Harbour," 117; "*In Honorem Doriani Creatorisque Eius,*" 38-39, 117; "The Last Music," 117; "Mystic and Cavalier," 112, 117; "To Morfydd," 117; "Plato in London," 191-192
Johnson, Samuel, 9, 149

Jonson, Ben: referred to in "At the Rhymers' Club: The Toast," 57-58
Joyce, James, 1; Yeats's advice to, 45-46
Keats, John, 84, 86, 158, 162, 164, 192, 193, 204; in *Daily Chronicle* review of *The Book of the Rhymers' Club,* 150-152
Kelmscott House, 19, 23
Kermode, Frank, 187
Kottabos, 17
Kropotkin, Prince Peter Alekseyevich, 23
Laforgue, Jules, 110
Lane, John, 9, 44, 93, 102, 144; dissolution of Bodley Head partnership, 94ff; effect of Wilde trials on, 99; rejects Symons's *London Nights,* 99-100
Lang, Andrew, 140, 141, 142, 153, 154, 157, 159, 161, 164, 169, 193; his review of *The Book of the Rhymers' Club,* 146ff
LeGallienne, Richard, 9, 12, 36, 67, 68, 79, 87, 95, 96, 99, 102, 140, 141, 146, 155, 156, 160; association with Oscar Wilde and London circle, 42ff; works: *My Lady's Sonnets,* 43; *Volumes in Folio,* 44; *The Romantic '90s,* 67
Lloyd, Constance, 36
Louÿs, Pierre: *Aphrodite,* 98
MacBride, John, 70
Mackmurdo, Arthur, 27, 28
Maeterlinck, Maurice, 190
Mallarmé, Stéphane, 30, 82-83, 164, 187
Malory, Sir Thomas, 155
Mantalini, Mr. (Dickens character), 63
Marlowe, Christopher, 55, 57
Martyn, Edward, 104
Mask, the, 4, 5, 14, 25, 41, 201, 206;

Yeats adopts from Oscar Wilde, 182ff; in relation to Yeats's idea of the dance, 189-190
Massinger, Philip, 29
Mathews, Elkin, 9, 21, 44, 93, 104, 138, 144; dissolution of Bodley Head partnership, 94ff; effect of Wilde trials on, 98-99
May, Arthur, 36
May, James Lewis, 42
Meredith, George, 33
Merimée, Prosper, 80
Mermaid series, the, 29
Miles, Frank, 36
"Missie." *See* Foltinowicz, Adelaide
Mistral, Frederei, 29
Moore, Albert, 73
Moore, Arthur, 60, 62, 67, 73, 79
Moore, George, 104
Moore, T. Sturge, 158
Morris, Jane, 17
Morris, William, 21, 23, 32, 35, 43, 150; early association with Yeats, 18ff; meter of "The Haystack in the Floods," 178-179; alluded to in Yeats's "The Statues," 186-187
Nation, 145, 146
National Observer, 35, 145
National Review, 29
Nettleship, John: attends Rhymesters' Club meeting, 55-56
New Ireland Review, 144
Nicholls, Harry, 13
Nineteenth Century, 140, 147
Oldham, Charles Hubert, 13, 15, 17
O'Leary, John, 15, 17, 26, 34, 55
Osborne, Churchill, 27, 29
Osborne, Walter, 19
Ovid: *Metamorphoses*, 193
Pall Mall Gazette, 37, 144
Parker, Gilbert, 32

parnassiens, 142-143, 192
Pater, Walter, 6, 9, 28, 35, 36, 37, 38, 40, 53, 61, 78, 79, 104, 109, 115, 118, 119, 121, 122, 190, 195, 201, 205; on Symons's work, 30-31; Yeats's early understanding of organic form, 33-34; influence on Rhymers' Club as reflected in Yeats's prose, 162-164; works: *Marius the Epicurean* 6, 37, 162; *The Renaissance*, 6, 35
Plarr, Victor, 9, 12, 28, 41, 53, 56, 61, 63, 67, 80, 84, 86, 103, 105, 146, 190, 192, 193, 204; on Dowson and Johnson's taste for French poetic forms, 72-73; letter from Dowson concerning "Missie," 109-110; poems in Rhymers' Club anthologies, 122ff; works: "Ad Cinerarium," 192; "Deer in Greenwich Park," 123-126; *In the Dorian Mood*, 96, 126; "To a Greek Gem," 192; "Twilight Piece," 192-193
Pennell, Joseph, 32
Phidias, 186
Phillips, Stephen, 59
Plato, 180, 186-187, 191-192, 198
Poems and Ballads of Young Ireland, 15, 17
Pollexfen, George, 200
Pound, Ezra, 1, 15, 31, 206
Pre-Raphaelites, 17, 20, 23, 32, 43, 163, 178, 187
Providence Sunday Journal, 15
Pythagoras, 186
The Quarterly, 151
Quinn, John, 68
Radford, Ernest, 9, 20, 23, 30, 107; Dowson's report on his verse, 62-63; reaction to dissolution of Bodley Head partnership, 95-97
Raftery, Anthony, 200
Ranking, Boyd, 25

Index

Rhymers' Club, the, 15, 17, 20, 21, 22, 23, 26, 27, 28, 30, 41, 64, 68, 71, 79, 87, 137, 138, 203, 204, 205; critical and historical overview of, 1-4, 6, 7, 8-10, 11-12; Oscar Wilde's influence on, 35-37, 61-63, 98ff; Yeats's conscious effort to meet and form, 44-46; founding stages of, 53ff; John Davidson and four Scotsmen incident, 72ff; dissolution of, 93ff; their anthologies as historical documents, 104ff; reviews of their anthologies, 139ff; Yeats's poetic treatment of, 194ff

Rhymesters' Club, 54, 55. See also Rhymers' Club

Rhys, Ernest, 9, 15, 16, 20, 32, 61, 68, 87, 140, 142, 204; background in London, 22ff; and Herbert Horne, 26-27; and Arthur Symons, 28-29; letter to E. C. Stedman, 55-59; works: *A London Rose*, 96; *Malory's King Arthur and the Quest of the Holy Grail*, 23; *Wales England Wed*, 23

Rhys, John, 25

Roberts, Morely: on four Scotsmen episode, 73-75

Rodin, Auguste, 30

Rolleston, T. W., 9, 55, 56, 61, 107, 140, 155; pre-London background, 17ff

Rossetti, Christina, 150

Rossetti, Dante Gabriel, 9, 19, 158, 163

Rothenstein, William, 12, 175

Ruskin, John, 5, 28

Rutenberg, Daniel, 54

St. James's Gazette, 139, 141-142, 145, 146

Saturday Review, 140

Savoy, 80, 101, 103, 104

Sayle, Charles, 43

Schreiner, Olive, 36

Scots Observer, 32, 34

Second Book of the Rhymers' Club, The, 68, 93-94, 122, 126, 130, 138, 154, 161, 187; analysis of poems, 104ff; reviews of, 143ff

Seiden, Morton, 3, 180

Shaw, George Bernard, 23

Shelley, Edward, 98-99

Siddal, Elizabeth, 17

Skipsey, Joseph, 25

Smithers, Leonard, 100, 101

Socialist League, 19-20, 21, 23

Southwark Literary Club, 20, 27

Sparling, Herbert, 25

Speaker, 143, 144

Star, 67, 79, 139, 156, 187

Stedman, E. C., 55, 59

Stevenson, R. A. M., 32

Swinburne, Algernon Charles, 42, 150, 158

Symons, Arthur, 5, 7, 9, 10, 12, 36, 54, 59, 61, 62, 63, 102, 104, 105, 107-108, 122, 137, 146, 156, 158, 173, 174, 175, 176, 190, 198, 205-206; background in London, 28ff; influence on Yeats, 75-77; his portrait of Ernest Dowson, 79ff; effect of Wilde debacle on *London Nights*, 99ff; poems in Rhymers' Club anthologies, 117ff; his symbol of the dancer as employed by Yeats, 187ff; works: "Being a Word on Behalf of Patchouli," 5, 100, 146; "The Broken Tryst," 117-118; *An Introduction to the Study of Browning*, 30; "Javanese Dancers," 121, 176-177; *London Nights*, 99ff, 121-122; "Love and Art," 117-118; "Music and Memory," 118; "Nora on the Pavement," 118-120, 121, 189; *Silhouettes*, 121-

122; "Song," 118, 120-121; *The Symbolist Movement in Literature*, 7, 30, 31
Synge, John, 168, 198-200
Taylor, John F., 14-15
Tennyson, Alfred Lord, 34, 106, 108, 122, 150, 152, 180
Thompson, Francis, 9
Thornton, R. K. R., 54, 55
Thuente, Mary Helen, 3
Times, 139, 146
Todhunter, John, 9, 17, 21ff, 61, 62-63, 106, 108; "In Westminster Abbey," 106-108
Tomson, Graham, 143
Tynan, Katherine, 15, 17, 19, 25, 27-28, 32-33
United Ireland, 144, 157
Unterecker, John, 3
Van Laun, Henri, 73
Verhaeren, Emile, 190
Verlaine, Paul, 9, 30, 86; symbol of the veil, 82-83
Watts, George, 186
Whibley, Charles, 32
Whistler, James McNeill, 63, 83
Wilde, Oscar, 3, 5, 9, 12, 60, 61, 67, 80, 93, 104, 117, 126, 173, 205; association with future Rhymers, 35-37, 37-41, 43-44; impression made on early Rhymers, 62-63; trials and effect on Rhymers' Club, 98ff; effect on Lionel Johnson, 102-103; his concept of the Mask as it influenced Yeats, 182-185; works: "Personal Impressions of America and Her People," 36; *The Picture of Dorian Gray*, 5, 35, 38, 41, 103, 182; "The Decay of Lying," 5, 184
Woman's World, 36, 37
Wordsworth, William, 180
Yeats, John Butler, 21-22, 141

Yeats, William Butler, 1, 2, 4, 5, 6, 7, 8, 9, 10, 11, 12, 13, 14, 15, 17, 18, 19, 20, 21, 22, 23, 24, 25, 26, 27, 28, 30, 37, 55, 56, 58, 63, 64, 83, 94, 96-97, 100-101, 102, 103, 104, 105, 105-106, 108, 123, 137, 138, 139, 141, 146, 147 150, 152, 204, 205, 206; and W. E. Henley, 32ff; and Oscar Wilde, 35-36; conscious effort to meet Rhymers, 44-46; founding of Rhymers' Club, 53-54; note to Horne concerning Rhymers' Club meeting, 60-62; influence of Dowson's "Cynara" on, 67-72; and four Scotsmen episode, 72-78; on Arthur Symons, 86-87; poems in Rhymers' Club anthologies, 126ff; influence of Rhymers' Club reviews, 154ff; influence of Rhymers' Club on his work, 173ff; his poetic treatment of Rhymers' Club, 194ff; works: "After Long Silence," 69; "Among School Children," 190, 201; "The Arrow," 70; *Autobiographies*, 2, 12, 13, 27, 44, 53, 56, 71, 73, 103, 137, 174, 190, 194; *Ballads and Lyrics*, 181; "Beautiful Lofty Things," 193; "A Bronze Head," 193; "A Bundle of Poets," 157-158; "The Cap and Bells," 131; "The Circus Animals' Desertion," 4, 69-70, 183-184; *Collected Poems* (1908), 180-181; "Coole Park and Ballylee, 1931," 199-201; "Coole Park, 1929," 199, 200; *The Countess Kathleen*, 146; "A Crazed Girl," 189; "Easter 1916," 183, 197, 201; "Ego Dominus Tuus," 162; "An Epitaph" ("A Dream of Death"), 126, 197; *Fairy and Folk Tales of the Irish Peasantry*, 22,

Index

37; "The Fiddler of Dooney," 131, 188; "The Folk of the Air," 126-127, 131, 188; *Four Years*, 2; "The Grey Rock," 2, 165-168, 195-197, 199; "The Gyres," 197; "Her Vision in the Wood," 188-189; "Hopes and Fears for Irish Literature," 105, 157, 168, 174, 176, 179; "In Memory of Major Robert Gregory," 3, 168-169, 198-199; "The Lake Isle of Innisfree," 176; "Lapis Lazuli," 192; "Long-Legged Fly," 189; "Magic," 7; "The Man and the Echo," 175; "The Man who Dreamed of Fairy Land," 127-130, 188, 203; "Meditations in Time of Civil War. (II. My House)," 191; "Modern Poetry," 174, 194; "The Municipal Gallery Revisited," 193, 199; "A Mystical Prayer to the Masters of the Elements," 130-131, 188; "Nineteen Hundred and Nineteen," 188; *The Oxford Book of Modern Verse*, 2, 137, 164ff, 173, 174, 194; "Pardon, Old Fathers," 179, 196; "Phases of the Moon," 191-192; "A Prayer for Old Age," 69; *Responsibilities*, 8, 165, 195, 196, 197; "The Results of Thought," 201-202; *Reveries Over Childhood and Youth*, 33; "The Rhymers' Club," 68; "The Rose," 181, 194; "The Rose in My Heart," 130-131; "Sailing to Byzantium," 183, 192, 193; "The Scholars," 69, 179; "Scotch and Irish Fairies," 34; "The Song of the Happy Shepherd," 187; "Song of the Old Mother," 131; "The Statesman's Holiday," 3; "The Statues," 186, 192; "To a Child Dancing in the Wind," 189; "The Symbolism of Poetry," 7; "To Ireland in the Coming Times," 77ff, 176, 177; "The Tower," 179; *The Trembling of the Veil*, 17, 35, 61, 73, 83, 161ff, 176; "Under Ben Bulben," 177-178, 183, 197, 202-203; *A Vision*, 179, 184-185; 206; *The Wanderings of Oisin*, 15, 20, 28, 33-4, 37, 177, 180, 181; "What Then?", 191; "While I, from that reed-throated whisperer," 197; "The Wild Swans at Coole," 198; "William Blake and the Imagination," 7; *The Wind Among the Reeds*, 69, 97, 130, 194

Yellow Book, 59, 101; effect of Wilde trials on, 98-99

Young Ireland, 17

Richard Hoffpauir

ROMANTIC FALLACIES

American University Studies: Series IV (English Language and Literature).
Vol. 31
ISBN 0-8204-0257-5   228 pages   hardback US $ 30.50*

*Recommended price – alterations reserved

As a contribution to a critical debate, this study is an attack, in the tradition of Yvor Winters and F. R. Leavis, on Romanticism in English poetry and criticism. It begins with an outline of the movement in eighteenth-century aesthetic thought that gave rise to several fallacious literary notions, doctrines, and procedures: mythic form, individual authority, inspiration, and dramatic immediacy. The argument moves from an extended critique of Meyer Abram's *Natural Supernaturalism*, through an evaluative comparison of William Wordsworth and George Crabbe, to intensive analyses of the critical reputations and poetic weaknesses of those two most definitive of Romantic poems, Coleridge's «Kubla Khan» and Keat's «Ode to a Nightingale».

PETER LANG PUBLISHING, INC.
62 West 45th Street
USA – New York, NY 10036

Maya Hostettler

D. H. LAWRENCE
Travel Books and Fiction

European University Studies: Series XIV (Anglo-Saxon Language and Literature). Vol. 135
ISBN 3-261-04021-1   286 pages   paperback US $ 22.50*

*Recommended price – alterations reserved

To what extent do D. H. Lawrence's life (long) journeys bear influence on his art? In order to find an answer to this question this study follows the artist through his fiction and his travel books. Minute textual analysis and juxtaposition reveal a traveller who turns from an angry preacher into a leader scholar. He finally discovers that the artist's quest for knowledge and understanding remains unsatisfied unless he is able to accept his own as well as the world's idiosyncrasies. This study shows that the influence of his travel experiences on his fiction and vice versa the influence of his fictionally achieved experiences on his travel books help him to come to this conclusion.

Contents: D. H. Lawrence and the Travel Book Tradition – The Doing and Undoing of *Twilight in Italy* The Lawrentian Relation to Nature – *Mornings in Mexico:* The Turning Point – The Etruscan Past.

PETER LANG PUBLISHING, INC.
62 West 45th Street
USA – New York, NY 10036

Lillie Jugurtha

KEATS AND NATURE

American University Studies: Series IV (English Language and Literature).
Vol. 18
ISBN 0-8204-0171-4   208 pages   hardback US $ 39.80*

*Recommended price – alterations reserved

John Keats loved the out-of-doors – flowers, birds, water, fresh air, the sun, the moon, and the seasons. The sight, sound, or touch of nature could send him into emphatic responses. Keats never stopped responding to the sensations of nature. But his letters and poems record a movement from thinking of nature as scenery providing sensations to seeing nature as a source of truths about how and why men live. In *Keats and Nature*, Lillie Jugurtha analyzes this philosophical evolution which climaxed in a metaphysical view of nature (organicism). Jugurtha shows how this conception of nature allows one to read *Endymion*, *Hyperion*, and *The Fall of Hyperion* with new understanding and pleasure – how it augments readings of minor poems, *The Eve of St. Agnes, Lamia*, and the great odes.

Contents: The work contains *criticism* and *literary analyses* of John Keats's major and minor poems. *Biographical* details, primarily provided by his letters, support the conclusion that the poet developed a *philosophical view* of *nature* called *organicism,* influential on his *poetic symbols.*

PETER LANG PUBLISHING, INC.
62 West 45th Street
USA – New York, NY 10036